Praise for Dave Ribble

(Taken from LinkedIn Profile Recommendations)

"In a world filled with noise, Dave Ribble is
a consummate listener and teacher."

"…His relationship building traits are top notch."

*"Dave Ribble stands out as a consummate marketing pro.
Dave indeed makes a difference."*

"Dave Ribble is a solution machine."

*"…A gifted communicator, skillful at motivating and
bringing out the best in those around him"*

"Dave Ribble is among the most honorable, ethical, genuine
people that I have had the privilege to work with. His intellect,
intuition and incredible insight allow him a vast array of tools
for solving challenges. Dave values positive relationships, honesty,
integrity and good will above all else."

The Way

Of

The Conscientious

Connector©

The complete paradigm-shifting guide to creating the most rewarding
and sustainable connections possible for business, career and life

Dave Ribble

ISBN-13: 978-0-9982383-0-2

ISBN-10: 0998238309

Library of Congress Control Number: 2017901316
StandOut Marketing Strategies, Long Beach, California

DEDICATION

To every person who will see themselves and others as the magnificent beings you truly are and to those of you who see the value in promoting this relationship movement to as many corners of this fragile planet as possible, I say…

"Let's do this."

CONTENTS

ACKNOWLEDGMENTS

Inspiration and Support Provided By

Gaye Kruger-Ribble

Dr. Wayne Dyer   Sheila Gillette

Mike Presnall   Paull McCoy   Ron Massman   Diana Williams

Bob Proctor   Sonia Le   Chris Brown   Tim Collins   Chellie Campbell

Zig Ziglar   Jerry Grant   The Theo Group   Benjamin Franklin

Napoleon Hill   Pam Grout   Jack Canfield   Elannah Resnikoff

Simon T. Bailey   Marcus Gillette   Keri Tombasian   Dan Ribble

The Breakfast Bar Gang   Og Mandino   Roni Wright   DeeDee Rescher

Rip Ribble   Erin Gray   Dale Murphy   Tom White   Deanna Tan

Christina Joy Ryan Rodriguez   Everette Laybourne   Ed Will   Joe Ribble

Blaine Bartlett   Kecia Wimmer Lyons   Deborah Jean Miller   Marvin Baida

Deepak Chopra   Barbara Niven   John Cofiell   Michael Kogutt

Adam Grant   Judy Nelson   Brian Miller   Lisa Lamazzi   Harvey Mackay

> **"Life is about connecting and connecting is about taking on other points of view. Our world is a shared experience, fractured by individual perspectives. Imagine if we could all feel understood."**
> - Brian Miller, Motivational Speaker & Magician (brianmillermagic.com)

Monika Lutz   Charlie Wright   Aggie Medrano   Karen Ribble

James Wedmore   Simon Sinek   Corinne Gelfan   Mom & Dad   Mel Ellis

Rik Middleton   Les Brown   Rumi   Sara Blatt Collins   Paul Brodsky

David Will   Katherine Ribble Powell   Mary Jean Valente   Michael Port

Ruby DeRuiter   Dr. John McGrail   Stephen Covey   Suzy Deeds Gunsauls

Jill Lublin   Erin Ribble   Joseph Murphy   Benztown Brigade   Gail Gust

Kathleen Deggelman   Helen Dolas   Danielle Ribble   Mark Heller

Glen Holt   Don Brown   Sherry Ribble   Rick Sessinghaus   Keri Murphy

Marilyn Ribble   Janet Switzer   Yogi Berra   Tony Robbins   Teresa Will

Dr. Miles Reid   Jason Powell   Fairmount High   Natalie Townes

T. Harv Eker   Michael Goldstein   Phil Glosserman   Dale Carnegie

Don Carkeek   Alex Ribble   Mary Brodsky   Mark V Hansen

Sarah Balkin   Brendon Burchard   Nicole Cavanaugh   Michael Gerber

Kirby Hasseman   Julie Aldrich   Uncle Joe Smith   Craig Sherman

A Grateful Thanks

Ashley McMahon, Editor/Content Strategist, Maple Street Media, LLC
(MapleStMedia.com)

Big Chief Creative Media
(BigChiefCreative.com)

Maureen Williams, Brilliant Publishing
(GetBrilliantResults.com)

Cover Design

Gaye Kruger-Ribble

MISSION

Always connected to Source, I enthusiastically encourage and facilitate others in reaching their highest level of desired achievement.

DEFINITIONS

Conscientiously Connecting

The process of connecting people because you sense there is a synergistic value available for the parties involved, regardless of whether you benefit personally or not.

The Conscientious Connector Culture

The infectious, conscientious mindset that permeates a group or organization after they've experienced the greater good that comes from becoming true Conscientious Connectors.

INTRODUCTION

This book is for you.

It may not be for everyone just yet, although anyone who reads it will benefit greatly no matter where they are on the spectrum.

I wrote it for you because your instincts tell you that if you could make the right connections, you could: Sell more products and services; or, accelerate your career; or, get that promotion; or, make more money and become more valuable to your employer as well as to yourself; or all of the above and more. And, I would agree because when you do formulate, then exercise the right connections to the right people, mountains can be moved.

Everything you need to accelerate your capability to connect this way is in this book, ready for you to learn, embrace, practice and enjoy. The good news is that it will take you a lot less time to understand and apply these principles than it took me to figure them out, test them, develop them and then put all this to paper.

One thing I can tell you, however, is that your ability to make all this happen for yourself is not going to be predicated on how many business cards you collect at networking events or how many networking events you even attend, for that matter. Yes. I said that.

When you learn and begin to practice the five necessary steps to becoming a *Conscientious Connector*, your life experiences will automatically start to broaden. Insecurities and frustrations will fall away and will be replaced by a new 'you' that is more confidant, much less frustrated and a lot happier. You will begin, as I certainly did, to build a database of the right, most rewarding and sustainable connections possible, connections that will enhance your business, career and life no matter what you do for a living.

As you will discover, the difference between networking and

truly *connecting* is vast. As you progress through this book you will notice how you begin to see the world through different lenses. No training in the world is this specific, focused and detailed on this subject.

I have asked many college professors to give me their opinion on the importance of these skills in order to have the best chance at a career and, to a person, they heartily agreed it is essential. Some have even placed the importance of these skills above the value of the diploma itself, especially when it comes to generic majors such as business or marketing. Yet, when I review their school's respective curriculums and course offerings, I have yet to see one semester dedicated to this most important skill set. Why? Perhaps it is assumed that everyone will figure this out on his or her own.

To be sure, there are great business and sales coaches who teach strategy and tactics for finding more customers, but very few concern themselves as I do with the non-sales related folks who also work for a living, support their companies and who routinely wield enormous influence on a company's bottom line. Creating relationships with people who will *never* buy what you're selling is just one of the many scenarios I will go over with you and why this is so important and valuable to your success and your career.

Historically speaking...

I used to think networking was a simple matter that followed an even simpler formula: *Figure out where your target market hangs out, go there with a winning smile and a business card and bring home a new customer.*

Simple. As I was taught years earlier, networking simply meant you 'go where the fish are biting' and pick up business. If you need more business, do it again and keep doing it until you have all the business you need (which, by the way, never quite becomes the case for most of us). I wrote this book for anyone in sales and everyone who isn't, so don't miss this.

If you are truly interested in developing better skills and

becoming a force for good in the workplace, whether in sales or not, this book is for you.

When people tell me they are challenged by knowing where to go to network, I have to smile, because as a *Conscientious Connector* I now look at the world differently than most. For me it is not a lack but more of an abundance of places I can go if my objective is to meet people.

- Thousands of Chambers of Commerce around the country represent and advocate for millions of businesses. They host breakfasts, lunches, mixers and evening events weekly so that you and I can find each other.

- Private networking clubs such as Le Tip and BNI, philanthropic entities such as Rotary and Lions Clubs and dozens of other well-known membership organizations that host networking events.

- There are over a million trade shows every year. The same goes for special events.

- Churches, coffee shops, your gym, bars and anywhere else where people congregate are places to go to meet people.

My first question to you, however, is this: Are you going there to pick up more business cards or are you going there to begin the process of establishing *relationships?*

My second question to you is this: Why do you continue to collect more business cards in the name of networking after you already have a desk drawer filled with them from previous networking events?

Mining the contacts you already have and building on that is where we need to start. From there, this systematic approach will kick in, broaden and accelerate your progress faster than you probably expect.

Three myths about networking

Myth 1-All we have to do to be successful at networking events is to simply show up. 'Just go to where the fish are biting, so to speak, walk in the door, cast our line, hook a new prospect, reel them in and voila, we have new customers!'

Just showing up might get you a new prospect once in a while, but at best that's an inefficient system. By following my systematic approach it will probably surprise you at how good you quickly become at collecting the best connections, the ones you can truly work with, in less time.

Myth 2-We must spend all of our networking time only with those who can write us a check or refer us to someone who can; talking to people who do not fit our preconceived definition of our target market is a waste of our valuable time.

My training will dispel this common myth quickly and you will marvel at how your whole world will change; how it will open up enormous new possibilities and potential by looking at everyone in the room from a new perspective.

Myth 3-We must continually attend networking events because we don't have enough connections to work with already.

My training will show you that who you are connected to right now may be all you need to build into a list of the right, most rewarding connections possible for business, career and life.

~~~~~~~

Are you reading these words yet still feeling that you already have this networking stuff figured out? I used to think I did, too. I played the numbers. I drove all over the area in search of that elusive 'perfect target audience'. I frequented those places where I could reasonably assume the person I was looking for would miraculously appear before me. I imagined I would find that person talking to someone else and I imagined I would step up and boldly peel that person away, spin my pitch, line up an appointment on the spot and head back to the office in record time, happy and satisfied that my work was done, here. Simple. After all, I was in sales. My job was to ferret out the person who could help me gain more business and sell more stuff. I worked on that with each person who fit my target profile until my efforts came to fruition.

As for all those 'other people', the ones who didn't fit the criteria, I avoided them because I had always been taught that my time should be spent only with the low hanging fruit.

Learn to Define The *Rest* of the Room

Taken from my personal experiences and the experiences of many professionals I have worked with, read and interviewed over the years, when you become a *Conscientious Connector* you will add an effective, systematic component to your efforts that will separate you from everyone else who still follows the old pattern.

- You will start to see the world in a broader, beneficial light.

- You will marvel at the good you can bring out in the people you meet and work with; people you probably ignored before.

- You will be surprised at how all this potentiality for greater collaboration has been there all along.

- The results of this new approach will continue to provide you amazing new referral partners and build your confidence to want to network this way all the time.

- You will start to see this same higher-level connectivity capability in others and the potential within whole companies.

In short, you will enjoy a greater presence at every opportunity and event you attend from now on. Your life will change, expand and grow at the rate you decide to devote to this practice.

One other important point I need to mention before we go further: There is a difference between being Conscious and being Conscientious.

The two words look similar, but the definitions are distinctively different. I want clear up any confusion.

Conscious is an adjective, defined as *'being aware of one's own existence, sensations, thoughts, surroundings.'* Being conscious is being aware of your surroundings.

Conscientious is a noun, defined as *'one's inner sense of what is right or wrong, as in being principled, careful, particular, meticulous.'* When you respond to certain things according to your conscience you are acting in a *conscientious* manner.

For example, let's place you in a networking setting. You might find yourself *consciously aware* that you can help someone you meet by providing a referral. Whether you decide to help them or not will be a *conscious decision.* If you choose to help the other person, it will be because your *conscience* told you it was, for you, the right thing to do.

Of course, if you look at it as an opportunity to gain advantage over someone else and just for yourself, that, too, is a *conscious* decision, but not necessarily a *conscientious* one. The difference between the two words has everything to do with what the rest of this book talks about: A much greater potential for accomplishment.

> **"Networking was a necessary evil; often awkward and forced and sometimes felt like a step backwards until I changed my approach. Now I treat each person I meet as a potential friend. It's fun and authentic and has made all the difference."**
>
> Jill Sands, Merch-Media

If you approach this practice as a 'necessary evil' that requires you to mix and mingle with others just long enough to get what you want from another person, that *conscious* decision limits you. It also limits everyone else in his or her capacity to help you. We will talk about this in depth, because you can change that and benefit greatly from doing so.

When you approach networking in this broader scope and you understand what you and I and all of us can accomplish together, you realize that instead of just looking for a narrowly focused target market of people to talk to, everyone in the room matters.

Moreover, you will add this mindset to your skills and you will understand, perhaps for the first time, that what we know about each other can often lead to mutual benefits not yet even explored. One of my favorite Zig Ziglar quotes comes up for me, more all the time:

"You can have anything you want if you will just help enough other people get what they want."

Are you ready to see what can happen when you take 'you' out of the equation long enough to focus on the person standing in front of you or the person you met before but never took the time to get to know? Are you ready to have a ton of fun building for yourself a stellar reputation as a 'connector' and to then experience the greater benefits that come from this level of professionalism?

It is a good day whenever we can learn new things, especially if this information can change your life while changing the lives of others. Read this book, adopt these principles, and test them to see where your challenges lie.

The Way of The Conscientious Connector says that everyone matters, everyone is valuable, everyone can contribute and together we can create success stories everywhere. This book and optional training series provides you a systematic way to build the best foundational database of the right connections you have ever created.

STEP ONE

CHANGE YOUR PARADIGM

**Even if you are already good at connecting…
this changes everything**

Imagine we're back in the 1800's. You and I rode into town, tied our horses to the hitching post and are sitting there sipping our sarsaparilla when a futurist guy walks over and starts telling us that before too long, relatively speaking, we'll be riding in horseless carriages, enjoying lighted streets at night and talking to people miles away over a funny looking contraption called a telephone.

Today, things are in an even greater state of change and there are ways for you to benefit. One example is to make your own significant adjustments to your method of communication and how you connect with people, which can and often will run counter to the current culture.

Rather than only focusing on your needs, Section One asks you to look at things from a different perspective. Before you go looking for your target audience, before you reach for your business cards and before you say one word to anyone, consider what can happen when you broaden your opportunities by expanding your connection network.

A shift is required to enjoy all the benefits of becoming a *Conscientious Connector*. One cultural constant that hasn't changed is people still want to do business with people they know, like and trust. But we often miss tremendous opportunities available to us through the many people who will *never* become our customers. We just have to step out of our own way long enough to see the potential.

Pull out your Journal and get ready to take notes, because your future is about to accelerate.

STEP ONE / CHAPTER ONE

LEAVE YOUR BUSINESS CARDS IN YOUR POCKET & YOUR EGO AT THE DOOR

The day everything changed for me and how it can change for you, too

There have been many instances in my life where certain information, circumstances and a modicum of accidental insightfulness somehow collide and I find myself gifted with yet another clue about how the Universe *really* works. It no longer surprises me when this happens and I am always grateful.

Several years ago, a bundle of insights and new understanding were granted me one workday morning in April. I didn't see it coming, of course; insights rarely announce themselves with a warning and they oftentimes only reveal at those odd, unrelated moments, kind of like when you're half asleep, trying to start the coffee maker without a full appreciation for how critically important it is to remember to pour water into the machine *before* you press the start button. There are always lessons in life and the lessons from this particular morning's events set me on the path to write this book and develop the training that I believe will change your life like it changed mine.

"When the student is ready, the teacher will appear."
Buddhist proverb

It was 2008 and it seemed the whole world was going to hell in a hand-basket. I hadn't slept the night before largely because our promotional marketing company seemed to be locked in a long dry spell. We had loyal customers who were still ordering from us and we were so thankful for them all, but for some reason the larger clients, the ones who wrote an occasional big order, weren't moving ahead. Whole campaigns to promote Warner Bros and Universal movies were delayed or shelved until further notice, all due to the crazy economy. Intensity was growing.

The wishful thinking that this couldn't last much longer was gradually being usurped by facts that clearly indicated this economy, whether manipulated or not, was nonetheless spiraling south so rapidly that no one really knew when, or if, the devastation would end.

The greatest economic downturn since the Great Depression was upon us. Every news program featured so-called sage advisors and no shortage of talking heads and their opinions of the cause, offering ominous recommendations for how to fix the problem. The foreclosure rate shot up 81% over 2007 and 225% over 2006, respectively. Banks repossessed over 850,000 homes, twice the number of repossessions from the previous year. Twenty of the largest companies in the country combined to lay off over 400,000 workers and some reports took that figure much higher. If you had a job, you were smart (or lucky) to keep it at all costs.

And, like so many others, our business was affected. The rules were changing rapidly. Costs for manufacturing many of the products we sold were increasing overnight. Suppliers were afraid to commit to inventory of their best selling items. Production times increased. Competitive prices for delivery fluctuated daily, at times leaving us with rate increases even *after* orders were already placed.

Many of our sources developed a *take-it-or-leave-it* attitude. The effects of the recession were palpable. Our loyal clients struggled too, yet most of them, fortunately, took our advice and stepped up their advertising and promotion.

This enormous pressure to make things happen made keeping

up with personal health difficult and it was really starting to get to me. My defenses went up. The erroneous notion that this was all happening to our business and no one else's clouded my judgment. It was becoming harder to stay cheerful in the face of so many unanswered questions. The stress of it started to negatively affect my wife's health. Just because you stare at a phone for an hour doesn't mean you can make it ring. We went for over a week without placing so much as even one order from any of our customers; something that had never happened before.

That Tuesday Morning...

Needless to say, I was in a pretty foul mood before realizing that this particular Tuesday morning was the morning for the monthly Chamber of Commerce breakfast. Up and dressed by 6 am, I was conflicted because my role was always to take the lead in finding us new business while ensuring our existing clients are watched over. That was always my specialty, my job. As a former Vice President of Business Development for a top ten distributor, I was affectionately referred to as 'The Hit Man" because of my talent for helping our sales people snag accounts they could not penetrate on their own. Finding more business had always been something I could do easily, until now.

This economic downturn was different, however, and something I had not experienced. Replacing the big orders from WB and Universal and the others that were now either on hold or canceled wasn't going to be easy, so why would I devote even a couple hours to attending a network breakfast, especially one that, for the past three months, had produced no new prospects or clients? I was certain the best thing to do was for me to stay home that morning and search for business.

> **"When you change the way you look at things, the things you look at change."** Dr. Wayne Dyer

As I paced the kitchen and drank another cup of coffee, Gaye, my wife and business partner, was also up early to make calls to east coast suppliers. She listened to my rant about the networking breakfast and, after hearing my concerns, told me she thought that I should still attend. She said that her intuition was telling her I should go. She assured me she would be fine and that I should hit the road.

Perhaps it was less intuition and more her desire to get my foul mood and me out of the house for a while, but since she is rarely wrong about such things, I grabbed the keys and headed out the door, still certain this would be a monumental waste of time. But, I needed to go and try to make things happen.

The Woodland Hills Country Club, site of the breakfasts back then, was a good 20 minutes from home. Traffic was heavy that morning. The usual speedsters and cranky, impatient drivers were prevalent. Of course, as I think back on it now, I have to question just what kind of driver I was that morning, as well. Foul moods and panic will do that to you.

I parked on the lower level and headed up. Adjacent to the steep, curved driveway, one can look down and to the left and literally stand above the beautiful 18th green. Still trying to calm myself, I stopped to watch an early golfer's approach shot that happened to fall 20 feet short. I remember saying to myself, *'Yeah, buddy, I know how you feel.'* I offered the guy an empathetic wave before finishing my climb to the main entrance and, as most golfers do who appreciate how difficult the sport truly is, he waved back.

There was no way to know that, what I was about to discover that would change my life, would serve to change yours, too. As I approached the heavy and beautiful front door, I instinctively reached into my jacket for my business cards. It was an old habit I had developed years before; a sort of ritual that prepared me: 'Move the business cards up to an accessible and convenient place, my shirt pocket, so that I can easily find one to hand to someone in the off-chance there will be *anybody* to give one to.'

This time, however, as I reached for them a quiet voice inside my head seemed to speak to me: *"Leave your cards in your pocket; you won't need them for a while."*

'What was *that?*' I wondered. As I took my hand off the door handle, two people coming from behind me who, rightfully so, had assumed I was going to finish opening the door and go in had to break stride and stop. I looked at them. They looked at me in an awkward glance. I smiled and motioned for them to go ahead of me while I stepped back. I remember it was a man and a woman and the man did a double take at me, as if to wonder why I did not open the door for them before stepping away.

I looked around, half-wondering if I was being played by a candid camera. It was one thing to be here against my so-called better judgment and quite another to be hallucinating. I moved off to the side and out of the way of others still coming up the steps. Walking back toward the parking area, that same quiet voice came again and this time it told me to take myself out of the equation and just help someone else.

Perhaps this was the result of too much caffeine or too little sleep? Frankly, I was dumbfounded. It was true that I had experienced intuitive thoughts before, the kind one gets when you just have a gut instinct about something, but I had never experienced anything quite like this. It was a directive this time, clear and concise. Moreover, this time I was being directed to behave in a manner that was quite opposite my typical approach to networking.

To take myself out of the equation, to leave my cards in my pocket and spend the entire morning just helping others in their quest for success wasn't normal. Given all the years I had aggressively gone after business, it was always a simple matter, really: Show up, quickly figure out who fits the description of a target market and spend time working to turn that person into a prospect and then a customer. In order to do that, I had always separated the few from the many; those I didn't spend time with were those who didn't qualify for being worthy of my time.

Most salespeople would agree - we don't go into events looking to help anyone else unless there is something in it for us. Rather, we go with the intention of finding whomever we need in order to boost our own business. Networking events are arenas designed to bring people together for the purpose of finding each other, exchanging information and seeing where it goes from there. Simple. Straightforward. It's the way we have always done things, so you can probably imagine that, for me, when this voice in my over-stressed head told me to approach that morning's networking opportunity with a totally different approach that took **me** out of the picture, I was more than a little skeptical.

I needed a moment. I was afraid to engage in any conversations until my head cleared. I walked around for a minute or two, pretending to check messages on my phone. I was experiencing equal measures of confusion and intrigue. Was I being asked to not care any longer about my own welfare? Was I being asked to go in there only concerned with the success of others and not myself? Really? It didn't add up for me. I was there to find us business and bring it home, period. That's what I came to do like I have always done.

I hoped for clarity. Perhaps the directive was misinterpreted and what the voice meant to say was that I should concentrate on whatever it was I needed in order to help get our business out of this damned recession.

I replayed what I had heard: *Leave your business cards in your pocket, your ego at the door and go see how many other people you can help this morning.*

I thought back to all the sales training courses I had ever taken, all the books on my office shelf I had devoured. Not once in those pages did I see any of the great teachers tell me the advice I was learning this particular morning on the run. Indeed, it was always about how to figure out my target and tracking them down so that I could try to win the conversation and convert them into a customer. *That* sales funnel took us to the ultimate outcome, I believed, and, if anyone fell out of the sales funnel along the way, well, that was good because after determining they were not a prospect, I would never again waste time on them. I could scratch them off the list and thank them for shortening my list on my way to my goals, etc.

Now? I wondered if I was supposed to discard all that I had learned and practiced for years. How much less productive would this morning be if I were to give in to whatever this voice was telling me?

I finally calmed down but I certainly wasn't settled. Gaye's intuition had told her I should be here and that something good would come of it, but I still grasped for what that could be. I decided, (mostly because people were wondering why I hadn't yet entered the building) that I had to try to figure this out. I would have to go in there and see what happens. I headed back up the steps, pulled open the door and got in line.

By now, the registration table had started to back up. I paid my 20 bucks, ensured my special Board of Directors nametag was right side up and headed into the main room. But, instead of joining several friends who had already found their familiar pockets of conversation, I pivoted to face the entrance, absolutely certain I would not see anyone new. I was uncomfortable, but determined.

The Shift Begins: John & Dennis

As I started to search for new faces, a couple of my friends walked by and asked me who I was looking for. My response of "I'm not sure" probably sounded flippant, but I didn't care. I was in the hunt for what I was certain wouldn't happen; someone new to talk to after months of no one new coming through those doors.

It didn't take very long. Over toward the left and along the wall, out of the way of everyone else still coming in was something I had not seen for a long time: An *unfamiliar* face. There was a new person in the room.

Or, was it just that I hadn't noticed before?

I wasted no time and headed over to introduce myself. His large, calloused hand quickly enveloped my own as we shook. His jeans and boots suggested that a suit and tie weren't a requirement in his profession and I felt a certain comfort level immediately, perhaps because I grew up around a lot of construction guys and farmers. The concerns I carried with me into the room that morning seemed to start to slowly dissipate as I walked toward him. Indeed, this was an interesting comfort level I had not experienced in a long time.

"Hey there! Good morning and Welcome!" I smiled. "I'm Dave Ribble. I'm on the Board of this Chamber and you are new here, are you not?"

He smiled back and nodded affirmatively. But, before he could speak I continued.

"Well, tell me who you are, what you do and, most importantly, tell me who you are looking to meet," as I overtly waved my hand toward all the other people in the room, "because I probably know them!"

My confidence level was rising and a better mood was overtaking the one I had walked in with. I was on my own turf. I knew most everyone there and yet it was quite uncommon for me to meet anyone without first thinking about and listening for the opportunity to control the conversation to my favor and for my own benefit. I mean *that's what sales people do*, right?

He smiled again and panned the room. His slow, southern drawl was about to surprise me.

"Nice meeting you, Dave. My name is John Oliver. My company is Oliver Construction, a little business I started up about 20 years ago after working for my Dad. I have to tell you; I've been to a lot of network breakfasts over the years but no one has ever greeted me quite like you just did and I appreciate that, Dave."

Joking that this must be his lucky day, we settled into a conversation as I asked him questions about himself and his business. I seemed to embrace just having this kind of conversation with someone without a hidden agenda and I let things flow wherever they were going to flow for a change.

I focused completely on learning about this new acquaintance while enjoying his accent immensely. It was a refreshing change. I learned a lot about John simply by remaining quiet and prompting him to do the talking. With each new morsel of information, his trust in me grew, just as did my confidence that I could help him.

He told me that he lived in a nearby city, had two grown boys in the business and a daughter in college. John and his wife ran things out of their home office. I thought back to my own roots growing up, recalling the many contractor families I knew and how nostalgic this conversation was for me.

He circled back to my offer. "Ok. So, you asked me who would I like to meet?"

I smiled and gave a wave again toward the room as if to say, 'your wish is my command.'

"Well, sir, I will tell you it would be great to meet a good Realtor, since I do so much work in getting residential properties ready for sale; you know, the repairs and the cosmetic stuff most realtors need someone to handle. I love doing that kind of work and I work with several realtors in several other cities."

I turned back toward the room and spotted Dennis Murphy, a handsome man in his forties whom I knew for a fact was successfully ethical, both in his profession as well as on the golf course. One of the more prominent real estate brokers around, this might be a match made in heaven and I was anxious to find out. I motioned for John to follow me and I took him right over to Dennis. I interrupted the conversation Dennis was having with someone and I didn't consider it rude to do so.

"Excuse me, Dennis. I have a friend here, his name is John and he specializes in working with real estate folks like you to help get a property ready for sale. He's been doing it for a long time now, knows a lot about construction, a lot about real estate, is a member of another chamber, knows a lot of people and is a heck of a nice guy."

Dennis just stared at me as I turned to John. "John, Dennis Murphy is a well-respected Realtor with four offices and a ton of great people working for him. He's a very good golfer, too, so bring your A game."

As they shook hands, I smiled and said, "Gentlemen, get to know each other. My work is done, here."

They both laughed and thanked me for the introductions, immediately launching into a conversation of their own. "Tell me more about you, John," I heard Dennis say as I stepped away.

From the moment I spotted John, welcomed him, learned about himself, his family and his business, found out who he was looking to talk to and then took him to meet Dennis required less than five minutes of my time. Everything flowed. Everything tracked. Everything seemed to be almost too easy, in fact.

Might John have found Dennis that morning without me? Perhaps. Maybe during introductions later Dennis would have heard John's 30-second intro and John might have heard what Dennis had to say and they might have then gotten together on their own.

It is also just as likely that it would have taken another network breakfast or two before they ever really learned much about each other. It's hard to say, but I believe it is likely they would not have learned that much about each other on their own that quickly.

Here's what I do know for sure: My actions expedited their

relationship. Dennis already knew and respected me; although before that particular morning, Dennis had never seen me go out of my way to help someone else connect to him quite to that degree. All he had ever seen me do is stand and talk about my company and my request to sell my products and services. For Dennis to see me, Dave Ribble, come right up, interrupt his conversation with another member of the chamber and be truly excited to introduce him to someone who wanted to meet him was well out of character for what Dennis was used to from me. By putting Dennis and John before my own needs, it caught Dennis by surprise (frankly me, too) and caused Dennis to adjust his personal profile of me.

Here I was, handing him what could arguably be considered the best personal referral he would receive that morning, and perhaps ever. I was doing it with enthusiasm, professionalism and a smile on my face without even a hint of requested reciprocity, implied or otherwise. Whatever I seemed to be smoking, Dennis was happy because there was no pressure on him. He benefitted directly from my actions; actions that would cause him to look at me in a different way in the future.

Think about it: The amount of time it took for me to meet John, learn a few key things about him by asking him direct, qualifying questions, then offering to introduce him to a key, valuable person he needed to meet took about five minutes out of my life. I listened. I prompted John to do the talking and it paid off for him.

This felt right to me. I was smiling inside. My shoulders were back. My posture was perfect and my confidence boosted; this felt really good. Waving off friends, I arrived back at my spot near the entrance with new enthusiasm. I scanned for new faces, not expecting to find any but hoping I would.

Mary Jean & Sara

To the right of the entrance was another new face. The first thing I noticed about Mary Jean was that she dressed very corporately in a business suit and heels. Positioned out of everyone's way, my first impression was that she was kind and considerate. People who walked by smiled at her but no one stopped to introduce themselves. I walked over. My enthusiasm for acknowledging her being there was met with her own enthusiasm for my spotting her and making the effort to meet her. Our conversation soon spilled over into learning about her 15-year old daughter, Paula, who wanted to be a dancer. Mary Jean told me she was a single mom and new to the area, and was looking forward to meeting people and getting to know everyone. She was a corporate events coordinator and shared with me that she had enjoyed a good business in Atlanta before moving west.

When I asked her to describe who would be 'home run' person for her to meet that morning, she said she wanted to learn about available meeting rooms and convention halls; someone in the hotel business would be perfect. As it happened, the General Manager of the local hotel and a solid member of our chamber, Sara Johnson, had told me months ago that she was going back to the early morning shift, which meant she wouldn't be attending the breakfasts.

I looked at Mary Jean, sorry to disappoint her. "You know...Mary Jean, Sara Johnson is the GM of the local hotel. It has great meeting rooms there. I've held some meetings there, myself. Unfortunately, Sara isn't here this morning because...."

Just then, Sara Johnson walked up to us.

"Dave Ribble! How are you my friend?" With a bit of a shocked look on my face, I said hello.

"Sara Johnson! What are you doing here? Didn't you tell me you had the early schedule now with Daniel and Michelle back in school?"

"Well, that's true. The kids are back in school. But I'm here this morning because the hubby and I are driving over to Vegas in a few hours for a convention this weekend. Grandma is staying at the house to be there for the kids. We decided to drop by on the way and see you all before we take off."

I then introduced Mary Jean to Sara and shared how the timing couldn't have been better. As I told Mary Jean about Sara, I could tell that Sara appreciated my kind words. She wasn't used to hearing that kind of well-deserved praise and I didn't hold back in my remarks. Sara ran a great hotel and was very good at her job.

Knowing that Sara's daughter was also into dance, I mentioned that Mary Jean's daughter Paula wanted to be a dancer, too, which gave the ladies additional things to talk about. It wasn't long before they headed across the room for coffee together and I headed back to my post to look for people I could help.

In the course of less than 30 minutes, I was able to connect five new people to five people I already knew. Five! Why five fresh faces decided to all show up that particular morning still puzzles me. After three months of seeing no new faces, was it just coincidence or had there been new people to talk to all along? Was I simply seeing with new eyes and hearing with new ears?

This particular morning I had helped expedite the process of getting to know people and people getting to know each other.

In all, ten people positively affected by my actions in less than 30 minutes would have been pretty darn cool on its own, but as I look back on it now, there is no way to calculate how many people those ten people ultimately affected by the actions that were initiated by yours truly. Think about that because there were additional lessons for me to learn.

The Voice Returns

The mixing and mingling time was ending and the formal part of the morning's activities was about to start. Diana Williams, the dynamic CEO of the West Valley Warner Center Chamber, announced it was time to grab our food and take our seats. The buffet line quickly formed and in short order the room settled into a muffled roar as people found their places. I scooted my plate and coffee onto the table assigned to me and got comfortable. I was about to receive another directive.

Diana approached the lectern and welcomed everyone as her assistants grabbed hand-held mics and headed to opposite ends of the room so the 30-second elevator speeches could begin. I was about to enjoy another rousing rendition of my private little game I call "let's see who is good and who needs help with their elevator speech" when that same small voice clearly directed me once more:

"Take Notes. Read the room."

I didn't question it. I was excited to see what else I would learn. I moved my plate over, opened my notepad and looked for lessons.

Comedian Jerry Seinfeld once observed that the average person's fear of public speaking is ranked higher than death, which means that if that person had to attend a funeral, he would rather be in the casket than delivering the eulogy.

Have you noticed that people with loud voices like to use them?

Some will conveniently tell you they don't need a microphone because they have convinced themselves their booming voice can be heard for miles, which happens to also be *an easily mistaken assumption.* Most every room has what we call dead zones, which means there are some places in most meeting rooms, especially in older facilities, where it is difficult for some people in the audience to hear what is being said unless the voice is amplified. If you are speaking and the key person you were trying to influence cannot hear who you are or what you do, is that really worth stroking your ego by not using the microphone? The fact is, anyone who is seated where they cannot clearly hear you loud and strong will mentally check out and talk to their neighbor or grab their phones to check for messages while they wait their turn.

It is equally amazing how some folks believe that the time restriction placed on everyone applies to *everyone else but them*. When Diana opened the morning's agenda, she politely but firmly asked for everyone to keep their remarks to 30 seconds or less, not 40 or 50. When people take advantage and go over that allotted time limit, it ticks off those who have already gone (the ones who endeavored to keep their remarks brief) and it also puts undue pressure on the ones still waiting their turn that now have to speed things up.

When you 'cheat' the time restriction, what kind of message do you send out to everyone else in the room? Does it mean you are selfish? Are you untrustworthy, even in a simple request like Diana's? Will you also be untrustworthy in your business dealings? Will you be someone to watch out for? Believe it or not, these are the things that will go through the minds of some in the audience. It's unprofessional. By contrast, however, honoring the wishes of the Host shows respect for the others who are there, regardless.

That particular morning of introductions started out pretty tame. The first few people said their remarks relatively quickly and succinctly. Handing the microphone off to the next person around the table was smooth, although for the life of me, I am still amazed that in preparing for one's turn to speak, people seem to forget to scoot their chair back ahead of time, making that mechanical requirement unnecessarily awkward. Moreover, it was interesting that by the time we reached the fourth table, people were already starting to stretch their 30 seconds into 60.

I recorded this note:

Always be respectful of the circumstances and the limitations of the room. If they ask for 30-second intros, give them 25 and be really good.

And never arrogantly put yourself above all others by going over the time limit. People are watching. Be humble. There will be plenty of time later to explain what it is you do to the right audience.

Having clever things to say in their 30-second allotment is the goal of some. Yes, there will be those who gain a laugh or two and some will win the accolades of others in the audience who thought they were funny or cute. I also noted that I would probably not buy a car or seek out a dentist based on a clever elevator speech. I doubt you would, either.

We finally finished the brief introductions. The room buzzed with opinions about who did well and those who fell short, but I was looking at the whole process with new eyes and ears. I felt for the first time those clever elevator speeches are just that: Clever. These speeches are not meaningful when it comes to determining whether someone gets my business. It might get my attention, but due diligence is still required, regardless.

The personal introductions ended and Diana was back on the stand to introduce someone we will call Bill Flaherty, the featured speaker that morning. Already in place was a big portable screen and projector. The owner of a garage door company he inherited from his father years ago and a solid member of the chamber, Bill seemed understandably excited about his opportunity to speak, especially after paying $150 for the privilege and waiting months for his turn. When there are only so many opportunities during a year's time to be one of the featured speakers, a certain amount of pressure comes with the privilege.

By the time his presentation was underway Bill was already sweating bullets. His slides were very hard to see due to the ambient light coming through side windows. Bill could have alleviated that problem by closing the curtains or choosing a different angle. As a result of poor positioning, most of his slides had little contrast, which made it even harder to stay interested in what he was talking about. The pictures told a thousand stories and were great examples of what Bill does so well, but we couldn't see them, at least from my table's angle. Bill knew his information, but it quickly became evident he was over-prepared and was trying to squeeze 20 minutes of power point slides into 10.

Lessons and More Lessons... Circling Back to *Me*

While Bill struggled, I looked around and continued to take notes. A couple of people texted under the table or checked their email. Others were whispering to the person next to them. The most blatant of the disengaged actually jumped up to get coffee or to go to the bathroom, which caused Bill at one point to lose his train of thought altogether. I thought about what I was observing and my gut feeling was that I was being reminded of my own behavior in times' past. I didn't like it.

Bill, realizing his time was up, hurried the last few slides and finally finished. Diana was ever cordial and we all applauded as Bill wiped his brow before returning to his seat. She then went right to welcoming anyone who had not yet placed their business card in the fishbowl for the door prizes and many seemed re-energized by the chance to spring from their seat and drop their business cards in the bowl before heading for the restroom.

Once the last bottle of wine, gift certificate and bouquet of flowers was awarded, Diana said there was still a few minutes left and invited the room to offer up any testimonials. This was a time-honored tradition if there was time left on the clock. One person shared that she had received great treatment from the local dentist, who half-stood at his table long enough to wave back to her from across the room. Another person said he loved his new car he purchased from a chamber member. A third person told us about the great food he and his family enjoyed at a new restaurant.

The Massive Multiplying Effect

With no one else raising their hand to give a testimonial to another chamber member, many wondered if Diana might dismiss us before 9 am but Diana prided herself in never doing that. Instead, she asked the room again if anyone had a special event coming up or anything else they wanted to share.

All of a sudden, a hand shot into the air and Diana's assistant hurriedly handed over one of the microphones. John Oliver, the first guy I helped that morning, stood at his table and scanned the room.

Pointing to me, he smiled and said… "Hi, my name is John Oliver. This is my first time to visit your Chamber and I just have to say that in all the years I have attended these, the way your Dave Ribble came up to me this morning… I mean it was really cool the way he welcomed me and then helped me find Dennis, here, and I just want to say, Dave, you're a class act."

Wow. Like at a tennis match, the whole room of people craned their necks in my direction at the same time, looking for my reaction. Some near me gave a thumbs-up and I admit I felt a bit of a flush coming to my face. I humbly nodded in John's direction and noticed Diana was grinning at me as well. Saying nice things about other people has always been fun and easy for me to do, but I forgot how great it felt to receive such praise from others.

As John sat down, Dennis, sitting right next to John, reached for the microphone and stood.

"I need to second that, Dave Ribble. You're right - John's a great guy and we're heading to my office right after this. Thanks, man. I appreciate you."

Heads turned toward me again. After nodding to Dennis, I kept my eyes on my notepad. Two nice compliments in a row was something I didn't want to spoil in any way; it was too sweet a moment to describe. Had that been the end of it, I was already feeling very good about what had taken place that morning.

But it wasn't over. Suddenly, Mary Jean popped up, the Event Coordinator, to also thank me and acknowledge me. She went on about her new friend Sara and how they were looking forward to a meeting the following week to talk about Sara's hotel and conference center.

"I too came here this morning for the first time. I didn't know anyone. Dave, let me thank you for helping me so much and for welcoming me the way you did. This seems to be a really cool group and I look forward to getting to know all of you."

And we still weren't finished. Another and another I had helped that morning popped up to say something good on my behalf. In fact, of the ten people I had positively affected, *nine of them* stood to thank me before Diana finally said we were out of time.

Perhaps at this juncture you are thinking, *'Wow, Dave, good for you, but how does this story relate to **me**?'*

That's an excellent question. I am glad you asked because I want you to think about how that morning might have otherwise gone had this all not happened the way it did.

Q & A's From The Observation Deck

1. Would all of those folks have found each other eventually?

    a. Hard to say. Perhaps it would have taken much longer, given the fact that the Chamber only meets once a month. You also have to consider that it may have been very difficult for the conversations to get that deep that quickly had I not been there to push past the typical non-relevant, "Hi, How Are You?" surface connecting, which is sometimes all that gets said when people meet for the first time.

2. Without my endorsement and help, would they have trusted each other as quickly?

    a. Maybe. Maybe not. A genuine third-party endorsement is as good as it gets to break the ice and launch into conversations. My third-party endorsement brought them together smoothly and quickly. It expedited things. It cut through the initial chit-chat and directed them right to the point, which enabled me to find the right person to introduce faster than it would have taken them on their own. It also gave me a way to say nice things about them that they would not otherwise say about themselves.

3. Was it risky for me to be the one to introduce someone I had only just met to someone I knew in the room?

    a. Some would argue that it could have had a negative effect on my reputation if the person I just met turned out to be of questionable integrity. My argument back to that is that if the people were already there to meet each other anyway, all I did was help expedite the meeting. Whatever happens after that is out of my control. It is important to remember to always speak only the truth of what you have been told by that person when introducing them. If I do not embellish or speak half-truths, I am not going to have anything to regret later. This does, however, leave me the opportunity to put initial faith into another human being and that is a good thing. If the person I just met turns out to not be of integrity, I also helped expedite that discovery, too.

These are profound lessons for all of us. I positively affected not just ten people that morning, but rather *ten times that number* when you consider there were 100 in attendance that morning that witnessed this and heard those remarks.

Did any of the new people that morning ask me about my business? Not one. Is that ok with me? Absolutely. Enhancing my reputation, long-term, became far more valuable. I somehow knew it would be all right. I knew some of them would circle back to me at some point, to either refer me to others or become customers themselves and, as it happened, they did. Some just became good friends and began their same journey to help others.

As I thought about it, the lessons of the morning continued to flood my head as I flipped open my notebook and wrote:

Encourage them to go first when you meet them. You never know whom you are talking to or their circumstances and you won't know until you engage in a conversation with them what they are all about. Approach everyone with consistent consideration. Remember, it's never about you. It's always about *them*.

While it was gratifying and humbling to have public praise heaped upon me that morning, it was the bigger lessons I learned in those couple of hours about creating relationships that would forever change how I connect and network with others.

I called Gaye before heading back, euphoric about what had just taken place that morning. I was laughing out loud because even with all the good that had happened, I was still coming home without new clients and it didn't seem to me to be a big deal anymore. She agreed.

"I told you something good would happen!"

"But, Gaye, I'm coming home again without new business! What about that?"

"It's ok. We just picked up three new orders this morning! We'll be fine. I am proud of you and what you learned this morning."

She paused and then laughed. "You should write a book about it!"

~~~~~~~

I did, these many years later, after further investigation, more interviews and a lot of practice in figuring out what has been missing when we network with others. When you adopt and embrace *The Way of The Conscientious Connector*, no matter what your occupation, you start going deeper with every conversation. You become the observer, the treasure hunter and the example for others to follow.

Spreading My Influence Through Others

I helped five new people that morning. The five new people I helped will always put in a kind word on my behalf unless I give them a reason not to. Those benefits are priceless. There is no way to know how far their good opinion of me will travel so I must always be worthy.

Of the five people I already knew that morning, my image improved in their eyes, too. I have no way of really knowing what their complete opinion of me was before that morning, but I suspect it was weary given that before that morning, I had a surface connector approach to things. I do know that I received 'good press' from everyone who was there that morning. Everyone.

As for the other 90 people who heard the positive remarks made on my behalf, some may have upgraded their opinion of me. Others who barely knew me at all may have formed a very good first impression of me. You never know who is observing you or who might be listening to you and who might already be forming a fair or unfair opinion of you. Protecting yourself by being a consummate professional in every way is always worth the effort. It will *never* fail you.

Seven Personality Types You Might Meet While Networking

After years attending networking events and thereby meeting perhaps thousands of people over the years, then subsequently developing the systematic approach that is *The Way of The Conscientious Connector*, I realized there are certain personality types that can almost predictably show up at networking opportunities, and I know this because I am almost certain that I have mimicked most of them at one time or another, myself.

Each one I identified has helped me develop a counter approach to them that I could use to get past the initial façade they might have and to the real person underneath those layers, because, as you will hear me say often, everyone matters.

In no particular order or preference, here are a few that you might also identify with, presented only for the purpose of our discovering how to help these folks get better and build true relationships that can benefit many.

• **The Aggressor** is the person who likes to quickly establish his/her importance to the group. Usually accompanied by a ready smile and a tight fisted handshake, the aggressor will be glad to tell you how good they are at what they do and leave little time to ask you anything about yourself. The Aggressor tends to look over you or around you, always seeking the next person they do not recognize. Their objective is to ensure you never forget them. Typically, the Aggressor will meet you three to four times before they start to remember who you are or what you do. **Whether they ever help you with a contact or referral is anybody's guess. Just be open, kind and do not dismiss them before you give them a chance. Sometimes, they don't even know they are behaving in this manner, so give them the benefit of the doubt and decide later what you want to do.**

• **The Wall Hugger** would rather not be there, but knows it is important, so they are already watching the clock and staying close to an outside wall when they arrive to ensure no one is coming up from behind. The Wall Hugger is ok with this because this way they can see the whole room at a glance, giving them time to avoid people easily. **They're comfortable if there is an exit door nearby, so stand there with them as you talk. Be a friend. Help them be comfortable. It's ok.**

• **The Categorizer** has an innate need to figure out what professional category to put you in so that they can keep moving through the crowd, searching for people to fit and fill their unclaimed categories. **If your category of profession is already taken in the Categorizer's database, you will likely be summarily dismissed, but courteously. It's likely your business card won't see the** light of day to this contact after the event. **If your category is not already taken, they will want your card because it gives them a sense of accomplishment. It may be uncomfortable to you, but remember that they might know people you want to meet and vice versa. Let whatever might develop happen at it's own pace and don't take offense.**

• **The Card Collector** isn't nearly as interested in you or what you do as they are in making sure they collect everyone's business card. Their measure of success of the event, in fact, is based on whether or not they were able to get everyone's card before the official part of the event starts and everyone has to sit down. **They're not likely to stop and tell you much about themselves because that slows down their mission to collect all the cards they can. Just call them later and see what happens when they are not on their 'mission'.**

• **The Polite One** sits on the fence for as long as possible. As soon as you mention what you do, you will be categorized but you will also be subject to a mental scan of whether they, like the categorizer, already have someone who does what you do. The Polite One will not tell you what they know. Rather, they will not want to risk offending you by mentioning they already have someone they know and like that does what you do. They will keep that to themselves in case anything ever happens to the relationship they already have established. **Like the others, when you offer to be of service to them without regard to your own benefit, they won't know what to do with you because no one has ever done that for them. Do it anyway.**

• **The Socialite** is that person who figured out that rather than look for opportunities to be a *Conscientious Connector* by trying to help people find each other, they prefer to not talk to anyone they don't know. They will arrive with two or three door prizes for the free drawing and simply stand with their closest friend and talk about other things until it is time to grab a plate and find their table. They take great pride in hearing their business announced over the speaker when it is time for the raffle. That is their objective each time and little else. Very little thought or emphasis is placed on whether they know people others should be introduced to. At testimonial time, the Socialite will typically promote his friend's business while holding the spotlight on himself for as long as possible because he believes that this is what is known as Brand Extension. **The approach to a Socialite might take some research, but there is a good possibility that if you help that person, they won't forget you did that and they will appreciate it and return the favor. It may take some time to receive a connection on their behalf, but they might surprise you with assistance because you surprised them with assistance, first.**

• **The Lyricist** is someone who waits for the 30-second introductions so they can recite a clever poem or sing a song about their business. They are usually well rehearsed and have won the "most clever elevator pitch" award many times. **At the event it will be difficult to have any conversation of meaning with this person, because they are more comfortable performing for the group than talking seriously with you about themselves. Try to get this person to go for coffee away from the audience or call them and see where it goes. Always be complimentary and respectful.**

Notice that with all the categories I made up, I see value in every one of those people. They are who they are and they have value, they matter and they are just like you and me, except they behave in predictable ways because that is all they have ever known. They have adopted their own personality when it comes to networking. It is how they approach everything, especially networking.

Until you have given yourself the chance to get to know more about them, can you honestly afford to dismiss them?

Take a look at your current database of the best connections you have right now. By what criteria would you rank them? By what they have done for you over the years or by what you have done for them? Very likely, your best connections developed because you showed just as much concern for their success as for your own, whether there was anything in it for you or not.

Simon T. Bailey, international speaker and author of *Release Your Brilliance* (Harper Collins, 2008, p.116) says it this way: "What is a meaningful relationship? I believe, first and foremost, it is one in which both people are authentic. Meaningful relationships strengthen your emotional alignment by inviting you to remove your mask and let down your façade that prevents you from being authentic."

The best relationships take time, effort and dedication and will always be worth the extra effort you put forth. Always.

HOMEWORK

1. Get into the habit of taking a small notebook or spiral notepad with you everywhere you go, and yes, I do mean everywhere. To work, to a networking event, to the dentist, because you are going to start writing down what you learn about people that can be then transferred to your contact data information. Have your notepad with you all the time for ideas, too, or to take notes on what a speaker talked about. It doesn't matter where you are as much as it matters that you assume the role of the 'Observer.'

2. Try leaving your business cards in your pocket, as I did, and go up to someone and start a conversation by saying "Hi, I'm (your name) and I would love to know more about you, what you do and how I might help you." Watch their reaction to this, because very few of us will do this; people are not used to it, yet.

    a. Record in your journal what their reaction to this approach is. How did they respond? In a positive way? Are they taken aback by this unusual approach? Do they smile from ear to ear? Do they act like this is something they've never experienced before? Are they curious?

    b. Are they taken aback by your boldness in stating that you want to help them? How does that feel to you? Are you feeling awkward or proud of yourself? Are you instinctively looking for places to switch the conversation back to you or are you resisting that temptation and just going with the flow?

3. Next, test some things out to further hone your observer skills. Keep your eyes peeled for the Wall Hugger, Socialite, Card Collector and the rest. You never know where or when they might show up and you are now much better prepared to talk to them comfortably.

STEP ONE/CHAPTER 2

THE MISSED OPPORTUNITIES OF SURFACE CONNECTORS EVERYWHERE

Replace old habits with The Way of The Conscientious Connector

LA's Largest Mixer is what it is called and it is just that. Over 20 local Chambers of Commerce combines their resources and invite everyone to attend this one-day event. Exhibitors spend anywhere from $650 to $2500 for their opportunity to be a part of this four or five-hour extravaganza and every attendee pays $20 for the admission.

Vendors, representing everything from insurance to spas, real estate to water systems and restaurants to garage doors absorb most of the 54,000 square foot expo hall, laced with ladies selling jewelry, Internet companies selling phone service and home care nurses handing out brochures. Full no-host bars anchor both ends of the long rectangular main room and servers carefully weave their way through the crowd offering miniature chicken kabobs, coconut shrimp and pizza slices.

No matter where you turn, someone is asking you for your business card or offering to exchange it for a chance to see what you win at their spinning wheel. Concussive music bounces off the walls as everyone tries to shout over the cacophony. Most conversations are short and sweet, like the answer to "how are you?"

The basic principle behind this networking event, like all of them, is the same: *Create an atmosphere where people can meet, and turn that opportunity into business and referrals. What you do with your time while in attendance is entirely up to you.*

The people who put on the Mixer do it right. They book the beautiful Shrine Auditorium Expo Hall, collect fees from each vendor, assign spaces, hire the band, provide security, pay the rent, buy in the license to serve alcohol, place the ads and campaign to get 3,000 people to show up so they can fulfill the promise they make to everyone to provide a huge crowd. As I like to say, they provide the arena.

The next question I have for you is this: If you are attending such an event, what will you do with this opportunity?

- Will you attend just to be seen?
- Will you go there with a mission to collect all the business cards you possibly can in the allotted time so you can follow up the next day?
- Will your expectations include having substantive conversations with just a few?
- Will you have any plan at all?

Let's assume you believe the best thing you can do is to collect all the business cards you possibly can before they close down the event. After all, if you cannot have meaningful, substantive conversations with people you are meeting for the first time, perhaps your next best bet is to collect every business card you possibly can.

There are 3,000 people in attendance, so if you plan on collecting all of them you will need to collect about 750 per hour. Since that is not a very logical or practical approach, how many cards *will* you collect? Of those collected, how many people will you connect with the next day or even next week? And, since you are going to the event to find people to buy what you're selling, how many of those will you actually convert into customers?

Some faithful defenders of this connection method will argue, *"Dave, all I want to do is go there to be seen! I'll find people and follow up with them the next day! Isn't it true that 90% of success is 'just showing up'?"*

The Sad Truth...

It's what I see at networking events all the time. I call it *The Typical 3 C's Mindset* and it is the default that most people go to in such an environment.

1. **Collect** - Collect as many business cards as humanly possible because you figure that the higher number of cards you have, the better your percentage of actually finding a few customers out of the bunch before you dismiss the rest. No real thought goes into collecting information or making notes as you go, even though ten cards with notes that follow a real conversation will always be incredibly valuable tomorrow morning.

2. **Connect -** You tell yourself that tomorrow morning, back at your office, you will pull out the cards from this event and begin the process of talking with everyone for the purpose of setting up lunches, breakfasts and conversations over the phone that will pave the way to new customers. If you do not have any other work to do and you have collected 25 or 30 cards, perhaps you will have time to make the initial calls and leave messages. But you didn't have meaningful, intelligent conversations with any of them and have few if any notes associated with the information on the cards, so you are going to be cold calling. Chances are, these connections won't remember you. Vendors and exhibitors who paid good money to be there talked to hundreds of people. You stopped by for five seconds to pick up their business card before moving on. Do you really expect them to remember you?

3. **Convert -** The third in the trilogy is that you are hoping some of those contacts you connected with will become clients. You are now into the ABC's of selling - *Always Be Closing.* Whether there is any substantive value to this new relationship remains questionable because last night's run-through to pick up their business card leaves a lot on the table.

Collect-A-Card surface networking is what most people do:

Collect the business cards of everyone you can, try to *connect* with them so that you can *convert* them to becoming customers. The ultimate goal of the Three C's is only one thing: converting them to customers. Of those who are not interested in becoming customers, it makes logical sense for you to not spend any time on them. Everything, therefore, is focused on making the sale because that's how it has always been done.

This approach is numbers-driven, so your best bet is to collect cards from as many as you can. I call it *hurry up networking,* much like a 'hurry up' offense in football when there are no timeouts left and the clock is ticking. Networkers arrive at an event hell-bent on collecting those cards, leaving little or no time to engage in any meaningful conversation. It is essentially surface conversations by surface connectors.

Should you stand and talk to someone at the expense of losing connections with all those other people, the ones you will not collect business cards from? Don't be surprised if you hear yourself saying, *"No, it's best to grab the cards, keep moving and we'll get to the follow up tomorrow"* as you go off into the feeding frenzy. *"I'll just put the cards in my special drawer until tomorrow."*

The Business Card Graveyard

Do you suppose those folks you are talking to have that 'special drawer' back at their office, too? Of course they do. It's the *business card graveyard.* This is where the cards that you told yourself you would follow up on are discarded when you get busy with other things.

(Press your ear close enough and you may even hear the cards calling you to let them out so they can be reviewed and appreciated.) Trust me: We all have a Business Card Graveyard.

If all we are going to do at networking events is collect business cards we tell ourselves we will follow up on in the morning, it will save all of us a ton of time and money if we simply agreed to package up 3,000 business cards and drop them off at the front door. Organize them and collate them with everyone else's. Then, stop back by a couple of days later and pick up your stack of cards from everyone else.

There's A Better Way...

Believe me, collecting data about someone at a networking event isn't easy for some in the beginning but I assure you it will get easier. Of course, I'm talking about information that goes well beyond just a phone number and email, by the way.

As a *Conscientious Connector*, you will continue to improve your skills in knowing what to ask and how to ask it. You will start to figure out your own brand of 'shorthand' in order to capture key points to explore for follow-up. It sure makes life interesting, fun and productive to pull those personal notes to study before making that follow-up phone call. Quite often you will have information to share with them about other connections you can make on their behalf. That's an attention-grabbing follow-up.

Taking notes on someone you meet not only provides you this advantage, it also demonstrates to the other person that you respect them, find them interesting and worthy of your time and attention. Everyone likes to be acknowledged. It is a much better approach than just grabbing his or her card on your way to another connection. In addition, you will develop better skills as you learn to ask questions that will benefit *them*, not just yourself. I have yet to find anyone I've talked to who didn't enjoy telling me about his or her needs. They also love to share with me whom they wish to connect with and oftentimes I can help with a suggestion there, too.

Anytime you find business connections or referral partners,

make sure to have an information-rich conversation with them, either then or as a follow-up. The more you know about the other person, the higher the propensity for creating a successful relationship. And, the better notes you take at the outset, the less work it takes to recall specifics later that can be rewarding for everyone involved.

The other day I was at an event and ran into someone I hadn't seen in several years. He didn't have a business card on him so I pulled up his old information on my phone to update the contact card. I showed him my notes, which told me that I originally met him at a Christmas Party on December 24, 2012 and I was able to tell him what we talked about. He was blown away that I had saved that much detail from our initial conversation and certainly looked at me in a different light because it told him that he mattered to me and that I valued his friendship.

Conscientiously Connecting goes beyond just showing up at an event and just collecting business cards. As my mentor and friend Mel Kaufmann used to say, *"The word networking includes the word 'work' in it for a reason."* I will add that once you become a *Conscientious Connector*, this won't seem like work. It will become a treasure hunt.

Changing Our Limiting Beliefs

Limiting beliefs are views about something we have come to accept as truth, whether right or wrong. When we develop a limiting belief about something or someone, we lock ourselves out to any other possibility. This can be crippling.

There are three limiting beliefs we will discuss in depth from many directions in this book:

Limiting Belief # 1- Networking is limited to the practice of capturing business cards and following up.

Limiting Belief # 2 - Networking is limited to the practice of identifying our target market and only spending time with those we have identified as potential clients.

Limiting Belief # 3 - Those who will never buy anything from us have no value to us or we, to them. Therefore, we should not spend any time or energy on them.

Looking for that Quick & Easy

Ever wonder how well things go for people who go to networking events looking for an immediate customer? What are their results after the networking event? I was curious, too.

According to The National Sales Executive Association, less than 2% of sales are made in the 1st contact with a prospect, less than 3% on the 2nd contact and less than 5% on the 3rd contact. That's not good news for sales people. In fact, they tell us the propensity to score sales doesn't go up much until there have been 6 or 7 'touches' with the prospective customer.

The same stats apply for non-sales people. We're all looking for people we can eventually know, like and trust and that doesn't happen instantaneously.

Their findings also tell us that 48%, almost half of sales people, never follow up with a prospect, anyway. Do you suppose it's because they can't remember the conversation or didn't have one in the first place while they were out 'networking'?

Further, do you suppose it's possible that while they were networking *they walked right by* valuable connections that could have developed into amazing, sustainable referrals over time? Will we ever know?

Who else was in the room at the last networking event you attended? Are there people you dismissed because you figured they would never be a good connection? What criteria did you use to make that decision? How many people will you never meet and get to know because you didn't recognize their potential? I promise you, most people miss golden opportunities every day and never know it.

Frankly, if you attend any networking event and you don't have a plan in place for what you want to accomplish, you shouldn't be disappointed with your results, or lack thereof.

If you believe that it's possible to gain useful information from every networking event you attend in the future, and, you are willing to let me dissect all of this with you to show you a better way, let's get started.

It's Time To Re-Evaluate Connecting

Embrace and adopt what this book teaches and your world will change forever. I am going to take the whole networking engine apart, see what's missing, make some adjustments to your game plan and show you how to turbo charge your ability to make right, conscientious and sustainable connections that will serve you for life. It won't be speed-dial networking though, so get past that idea.

Instead, you are about to see how much you can accomplish in the world of connecting with people on a mutually beneficial level and win. You are going to see a bigger picture of how you can walk into any networking event and be recognized as a 'connector.' You'll understand how others will begin to regard you as a professionals' professional, whether you are in sales, accounting or any of hundreds of other occupations.

We'll also explore the many places you can network, along with the pros and cons of each. We'll talk about the lessons I learned along the way and the lessons I want to pass along to you. In turn, you will want to pass these lessons along to others.

This Is For *YOU*, Not Somebody Else.

This goes far beyond just your casual conversations with others. In fact, it's just as much about your image, your reputation and your stature amongst your peers and the regard others will develop for you.

And, it works for everyone. No matter what you do for a living, you will benefit from this information. Stay with me. If you are in sales, that's great. So am I. I have also worked in marketing, promotion and management at different stages of my career, which is to say I have experienced many different roles and the inherent responsibilities of each. I've also cleaned toilets, painted houses, sold shoes, driven a tractor, baled hay and had my heart broken, just like you.

I have experienced rejection from clients who downsized or merged with others, only to learn that our services were no longer required. I've been fired by individuals who were uncomfortable with my ability to better connect with people at every level in a company when they could not. I've attended and paid for expensive real estate school education, sales training courses and leadership classes. I've won contracts and opportunities when it seemed impossible. I've also experienced what it's like to have the business still go to some other company because of politics and nepotism. I know what it feels like to invest thousands of dollars into a project that never comes to fruition. I know first-hand what being lied to straight up can do to one's ego.

I didn't finish Chapman University (awesome school) until I was 30, with two of my three children already present and accounted for. I've experienced bankruptcy. At one point I had three jobs and one of those involved getting up at three in the morning to deliver newspapers and return in time to go to my full-time job before I worked weekends at a department store. I've experienced being divorced and then getting married to someone new and all that it entails, especially when three beautiful children are involved.

I've screwed up and I've triumphed. I've enjoyed a well-earned reputation for being creative and for walking my talk. Over the years I've interviewed many other professionals at every level of sophistication, largely due to my never-ending fascination with the human spirit. I've been in several multi-level marketing businesses, so I know what that is about. I've delivered talks and training in front of many networking groups and have been a member of three. I've served on the Board of Directors for two Chambers of Commerce. I've taught networking to returning Disabled Veterans through a program through Syracuse University.

You may be a student or work in what you consider a non-descript department. You may be a teacher or drive a truck or you may be CEO of the world's greatest logistics company. There is something here for all of you, I promise.

All my years of highs and lows have greatly contributed to the information that I am pouring out in this book and training. It is pure and yet imperfect because everything and everyone is pure and imperfect. In other words, I am you. I understand some of the things you deal with every day because I have a stack of similar experiences to draw upon. You and I will take these basics that I've learned and together, you and I will come to understand how to put *your unique style and personality* into this so that you *own* it.

For me, it's what I call *The Ribble Effect*, which is a cute and clever phrase that lends itself well to my last name. If your name is Michelle, then yours might be called *The Michelle Effect*. If you prefer using your last name and your last name happens to be Harrington or Johnson or Cramer... well, you get the idea. Whatever you want to call your 'Effect,' it will be according to your own unique personality as well as proclivities.

I am not interested in you becoming me. I am, however, most interested in helping you become the best communicator, connector, networker and unique you that you can be.

Of all the lessons I continue to receive on a daily basis, one constant is about the human spirit; *how much we are all alike and how much more we can all accomplish when we get on the same page.*

By the time you finish this book, adopt and embrace what I have learned and then adopt it for how you think and act every day, you will start to see your reputation and your database of great connections rapidly expand. I am excited for the opportunity to facilitate this phenomenon and assist you in improving your life in the same way these principles continue to improve mine.

HOMEWORK

1. The next time you attend a networking event, go with the express purpose of interviewing others without revealing your personal information. Hold off talking about yourself for as long as possible. Many you interview will continue to talk for as long as you will show interest. We'll talk about asking questions throughout the book, but, for now, just be the observer. Are they enjoying talking about themselves? Are they embarrassed that you continue to prompt them? There's a lot going on we will discuss.

2. Journal your observations. Think about how you felt as you were doing this exercise and what you learned. Is there a better balance to all this networking stuff that you can engineer in a better way? Going through this exercise will tell you a lot about what is really going on at most networking opportunities and you have the power to make this a very rewarding experience.

STEP ONE / CHAPTER THREE

STOP DEMANDING RECIPROCATION

You don't have to worry about that anymore.

One of the very first things we must discuss is whether we should obligate each other in the process. Here's the question: Once you have successfully connected with someone and can offer them your support, your help, your products and services as well as a referral, should you obligate that person to give back to you in equal measure or better? Is that realistic?

The fact is that it rarely works out that way. If you sell expensive cars and the person you give a referral to cannot provide you a good candidate who is looking to buy an expensive car, will you think that your referral to them was wasted time and energy? Will you be disappointed?

There is a certain prevailing attitude out there that says that if I do something for you, you will need to do something for me in return or you are not playing by the rules. Here's an example:

Sam: "Hey Dave, I ran across someone the other day who said she was looking for help with her promotional marketing and I remembered you do that sort of thing."

Me: "Thank you. Yes. We have been in that line of work for over 30 years now and we love helping our clients capture additional market share."

Sam: "Well, I told her that I would tell you about my conversation with her the next time I saw you."

Me: "Thanks again."

Sam: "But... before I give you her contact information, what do you have for *me*?

To some, the above conversation sounds perfectly reasonable. For others it is a bit off-putting because there is an implied, if not downright explicit condition placed on whether Sam will release his referral to me.

Should Sam offer this conditional demand before passing along a referral that has all the earmarks of someone who could use my help?

Adam Grant's bestselling book *Give and Take* (Penguin Publishing 2013) states there are three distinct types of people: Takers, Matchers and Givers. I highly recommend you read his great study because you will see, immediately, how those roles come into play on a daily basis. Takers, he says, will simply take everything you offer them, from referrals to money to the keys to your house if you offer, and then dismiss you when they think there is nothing left they can take from you. Matchers will be Givers up to that point where they no longer feel you are reciprocating to them what they have done for you, or better, and at that point, Matchers will become Takers. Givers, on the other hand, simply give and move on. They don't worry so much about reciprocation; they just do it and keep going. According to Adam Grant, Givers, as you might expect, are more successful.

Reciprocity refers to paying back, returning the favor, doing something for someone because they did something for you. Dr. Robert Cialdini, author of *Influence-The Psychology of Persuasion* (William Morrow & Co) points up that it is our nature to hate being indebted to others.

James Wedmore, the online video expert (JamesWedmore.com) and fellow graduate of Chapman University sees this as why free online content is welcomed by most only after giving up their contact information in trade. It is a principle that works well for this.

Offline, however, in one-to-one personal communication, it's easy for me to tell you that if someone gives you a referral, you should bust your backside to return the favor as soon as possible. That is a good idea and you should do that if and when you can. *But do that when you can provide them a truly good referral they can use*, rather than just to fill a quota by offering up an unqualified referral.

Unfortunately, I see a lot of folks living and dying by the creed that if they do something for you, the clock is ticking for you to come up with a gesture that is equal to or, preferably, better. Sadly, I see many times people place a higher emphasis on your returning the favor quickly rather than whether the favor you return is a qualified and valuable referral for them. Some even expect a referral fee.

Perhaps you are a member of a private networking group. Most groups rely on its members to contribute in monetary terms, attendance, support and referrals to other members. The Rotary organization depends on its members to show up and help with the club's choice of charity work. The work won't be accomplished unless the membership steps up to do the work. The same is true for the great work of the Lions Clubs of America and the other wonderfully dedicated organizations. Every one of them is only as good as the commitment by the members. Without that, there's no organization.

The same is true of private groups who have formed for the purpose of networking. Members join and take an implied oath that everyone in the group will help each other find business, referrals and the like. Most, if not all of them, are organizations based on the law of reciprocity, which means members are expected to help bring business to the other members. Generally speaking, the methodology is explained to a new member this way:

Turn in your leads each week and the rest of the group will do the same and everyone will eventually end up with referrals! And, if you haven't turned in enough referrals after a certain period of time, we will need to replace you with someone who will, because referrals are what drives this networking group.'

I have been a member in good standing of several networking

groups at various times over the years who follow this credo and there are national and international organizations that can certainly boast success with this model. Everyone needs referrals so there are many organizations that have been developed to help its membership speed up the process of finding business. Many who join become lifelong members, while some groups have members who join and leave on a yearly basis because they believe they improve their chances of success if they continually move to new groups.

Whatever networking group(s) you decide to join, I want you to be fully aware of the fact that a group dedicated to networking will rely on each other to bring them referrals. It is also fair to say that members of these groups, just like the people who attend other networking events looking for business, will expect you to send them prospects, not just acquaintances, because they're not used to understanding how people who will never be customers of theirs can still be valuable referrals. It is the way things are.

Equally true, to expect reciprocity, whether it is implied by your membership or attached to someone independently providing you a referral, simply means there is an implied expectation. The expectation is that the referral from the first party to the second party now has every right to expect the second party to come up with a referral for the first party, preferably soon. It is also implied that if the second party fails to do so, the first party has every right to feel gipped, abandoned and taken advantage of. That's a lot of unspoken, implied guilt that comes with the first referral. When reciprocation is *expected immediately* from the other party involved, things can get muddy pretty quickly.

An Alternative Way To Look At This

Let me say it this way: If you send me a referral, you have every right to *hope* that I will return the favor and you have every right to hope that I will do so sooner rather than later. Most of us would agree that it's always nice to get referrals. It implies that someone is looking out for us and not just himself or herself. That very principle is at the heart of becoming a *Conscientious Connector*.

But, having said that, it is very possible that my returning the favor of a referral to the person who sent it to me will take longer. It won't be immediate, necessarily. If you send me a referral and I have no one to immediately refer back to you, no one that truly needs what you offer or no one who might be someone who can lead you to *someone else* you would like to talk to, what we are left with is whether there is anything I can do for you at the moment. Sometimes, additional development time is required.

Good referrals require breathing room. If we ignore that fact, all we are doing is shuffling business cards, similar to how some real estate agents will slide their business card under a locked door. It may eventually pay off, but don't hold your breath.

To reciprocate in a thought-filled way may take days or weeks, even months, before the right person comes along, if ever. If I wait that long to reciprocate, will you trust my judgment or will you believe that I have taken something from you but didn't return the favor and, therefore, I am an unreliable source?

You don't have to worry about that stuff anymore.

For referral groups who demand that every member turn in a certain amount of referrals each week or each month or they will be replaced, my hope is that *Conscientious Connectors* will rapidly multiply, so much so, in fact, that most networking groups won't be able to keep up with the number of referrals coming to its members every day and every week. The difference, however, is that these referrals won't necessarily equate to an immediate sale but will be solid, well thought out and valuable for all parties involved. That's what we're missing, folks, and that's what will instrumentally contribute to added success stories across the board when we finally get it together and make this a common occurrence.

As for how you operate in the general terms of day-to-day with others, I suggest you take worrying about reciprocation out of the equation for both yourself and those with whom you associate. Build your database with solid connections and, should you decide to join a networking group, you will have an enormous library of great referrals to meet your quota, assuming those are the rules you have to follow. Ideally, the networking group you decide to join will understand and appreciate the bigger picture and be a little flexible in how you can support them.

In the interim, continue to refer people to others without a concern for reciprocity. Life's too short and, in general, reciprocation is one heck of a lot of work. I have actually found it *easier* to refer people to others when there is no implied reciprocation.

HOMEWORK

You need to take the pressure off yourself about reciprocation so that you can simply concentrate on looking for ways to help others in their quest for success. The best way to do that is to get better and better at collecting information about people as you meet them.

Assuming you have at least a few contacts already in your database, let's start with beefing up the information that you already have and start adding to it.

1. Take a look at your database of contacts and look for how much information you have collected on each person you have added over the years. Leave out no one, for if you took the time to add him or her, there must have been a good reason at the time.

2. Next, see how many you have entered in your database but without any notes related to when and where you met them, what you talked about, and their specialties and professions. This part of your homework will be enlightening.

3. Now, think about how you can categorize those contacts into the type of work they do, their personal profiles and anything else you can 'load in' to your database that will help you find them. For example, you may only have my brother Dan's name and phone number but didn't list other information you learned, such as the fact he is a painting contractor, he was a boy scout, he is a grandfather, he loves gardening and building things from wood.

4. Journal your thoughts about reciprocation as you do this, for you are changing your point of view. By getting into the habit of listing these extras your contact software will allow you to plug in certain key things like this and all of the people who fit the same criteria will come up. Then, when you meet someone who, for example, is looking for a painting contractor, your database will tell you whom you might refer.

As you start to practice this new approach for referring people, take the time to add notes in the history of those profiles involved, not for the purpose of expecting direct reciprocal benefit, but to create a greater number of talking points. You will be amazed at how little time and effort this requires yet how glad you are you recorded the information. I laugh out loud when I go back and see I have added great talking points to my database, rich information I had forgotten, and how that information continues to build. Talking points can include business information but also it can include personal information, and should. Kids names and ages are always fun to include, for if you talk to your contact two years later and you have information about Tommy, age 8, who is now Tommy, age 10, I guarantee Tommy's mom will love that you remembered and will want to tell you all about her son.

Think of all the great conversation starters you will have and all the rich information about someone you can pass along to others as you help promote them. That's the systematic way you will build a tremendous database of the right connections while honoring the very human spirit of the other person, at the same time.

That's *The Way of The Conscientious Connector.*

STEP 2

UN-LIMIT YOUR SUCCESS POTENTIAL
STOP PURSUING JUST YOUR 'TARGET MARKET'

The first section was dedicated to helping you see that the way most of us go about this is what I call surface connecting. We show up, look for specific categories of contacts and summarily dismiss the rest of the crowd because they aren't on our mental list of those we should spend time with. Once you see the potential for a much larger pool of people and once you understand that to worry about reciprocation is a huge energy drain, you are well on your way to becoming a *Conscientious Connector*.

This second section of five helps us see just how valuable everyone we meet can be for our growth and expansion. For far too long, we've continued to isolate ourselves, certain that we need to play things 'close to the vest' in order to outrun our competitors. At networking events, we've conveniently believed that if we simply show up enough times, we will gain our share of contacts to propel our careers. The fact of the matter is this: The world is moving far too fast. Unless we start recognizing the value in everyone, not just our target audience, we are missing enormous opportunities.

Know your ideal target. If you happen to run into them, do what you know to do. But, don't be so quick to discount or dismiss the rest of the room on your way to the one or two people who represent 'potential prospects,' especially when there may be dozens of others there that represent an enormous mutual benefit once you've given them a chance and yourself permission to explore what's possible.

NOTES

STEP TWO / CHAPTER FOUR

EVERYONE MATTERS

*The story of a naïve, knobby-kneed nine-year old boy, an out-of-control fire
and what I learned from that experience about people*

"My God, David! What have you done?!" still resonates with
me these many years later. There is nothing she could have said that
would have penetrated my heart as deeply. The screen door on our
farmhouse slammed open, nearly taking off its hinges as I watched
Mom running toward me, still wearing her apron, her hair swirling up
from the cross breezes as she screamed my name. Dad came right
behind her followed by my older brothers, Dan and Jon.

I searched for reassurance from any of them that everything
would be ok but it was not forthcoming. Frozen in my tracks, my
whole body started to shake. I was helpless and tears streamed down
my face. The only amount of humiliation that can be worse than a
parent voicing disappointment in their child has to be when that
feeling of humiliation is coming from everyone else in the family, too.
Dan grabbed one of the shovels and yelled "Nice going, dumbass!"
as he ran by me. He was right. That's how I felt. But the terror in
Mom's eyes said it all. The fire behind me was big and growing
rapidly out of control.

There is no way I could have known how that day would so
profoundly affect me and the lessons I would learn. The five-acre
field in front of our house had been allowed to go fallow for a
season. Knowing the dead grasses, old cornstalks, dry weeds and
thistles would soon be plowed under for the winter, Mom had been
after us to clear the dead grasses along the fence line, arguing that
once the field was cleared the fencerow would look much better for
the winter. The unpredictable Indiana rains were coming later in the
afternoon so Mom was bound and determined to keep us at it until

we finished the job to her satisfaction.

Naturally, my brothers and I began to look for ways to get this chore over with in as efficient a manner as possible so as to salvage as much of the rest of our Saturday as possible. My brothers, in their typical creative ways, talked our parents into using a 'controlled burn' to help expedite things. My brothers were deemed old enough to use the matches but everyone told me I was too young, so my job was to help put out any flames that drifted over into the field. My brothers convinced me I had the best job because I could be the honorary 'fireman' who could come to the rescue.

I was disappointed, however, because I was quite certain that my family didn't fully appreciate how mature and grown up my nine-year-old self had become.

Lunchtime came and Mom, pleased with our progress, called us in for egg salad sandwiches, chips and Pepsi. While my brothers argued over who would get the last of the chips, my thoughts were on how to prove to my family that I had become a responsible young adult and I decided this would be a good day to show them.

If I were to head out and finish what was left of the fence line before the rains came, I reasoned, and if I did it by myself, I would not only win the eternal gratefulness of my entire family but I would earn their respect for being old enough to handle such a responsibility!

My brothers and I cleared the table. Dad headed for the living room to rest and catch part of the White Sox game and my brothers joined him. I, on the other hand, decided this would be a good time to head out and inspect the project to see for myself how long this chore would take while ignoring Mom's last remarks to me as she headed upstairs. As I recall, she said something about staying away from the matches and not doing anything until someone was out there with me.

The air had cooled a little when I walked back to the field. Our family dog, Sass, followed me but didn't stay very long, electing to go to the back door in anticipation of being fed any leftovers from lunch. I suspect, too, he wasn't that interested in appearing as my accomplice for what he sensed I was about to attempt. Who could blame him?

True to what you might expect, my nine-year-old ambition got the better of me. I was far more interested in proving all of them wrong and besides, with the breezes starting to stir things up, I needed to get the project finished. I was certain they would thank me for it.

Dan had left the matches on top of one of the fence posts and I grabbed them and a shovel and headed to the next section that needed to be cleared. I struck the match and the grasses started easily, promoted by the increasing breeze. I remember being fascinated at how the dead grass would coil in on itself before going black and dropping to the ground, sometimes sparking a little flame. When that happened I was able to stomp out the small fires easily.

In fact, everything had gone so well I decided to start additional 'burns' you know, so as to expedite the process, and that's when things started to get out of control. The breeze lifted sparks and dropped them into the field where they easily caught. I rushed to pound them out and pour dirt over the flames, but the faster the breeze kicked up, the faster additional pockets of little embers made their way into the field. I looked back toward the house and noticed that the tops of the trees in our front yard were starting to really sway and the sky was getting darker by the minute.

Not wanting to admit there was a problem, I remained quiet while I raced to catch up. In a matter of just a few minutes, however, there were a half dozen fire pockets, which quickly turned into a dozen. Dust started to spin the embers and, as I looked around, I could see that a full line of fire had developed. *The field was on fire.* Worse, the wind seemed to be pushing the fire as the embers played hopscotch, dancing ahead of the main fire line and igniting fire pockets everywhere. It was pure fuel. The field and fire were coming alive.

Finally, in desperation, I yelled and ran half way toward the house then came back to the field, all the time hoping I could be heard inside. No one came at first, so I ran toward the house again. That's when I met them as they poured out from the back porch. By now a full one-third of the field was engulfed and the wind was sending the flames in the worst possible direction: It was heading toward our neighbor's barn and house just across the road. Could the fire actually jump the road? If it could, would it take the barn and then the house? Why wasn't he coming out with a garden hose or something and watering things down? Was the neighbor even home? Why was this happening? Why did I ever want to try this? What was I thinking? Will my parents ever forgive me?

In less than a minute, half the field was gone. My continual prayers that it would start raining immediately didn't work, either. Ominous crackling sounds were all around. Old thistles became tiny landmines. The fire was hot and the swirling wind seemed to enjoy its part in helping advance the flames.

Suddenly over the crackling, I heard voices. Uncommon voices. I heard shouting and doors slamming. There was yelling. I looked up through the dust and smoke and could see people jumping out of cars and trucks. Some rode in the back of pickups, hopping off like my cowboy heroes coming to the rescue, shovels in hand. Others had blankets and everyone ran toward the field. Farmer's wives piled out of cars. Some were our neighbors who lived just down the road but there were others who I knew lived further away. Some I had never met before. One man was dressed in a suit. I remember he went to the trunk of his car and exchanged his suit coat for a blanket and ran to help. Neighbors, friends and perfect strangers showed up. The people in and around Fairmount, Indiana might live modestly, but there is no way to measure just how big their hearts are until you see how they come together in an emergency.

We fought hard. The dirt, dust and heat were unbearable. The hum and crackle grew louder. The ground was so hot with live embers that the blanket I was using caught on fire. We kicked and shoveled dirt, pounded the ground with whatever means we had, but each time I looked up, the fire seemed bound and determined to jump the road and head straight for our neighbor's barn.

What was in that barn, anyway? I was certain it contained his tractor, his pickup truck, probably gasoline, along with bales of straw and hay for his cows. Were there family photos and other keepsakes I was now going to be responsible for destroying? And his farmhouse, not even a hundred feet from the barn, was on the same trajectory. The guy wasn't even home to defend it and, thanks to me, would be coming home to nothing left of his time spent on earth.

It was the greatest feeling of helplessness I had ever experienced. To this day, the chilling memory of a situation being that out of control still surfaces. We all have watched reports of others getting caught in unexpected emergencies and I had heard many stories at the kitchen table about people being flooded out or their places burning to the ground, but they were strangers to me and until this day, nothing like this had ever happened to my family. My prayers up to that point had been for stupid things like a favorite toy or a baseball glove for Christmas. Now I was asking God to intervene for something truly important and although I certainly didn't deserve the rain I was praying for, my neighbor certainly did.

By now, over a dozen of us fought the fire but knew we were losing the battle. That same sense of hopelessness, I am sure, was running through everyone's mind. How do you stop a raging fire with just a few blankets and shovels far away from any water hoses? The impossibility of it all loomed. The sky became darker and the promise of rain was imminent but still not forthcoming.

Suddenly, there was another sound above the shouting, a distinct sound that caused everyone to look in the same direction; a sound that seemed to pierce through all other noises, coming from further away. It whirred from a low growl, slowly moving up the scale like you would hear just before two cats start to fight, growing louder with each breath. We could see the dust clouds of something big, still hidden behind a final hill as it made its way over the top we all cheered. Heading toward us was the Fowlerton Volunteer Fire Department's old diesel fire truck, spewing black exhaust from the chrome pipes and bouncing down the road like a bulky, slow moving linebacker looking to tackle anything in its way. Unbeknownst to us, someone had called in the emergency and here came the two guys on shift that day, driving that beautiful, two-decade-old water cannon.

I immediately looked over toward the barn and, sure enough, that fire had jumped the road and was starting to eat away at the dead grasses just inside our neighbor's property line. We all wondered if that big, clunky old machine would get there before the fire reached the barn and my heart skipped a beat when the firemen stopped at the highway before turning right and the engine sputtered and coughed, almost shutting down. The engine fired up again, though, as they lumbered on, able to kill the flames nearest the barn before turning around and finishing off the field on our side of the highway. It only took a matter of minutes to empty the tank of the water it carried. Had the fire made it to the barn, even that old warhorse wouldn't have had enough water to put it out.

White smoke began to join the rest of the swirling dust. Everyone cheered our conquering heroes who had come to save the day. Mom cried as she hugged everyone she could. I cried, too.

Neighbors laughed and clapped their hands, then waved to my parents before they walked back to their cars and trucks. A few of the old farmers and their wives stood with us in the field for a while, shirking off my parents' sincere offers to fix them dinner or bring over a freshly baked pie the next day. The guys who brought the water cannon stuck around for a while, too, as my brothers and I combed the field for any remaining embers, although there was little left that hadn't already been extinguished. Finally convinced the fires were out, the two volunteers hopped up into that beautiful old contraption and waved back to us. Black smoke billowed from the stacked exhaust pipes as they bounced along the field, then up onto the highway and headed back to the fire station five miles away.

After watching the last of our friends, neighbors and strangers pull away; we waved gratefully one last time. As we turned toward the house and started our back up the lane, I had only taken a few steps before I felt my Dad's hand on my shoulder, slowing me down so that we could walk together behind the rest of the family. Mercifully, he kept his voice lower so as not to add further embarrassment to me and asked me what I had learned. I was quick to tell him I would never again underestimate the power and danger associated with fire. I had learned my lesson about not doing something like that by myself. Good intentions notwithstanding, I screwed up and I was forever sorry for what I had put everyone through. Mom, who was listening too, never turned back toward me but added, loud enough for me to hear, that she certainly hoped that lesson would stay with me. "Yes, ma'am," I answered.

And, as if to put a post script on all that had happened, God's good humor showed up. Halfway back to the house, it started to rain.

Lessons I Learned And Continue To Be Reminded Of

It's been said that a lesson will repeat itself until we learn it. I think that's true. The story I just relived for you contains lessons about a boy's misdirected desire to prove himself to his family, but the bigger lessons I take with me are about other people.

Here are the five most prominent lessons I'm reminded of when I am out there meeting folks from every profession and background:

1 - Everyone has things they are dealing with. You certainly have your own challenges you deal with each day, and whatever that entails and includes is your business. Everyone else has to deal with their own circumstances, goals, dreams, setbacks and conditions, too. The people who came to our rescue put their own lives on hold and came running to help. Do you suppose I will ever forget what they did for my family, as well as what they tried to do to save our neighbor's barn and house? If this story moved you in any way, will you ever forget it now, either? When meeting people for the first time it's easy to believe that our challenges are greater than theirs, but as my Dad always told me, *"Anytime you think you have it tough, look around because you will always be able to find someone else who has it tougher than you."* Good advice from a guy a lot of people loved.

2 - Everyone you meet is worthy of your time and energy until proven otherwise. When the field was on fire and there was a need for neighbors, friends and strangers to drop what they were doing to save a guy's barn and house and who knows what else, they didn't prequalify my family or our neighbor as to whether we were the right ethnicity or had the right education, whether we were with the right religious affiliation or drove the right car. It didn't matter to them how my parents voted in the last election or whether we were of a certain pedigree. They came because there was a need. In your own life, remember that you and your new connections were cut from the same perfection that created our world. When you walk into a networking event, resist dismissing people, just as you would resist people dismissing you before getting to know you. Give them your best professional benefit of doubt and see what develops before you make premature assumptions you will very likely regret.

3 - Conscientious people don't worry about payback. There was no reciprocation expected or even wanted by the people who came to help us fight that fire. Mom practically *begged* them to let her bake pies but had no takers. *What goes around comes around, so maybe one day someone who helped you will need your help too. Just glad you are ok* was the prevailing attitude. In other words, if you find that you want to do something for someone who did something for you, great. Do it and keep moving. Payback is good when it comes from the heart and right timing. But when it is given to even a score or as a burden you are ridding yourself of, that's reciprocation tethered to an obligation, which is an entirely different condition. Keeping score will exhaust you.

4 - Character comes in many disguises. I am fairly certain the stranger who pulled off the road wearing a suit and tie, got out of his nice clean car and fought that fire right along with the rest of us, didn't dream that morning he would end up traipsing through a dusty, hot, muddy Indiana cornfield hours later. Neither did the farmers in overalls or the housewives still wearing their aprons. True character quietly showed up that day in each and every person who came to help. Quiet character like that doesn't come with a neon sign, but resides internally. You have to recognize it when you see it, just like everyone else will hopefully see the same in you. Yes, I want you to always make a good first impression and there is no excuse not to wear your best whenever possible, but remember that trust and respect are what people look for the most. That's character. I look for character.

5 - Those deserving praise should hear it. It is easy for me to tell you that they don't come any better than the folks I grew up with in and around Fairmount, Indiana. That said, I must also add that there are many of those same great people wherever you are, too. You just have to look for them because they are there, guaranteed, quietly disguised as everyday folks just working to raise their families and meet the challenges of life, the same as you and me. I praise the folks who came that day to help.

That morning at the network breakfast, after I singlehandedly managed to positively influence ten of my peers and ten times that across the room, little did I know that nine of them would stand and say something nice about me before we were adjourned. It took, collectively, about five minutes for those remarks to boost my image and my reputation. Third-party endorsements like that are *priceless*.

Why Unexpected Praise Is The Best Kind

You simply cannot go wrong in offering to say something nice about another person. Praise is in short supply but it doesn't have to be.

Another way I praise is when I go to a restaurant or coffee shop. If the person who waits on me is good and attentive, I will tip generously. But the kicker is that I will also write a note on the restaurant copy of the receipt that stays behind, stating something like, "Stephanie was great!" and I write my initials so that the manager who goes through the receipts will see it. I've done that for years, when warranted. Those folks are working hard for tips to go with their minimum wages. Perhaps they are going to school or trying to start businesses. Maybe they have two or three part-time jobs just to make ends meet. While I cannot just give them a huge tip every time, I can give them a huge boost and it doesn't cost me an extra dime to do that. I rarely hear from them about it when I return to that restaurant, but I sure do notice all the smiles I get from those who have served our table in the past and I think that the note sometimes goes a long way to their looking forward to seeing me again. There are many ways to praise someone and most of them cost nothing but forethought.

The Way of The Conscientious Connector is to always look for ways to praise. My wife and business partner Gaye read book years ago called *Try Giving Yourself Away* by David Dunn that positively and profoundly affected her. The simple act of taking time to praise someone has so many great rewards for everyone involved that it deserves a mention. Our good friends Sara and Tim met us at The Americana in Glendale one night for dinner and shopping. As Sara and Gaye walked along they came upon a beautiful window display of women's purses. The lighting and the backdrop were so bright and beautiful and the way everything was laid out was extraordinarily attractive. Gaye walked in and asked to see the manager. The first concern, of course, is that there was something wrong and Gaye was there to make a complaint. The manager came to the front of the store and Gaye launched into carefully chosen remarks about the window display.

"I know you probably hear this all the time, but I just wanted to tell you that your window displays, the lighting, the fabric, the items you chose to feature... well, I have to tell you that it is the most beautiful window display I have ever seen. Who is the person that did this for you?"

The manager blushed. *"Well, to tell you the truth, it was me"* she said. *"Well,"* Gaye said to her, *"You have a gift for this and I felt you needed to hear it."*

The Manager was clearly taken aback and thanked her several times. Sara spoke up and concurred with Gaye and it seemed the Manager was struggling to catch her breath from all of the positive attention that was being thrust upon her to praise her talents.

Simple. Straightforward. Timely. It took very little time to hand out that honest praise of the work the Manager put into decorating that store window. Here's the interesting side story: Because all of us love to see nice things said about another person, the immune systems for Gaye, Sara, the Manager, the Clerks and the other Customers in that store who heard Gaye's praise also felt uplifted. Everyone smiled. Some took a second look at the window and offered their own praise. Good vibrations all around are downright *addictive*.

Try Giving Yourself Away

Find your moment to try this. It might surprise you at how good you feel helping someone else with a little praise that costs you nothing. It will not only improve your health by the way it makes you feel, but also by the improvement of your image in the eyes of others.

HOMEWORK

In order for you to really slow things down long enough to realize what I'm talking about, I ask you to step outside yourself just long enough to try some things that will help you begin to adjust to this new thinking and of being a *Conscientious Connector*. Try these exercises then write down for yourself what you noticed, for it is in the noticing that you start to change your approach.

1. Notice what you're noticing when you walk into a store and meet a perfect stranger. Do they look you right in the eye? Is their response to you short and sweet or short and reserved? Is there a sense of trust from you right away? Is there a sense of trust from them right away? Write down your thoughts and journal them for later review.

2. Try to strike up a conversation with someone you don't know. Will they engage with you? Is your attempt to get them to talk to you being met with polite aloofness? Are they guarded? Do they seem to want to keep moving and not stand there and converse with you because they (1) are on a timetable and they have their own agenda and simply cannot waste time with you? Or (2) are they moving on because they simply are not comfortable with this? Or (3) are they willing to engage in a conversation with you because they seem to like meeting new people? Write down your thoughts and observations.

This exercise is *cold calling in person*. It serves to remind us about how people like to be treated, how they typically might react to you and why it is so important to get good at knowing how to strike up conversations and engage with people in a way that suits *them*.

I remember after 9/11, everyone across the country seemed to be more considerate, forgiving and trusting, at least for a while. It was nice. We were all supporting something bigger than ourselves.

It shouldn't require a national crisis to get us there again.

STEP TWO / CHAPTER FIVE

THE WISDOM OF UNCLE WALT

Anyone can have a good idea.

While it is only 2,200 miles from our Indiana farm to Burbank, California, it was light years from where I grew up the day I joined other budding young management-in-training people from Disneyland for a field trip and tour of Walt Disney Studios. It's something I will never forget. I have always been curious about what's behind the curtain, how things are done, how things are made, etc., so to see the sound stages, props, actors and actresses walk around in costume and the framed pictures of famous people on the walls of the Disney commissary was nothing short of thrilling for me.

The lessons I learned that day included stories told to us by Dave Smith, the now retired chief archivist who was, shortly after Walt's death, granted the opportunity to collect and catalogue the hundreds of thousands of Disney artifacts and memorabilia that would otherwise have been tossed out or destroyed.

The end of our tour brought us back to a small welcome center near the entrance. Many of us picked up a memento or two while we waited for our chartered bus to take us back to Anaheim. I remember how we were tired from all the walking but each of us felt we were privileged to learn so much about this company we had come to love.

Some in the group walked back outside to wait. It was a warm summer day and the California sun felt great, a cool breeze accompanied by the scent of the familiar orange trees nearby. But I elected to stay inside with a few others, hoping Mr. Smith would regale us more insights, tales and stories about this most amazing place we found ourselves a part of.

He invited us to look through the window as he pointed to the two rectangular, salmon-colored buildings not far from us and asked if we agreed they looked rather out of place, especially when compared to the creative décor all around them: Evenly-positioned square windows all along, and one door to the outside with deco aluminum handrails didn't seem to fit what one would expect from great creative minds. Those two buildings, he explained, were the first ones built on the Disney lot and their architectural style was purposed to match the specifications of what could easily be converted into something else: A hospital.

According to Dave Smith, after *Snow White & The Seven Dwarfs* experienced critical acclaim and worldwide success back in 1939, Walt and his brother Roy went to the Burbank planning commission and asked for help in funding the purchase of the fifty-one acres that would become Walt Disney Studios. The Burbank representatives were more than a little skeptical and only agreed to the deal if Disney would build the first two buildings according to the specs of a hospital. The reason: While Burbank knew they needed a hospital, they weren't sure Disney would be successful.

So the first two buildings on the lot were designed as a series of hospital rooms. Halfway down each hall was an area designated for a nurse's station. Fluorescent fixtures, additional electrical outlets and everything else had to be easily converted the minute the Disney organization went under. This was a take-it-or-leave-it proposition. Unless Walt and Roy agreed, no deal would be struck.

We don't always get what we want the way we want it, do we? Sometimes the world opens its doors to success only to close them when you decide to stretch and grow, which then requires a whole new set of challenges.

Lessons abound, here. The fact that Walt was undeterred is a life-lesson in itself. He didn't back off. If they wanted the first two buildings built to those specifications because the planners didn't trust he would make it, so what? At least they were willing to give him his shot. Whether Walt already had in his mind what he wanted to build there instead is irrelevant. The much bigger lesson to share with you is about what he did to make that situation work for him after the buildings were built.

Walt Disney: Everyone can contribute!

Walt instinctively knew if he surrounded himself with creative talent he could be successful no matter what. After all, Walt Disney was born in 1901 and started his company in 1923. By the time 1939 rolled around, he was already 38 years of age. He had already gone through many ups and downs and had learned many experiential lessons about business and life. By the time he arrived in Burbank and stood before that planning commission, he knew how to make things happen and he also knew that he could not do this alone.

Walt needed his animators to consistently churn out hit movies and cartoons and he knew he needed everyone's input. It was common for Walt to walk the halls at night and check the work his animators were turning out and it was not unusual for there to be a note from Walt waiting for them the next morning with questions and suggestions. He was constantly looking for answers, solutions and creative input wherever he could find it and he understood something better than most: *Anyone can have a good idea.*

Blackboards, Chalk and the De-Compartmentalization of Creative Potential

Walt noticed that his animators and storytellers would go to meetings to discuss the projects but after the meetings were over, the people and their challenges would again disappear behind cubicles. No one else could offer any solutions because they were not privy to the challenges. Could more access to those challenges by others who worked there contribute to perhaps even better ideas and suggestions? Could the company benefit from this input anytime, on-going?

Decidedly yes, but the challenge was in how those challenges could be seen by everyone else so that creative juices could flow?

Remember, this was way before computers, social media and immediate live-access-linked people.

One day Walt noticed the enormous amount of wall space available in the rooms and hallways and hit on an idea. He ordered blackboards installed along the available walls so that every challenge could be seen by anyone walking by.

When the project was complete with plenty of chalk and erasers, the animators, storywriters and everyone else were told to put their challenges up on the board so that others could read them and offer suggestions and recommendations. One of the artists might be looking for feedback on colors to use for a background scene. Another artist might be researching the history of a region of a country in pursuit of authenticity in costumes and props. A storywriter searched for colloquialisms and books on certain subjects. By putting challenges up where everyone else could also see them, anyone from any department could contribute or lead them to more information, even the guy sweeping the floors after everyone else went home.

Walt took away restrictions. *He de-compartmentalized creativity* and encouraged everyone to work more closely together for the greater good that could come from collective collaboration and input. My impression from this story is that Walt didn't care nearly as much about the pecking order of executives as he did about getting the creative juices of his talented workers flowing.

The same can be true for you wherever you work. For example, just because someone's specialty is accounting shouldn't exclude him or her from having good ideas that might help your marketing or human resources folks. Think about it. Accounting people are inundated every day with advertising and marketing messages. They are influenced by outside stimulus just like you. So they clearly know more than just about their own discipline. Who's to say they couldn't have a good idea? But if they are told to remain in their own area of responsibility and are never encouraged to throw in their thoughts about other areas of the company, it's anyone's guess as to what your company might miss as a great idea that leads to an opportunity.

Creativity of thought, inspired thinking and the innovative process should be encouraged from everyone, not just from an isolated few.

Walt Disney, arguably one of the greatest creative minds of the 20th century, put blackboards up on the walls to tap into every possible resource he could find. He didn't rely just on himself and a few others to handle the creative process. Why should you?

Take another look at your company. Look for 'walls' that are blocking creative minds from providing input that your company could use and take the walls down. Invent new ways that allow everyone access to challenges and encourage creative input. You never know what will happen. If you are applying for a position with a company, remember these stories and start right now to figure out how else you can become more valuable. Get ahead of the curve in how you can contribute.

Oh, and remember that hospital that Burbank desperately needed, the one they provisioned in case Disney failed? The Providence St. Joseph Medical Center was established in 1943 and is right down the street from the Walt Disney Company, which happens to be one of the hospital's biggest supporters. Burbank got their hospital and a whole lot more.

Anyone can have a good idea. Everyone has contributions they can make if they are encouraged. Keep those doors wide open. Think up great avenues you can create so that the creativity never stops flowing. Yes, let the creativity flow. Encourage everyone, even the people who are friends of the company, like supplier partners, to feel free to make suggestions. Success and creative thought comes in many forms and should never be stifled or compartmentalized.

HOMEWORK

1. Get out your journal and write down your thoughts about how you can pull from all of the creative talent that surrounds you. It may be people with whom you work that you can get to know better. It may be outside people you have known or been associated with but you never really explored what and whom they know. The example you can use for how to approach this is none other than Walt Disney, himself. Write this question out, then respond: *"What would I see if I were Walt, looking to expand my business or boost my career? What would I outline as steps to enlist and engage everyone I ever meet in helping me as I help them?"*

2. Record your thoughts as fast as you can write, for the answers will start to come and, when they do, it has been my experience they will come faster and faster. Connections will come to mind. Opportunities to collaborate and to bring others into your arena for the purpose of **mutual** benefit will start to show up. Don't worry about grammar, either. Just write!

3. Add the new potential of your information back into your contacts. Make notes and start building steps to your new future. It's there, waiting for you.

4. If you are a CEO, check to see if you have 'walls' around certain departments that need to come down so that you can tap all the creativity and connections that are already in your presence. Journal a new game plan. Write down what you find.

5. See what you can do to expand this, permanently, into your activities, every day, moving forward and don't limit yourself to focusing just on the salespeople, anymore.

6. Share what you will with me so I can pass it along in subsequent work I do. It will begin to surprise you at how this process can bring

out good ideas that come from people you may have not thought would be contributors. When that happens, celebrate it! It may very well be they read this book, too, and have been walking around a long time with good ideas to share but because of the compartmentalization of things, they kept their ideas to themselves.

NOTES

STEP TWO / CHAPTER SIX

PEOPLE ALL AROUND YOU HAVE CONNECTIONS

And most have information they'd love to share.

I grew up in a family of marvelous storytellers. I guess that's why I love to write. My brother Dan regales me with truths and an occasional fable about people he knows or people he met when we were growing up on the farm. It doesn't matter if I visit him once every five years or once every five weeks; he will have new stories.

Dan, who seems to know pretty much everyone in five counties, will call me in California to tell me the latest news from home. I appreciate his willing intention to keep me informed with the latest but because I haven't lived there for over 40 years, the conversation usually goes something like this: (Some names have been changed.)

Dan: Did you hear about Charlie Burrell?

Me: Who is Charlie Burrell?

Dan: Didn't you play ball with Charlie's stepbrother Bill Martin?

Me: Uh, I remember the name, Bill Martin, but I think he was a couple of grades before me. Was that the guy we called Spud? Why?

Dan: Yeah. Spud Martin ended up marrying Cheryl Jones.

Me: And... I should know Cheryl Jones?

Dan: I thought she was in your class in high school.

Me: No, Dan. Cheryl Jones was in the class with our brother Rip when he used to go by Jon Ribble and before he, too, moved to California *over 40 years ago*.

(Exasperation to get to the point is starting to override best intentions)

Dan: Oh yeah, maybe you're right. Well, anyway, Spud's stepbrother Charlie had an operation the other day and he is doing much better now.

Me: Well, good to hear, Dan. Thanks for telling me.

~~~~~~~

Dan finds people interesting. It is this virtuous, well-meaning fascination in other people that my brothers and I gratefully inherited from our parents and other family members.

The more you get to know people, the more interesting, and quite often, the more *valuable* they become in this quest. What is so intriguing to me is how much we miss when we narrow the field of potential influence without realizing what we are missing.

Paul Brodsky (epbcpa.com) has been my friend and our CPA for over 25 years. He's really good. Every so often Paul will venture out to a networking event and I am always fascinated by how many meet him and briefly say hello before moving right past Paul on their way to whomever they think will be more 'fitting' for them to spend their time and energy talking to. Why? Because they already have a CPA and, therefore, they feel they can move on.

From my perspective, the irony is almost comical. Paul's list of clients and the industries he serves is vast. Therefore, his connection to others is vast. As a practicing *Conscientious Connector,* Paul has the full grasp of the value of matching people he knows to the right people they're looking for and I assure you he is ready to assist those who ask. Why don't they ask?

Target *Audience* versus Target *Market*

People you meet aren't just customers or stepping-stones for your career. Some can become advisors, mentors, coaches, connectors, facilitators, and encouragers for your success. In many instances, I've picked up lifelong friends in the process who will never have a need to buy anything from me and that's ok.

"But, Dave," I sometimes hear, *"If I am going to go to a networking event for the purpose of finding a customer or a career connection, I can hardly afford to stop and talk to just anyone I run into. I have to keep moving to find that key target if I want to use my time wisely, right?"*

Ok, let's talk about that because this is where pure logic might seem to take a bit of a hit. On one hand, it might seem logical that if you only have two hours to find your target market at an event, talking to anyone else is a gross waste of your time. After all, we know that time is money, right?

But, let's break that down a little further and let me give you a hypothetical that will help demonstrate what I want you to re-think and why, because what might seem logical on the surface isn't always the best way to look at it:

Q: If you spend two hours searching for your target market and you do not find the perfect person to talk to, did you waste the two hours?

- Standard logic would say you did.

- *Conscientious Connector* logic would ask whether you spent any of your time with anyone else to discover *his or her* needs. Did you spend any time focused on anyone else?

Q: If you spent your two hours and ended up having ten solid conversations with people while you also searched for your target, that's one conversation with someone other than your supposed target market every 12 minutes. Would that be a better use of your time?

- Standard logic would say, "Go home, because this event's attendees didn't include the right people for you and, therefore, no value. And don't attend this event in the future."

- *Conscientious Connector* logic would say you opened up the potential for tremendous opportunities for yourself and the people you met at this event and that your two hours were spent *brilliantly*. Targeting your market is one thing. Targeting your audience to gain information about them is quite different and will always give you more to work with.

Dating versus Connecting

Some folks will approach this like they do the dating process. Initially, there is something that attracts you to someone else and you move closer to see what might develop. Great. But if you are only interested in people with red hair who are 6 feet tall, the possibilities are severely limited. What if your perfect match is someone who has dark hair and is 5'9"?

If you approach a networking event like you would pursue a dating opportunity, you run the risk of eliminating a very high percentage of other connections that could prove to be even more valuable than those you seek.

When you move beyond the obvious and dare to delve into getting to know someone for the purpose of discovering *how you can help them as well as how they might help you*, the numbers go way up in terms of where and how you can be a successful connector.

Once you have crossed this threshold and you no longer focus on your preconceived notion of the ideal target market, and instead, look at others as potential partners in your ever-expanding audience of solid connections, the shift begins to happen that will change your life forever.

For some of you it's not easy to go up to a perfect stranger and start a conversation. I know because I still come across situations where people are clearly nervous and create an uncomfortable scene when trying to meet people. One of the telltale signs of this is when someone comes at you totally over the top, talking loudly and getting right in your face. Are those people like that all the time? Most of them are not, but they use that persona as a shield to protect themselves from being found out that they, too, are nervous.

If that happens to you, and it will, just know that underneath the nervous bravado is someone just like you and me, trying to do the best they can. They are still worthy of your attention and consideration and you should resist dismissing them before you find out more about them.

Conscientiously connecting with anyone you don't know requires time to learn new information and to develop a relationship. For us to expect more than that when we meet a stranger at an event is tantamount to going on a blind date and heading straight to the jewelry store to pick out rings. Sure, some people do that, but very few.

Unlike what your parents probably taught you when you were a kid, I want you to become comfortable introducing yourself to strangers, because strangers are new friends just waiting to be developed.

How do you instigate conversations without coming across as cheesy, pushy or self-centered? How do you represent yourself in a way that tells the other person that you are worth at least talking to for a minute or two, just to see what develops?

Shift To Neutral - Help Them Go First

Here is what works for me. Take what I say here and modify it to your liking if need be. It only matters to me that you start off the conversation by encouraging the other person to go first.

This means that you *leave your business cards in your pocket and your ego at the door*, just as I talked about in the first chapter, and demonstrate genuine caring and empathy for the other person regardless of how they look, how tall they are, their ethnicity, their clothes, the way they comb their hair or any other superficial characteristics that might try to become an identifying part of the profile of that person, fairly or unfairly.

When you are authentic, new information from the other party is free to flow to you, information that might lead to mutual success. While it may or may not lead them to help you in return, that's ok because it doesn't have to be a two-way street. Like we said earlier, reciprocation isn't a priority.

The first step in seeing what develops is for you to go immediately to a neutral corner, metaphorically speaking. It might be as simple as an opening statement like, "Hi. Looks like a great group of people here tonight." Or you might want to open it with a reference to the facility, such as, "Wow, I am really glad they held this event here today. It is a beautiful room and it has plenty of good lighting for all the vendors."

Pick an opening remark that cannot be taken as a pitch, a push or a challenge. Talk about the weather, the traffic, the day of the week, your experience the last time you were there. Go to a neutral corner first, then into an opening remark about them, not you. You can open with any neutral reference but the next step is to move toward a conversation about *them*.

This neutrality statement allows the other person to hear your voice, hear your opinion on something, hear that you are not coming after them right out of the gate, hear that you are willing to take it slow for both parties' benefit and know that you are someone who is not desperate for business.

'Neutral zones' allow you the opportunity to stand in the presence of someone you have never met and not rattle them or be rattled.

It's also a testing ground for whether they wish to engage in a conversation with you. It's been my experience that you will usually learn your answer to that question relatively quickly, which is a good way to prevent wasted time with people who are not interested in engaging in a conversation with you. Maybe they are busy. Maybe they have other reasons for not wishing to engage at that moment, like a desperate need to go to the bathroom.

For the most part, if you remain in the neutral corner, the person you are speaking to will generally lead the conversation and that is perfect. You just have to be patient and wait for it.

Remember, too, there are no shortcuts. Trust develops over time in relationships. It's never instantaneous and information about someone always floats to the top at its own speed and in its own way. I think of it like pouring resin onto an uneven piece of wood and watching it seek its own level; some things take a little longer to settle in.

Open with neutrality. Move in the direction your subject wants to take you and be ok with that because you are learning volumes about that person no matter what direction the conversation takes.

You'll have to throw out the old sales coach directive of Always Be Selling and replace it with *Always Be Listening* and *Always Be Learning* about potentially valuable resources for others. The more you know about the needs of others, the better able you are to help them. I see an inherent potential for good information to come from everyone I meet. Just as Walt Disney taught us that *anyone can have a good idea*, it is equally true that *anyone can have a good connection.*

A Brief Encounter-Another example…

Just the other day Gaye and were finishing up an appointment with Dr. Miles Reid, (energylifesciences.com), a fabulous health practitioner in Santa Monica we met years earlier when we were members of the same Le Tip networking group, Westside Referrals. As we were saying goodbye to his awesome Office Manager, Amanda, a new member of that same Le Tip group walked in and Miles introduced everyone.

I asked her how it was going in the networking group and she said she was having a tough time making connections and that it was slow going. I suggested that the best thing for her to do, whether at Le Tip or at any networking opportunity would be to relax about trying to force things to happen and take a different approach: "*Leave your business cards in your pocket and just try to see how many other people you can help next time and see what happens,*" was my advice to her, which should sound familiar to you by now.

She said she had never looked at it quite like that and thanked me for the great advice. Miles laughed and told her that I was an expert and that my book would be out soon. She told me she would love to read it and to have the opportunity to learn from me. Is she any different than many others you know?

What Happened Here? Review of that Brief Encounter

Note: I began my remarks with information that would help her be more successful, not just information about me. In that process, I (1) encouraged her to go first and to tell me how she was doing, (2) offered her good advice that would benefit her immediately and (3) received a third-party endorsement from Miles, all in less time than it took to walk to our car. After she learned of my expertise and asked about my book and training, I left her with a smile and a handshake and a promise that I would let her know through Miles when the book was published.

There was no push, no agenda, no reciprocation expected. I gave myself away and there was no expectation on my part to receive anything in return. Simple. Honest. Authentic.

Where do you suppose that brief encounter will lead? Will she take my advice? Will she want to read the book and take the training? Will she tell someone else about it? I didn't meet her at a networking event. It was in a doctor's office. I will trust this approach with everyone I meet because I love people and because it is rewarding for me to help others be more successful. Whatever comes of that encounter for my own wellbeing is left to the Universe to figure out on my behalf.

Oh, and one more mention: When I said those things in front of Amanda and Miles, they, too, upped their good opinion of me. That's the life I wish for everyone. It's living at the higher frequency, *my higher self*, that helps others and it never fails to help me, too.

Connections: Yours + Others' = Mutual Success

By developing an attitude that says *'people all around you have connections,'* you keep the door open to possibilities. Therefore, always inquire, always ask and always offer to help if there is something you can do for someone. The rewards are always positive and, more often than you might think, surprising, because you never know what can happen when the right people connect.

The same can be said for where you work. Do you know everyone you work with? Have you slipped below the typical surface existence in most companies to find out who people are and whom they know? Do you have a good feel for what connections, experiences and talent might be staring you in the face, undiscovered, in the people with whom you work and associate?

When you meet someone for the first time you are meeting another key part of the Universe just like you. It's a big deal. You are coming into contact with that person, his or her pathology, hopes, dreams, experiences, ancestral makeup and so much more. Respect that and appreciate it.

Who is Already in Your World?

Here's another story, an example of how we sometimes have people of influence sitting next to us but because we haven't explored getting to know them, we never knew who they know or how they can help us.

Charlene is the VP of Purchasing at Acme Company. (Acme is a throwback name I use because I saw it so many times in Road Runner cartoons, ok?) John is the warehouse foreman and the company is located in Los Angeles. John has worked for the company for 12 years. Charlene came from another company a couple of years ago and is very good at what she does. Today, John received an email from Charlene to let him know about a large shipment of maintenance materials she ordered that will be arriving in the coming days so that John can alert his night crew to make space for all of it. John acknowledges receipt of said paperwork back to Charlene and both go on their merry way, doing their jobs. Neither of them has ever carved out time to get to know each other. The conversations have always been about their respective responsibilities in the day-to-day operations of the company.

The CEO of the company, Susan, wants to expand their business by having a second distribution facility closer to the East Coast but doesn't want to alert the media or anyone in the company until solid information has been quietly collected. It is hush-hush for now because Susan knows the prices for real estate will rise if word leaks prematurely. Charlene is told to take a week off and travel to Memphis to scope out opportunities for expansion and to report back to Susan with her best recommendations. Susan also directs Charlene to become fully knowledgeable of the pros and cons, advantages and disadvantages of building something new versus rehabbing existing buildings.

Charlene's trip is good and things develop quickly and quietly. After Susan's third trip, she and Charlene determine the best route is to take over an existing warehouse rather than build a new one. Charlene signs lease contracts on behalf of the company. Only after the transaction is complete and announcements to the rest of the company are made do Susan and Charlene learn that John grew up in Memphis, has many good friends and family there, knows the mayor and that one of John's brothers happens to specialize in commercial real estate. John never had the opportunity to help with this project because no one got to know John.

~~~~~~~

It's the same 'compartmentalized', limited thinking we talked about earlier, where everyone is supposed to concentrate on his or her own responsibilities and not weigh in on anything outside their respective area. Add this kind of prevailing approach to the day-to-day of business demands and what we create are unnecessary limitations on the whole organization.

By contrast, *Conscientious Connectors* love to continually engage and interview other people inside and outside the organization because we know the possibilities. We are always in the hunt-and-gather-information mode. We're curious and we ask people to tell us more about themselves. We look from a broader perspective because we know we will always turn up useful information for both others and ourselves.

Remember, too, that what we learn about people doesn't necessarily have to serve us directly, but may very well serve someone else. Here's another example of what I mean.

Don & Chris Brown

It was late afternoon on a Friday and the first week after we moved into our new condo. We were still getting settled and I met a guy out in the parking lot who frequently comes to my building to do carpet cleaning. He introduced himself as Don. We struck up a friendly conversation and by the time we finished talking, Don asked me if we liked sushi. I told him that Gaye loves sushi and Don invited us to join him and his wife Chris at one of the best sushi restaurants around.

When we walked in, Don and Chris were welcomed and treated like royalty! I only learned in subsequent conversations that Don grew up in this area and knows just about everyone, which led me to meet other people from companies we now serve and to make new friendships. Chris, for example, is the amazing Manager of the bank we use.

Don demonstrated the attributes of being a *Conscientious Connector* because he genuinely loves people and is a living example of how those you come into contact with every day have more to their story. To this day, when I meet friends of theirs, I am always asked if we met Don and Chris the same way they did, over sushi, because, as it turns out, Don's been inviting people to join them this way for years.

Keep this in mind, too: When I met Don, he was putting his carpet cleaning equipment back into his truck. He was drenched in sweat because he had just worked three hours straight on someone's carpet in the building and was heading home. I was walking by. We said hello. Our conversation soon revealed authentic, welcomed interest in each other. That is how it all started and, for the record, Don said hello to me first. Don and Chris have been good friends of ours ever since.

Explore talent and connections everywhere you go and encourage everyone in the company to think this way. Don't make assumptions about anyone but do tap all the resources available to see where they may lead you. Make it part of the culture.

Sometimes, the most obvious information is hiding in plain sight, similar to when I have to ask Gaye to help me find the pickles in the refrigerator after I have stared right past them. Unless we have a firm grasp of all of the connections and references that people we work with happen to own, how can we possibly tap into that for the greater good?

These potential connections that go undiscovered cost all of us when they shouldn't have to. Take Patricia's story, for example.

The Story of Patricia, Brenda and Steve

Patricia has worked for an accounting firm for eight years. She is an excellent bookkeeper. She likes the people she works for but also sees that any advancement to a higher position and higher salary is going to take a long time. A single mom with two kids, she regularly frequents a particular hairdresser and has been going there for a couple of years but only knows that the owner of the hair salon is Brenda. The relationship between Patricia and Brenda is professional, friendly and surface-oriented at best. Patricia comes in for her hair appointment and the conversation always dwindles to talking about the weather and the tabloids. Brenda doesn't really know much at all about Patricia.

Interestingly, Brenda and her husband, Steve, are quietly looking to expand the business to multiple locations and are having a difficult time with their bookkeeper and are looking for a replacement but are hesitant to take on someone they have never met. They have budgeted more money for freelance bookkeeping services than Patricia currently makes and that position promises to be expanded as Brenda and Steve continue to expand the business, which would be perfect for Patricia and for Brenda and Steve.

In addition, Brenda and Steve's plan for expansion happens to include places where Patricia has friends and family who could help with referrals and business. None of this will happen, however, because they didn't get to know one another. Brenda and Steve will find someone else and Patricia will continue to look elsewhere for her opportunities to make more money and start her own business.

~~~~~~~

Think of *this process as* **Prismatic Discovery**. When you shine a light through a prism, a relatively clear piece of glass that has been cut with angles, the light coming into the prism is clear and not really noticeable. But, when you do this just right, you can see all the colors of the rainbow projected out from the other side of the prism. The colors of the Universe were there all the time but until there is a concentrated effort of light, we don't see them. *Conscientious Connectors* concentrate their efforts the same way and what very often happens is a full color spectrum of possibilities and potential that comes back to you for your efforts.

Do not assume that someone in another department or division in your company represents little value in terms of connections and information until you've given yourself a chance to know more about them *and them about you.* Don't pass uninformed judgment. Instead, bet on the other person as having value, as having stories to tell and experiences to share. Wonder about them and about what you might do to help *them* be more successful, then explore the possibilities with them. No matter what, you will add at least one more person to your database that might help you down the road.

Getting Down Some of the Basics

For those of you who like to follow certain steps in the beginning stages of your meteoric ascendance to becoming a *Conscientious Connector*, here are a few questions you can ask coworkers and associates just to get the ball rolling.

While they're not invasive, they provide a starting point that will very likely lead to other discoveries, considerations and matchups as you go. Be sure to record what you learn, on-going, because this kind of attention to the process will take off like a rocket and you will want to not leave out information simply because you didn't bother to write it down. Writing it down reinforces your memory and you will be surprised at how much of what you record comes back to you quicker in later conversations.

1.   **Name of the person.**

2.   **What they do?**

3.   **How long they've been doing it?**

4.   **Where they worked before?**

5.   **Where they went to school?**

6.   **What they studied in school?**

7.   **What military experience and where?**

8.   **Where they grew up?**

9.   **What they like to do for leisure?**

10.   **What is their family makeup?**

Take an index card; place that person's name at the top and write down what you learned. Studies have shown that if you will hand-write this information, your memory will lock it in much better than if you type it into a document. There is something about that cursive, tactile process than helps you retain information more readily and that is the ideal.

If you feel you will retain the information by typing it into your computer, great, too, so type away. Just get it down. Most important to this exercise is to gain information you can review again and continue to add to as you learn more about that person. You never know when the dots will line up and there suddenly will be a connection between this person and a conversation you happen to have with another.

More examples – Creating history

I was on Facebook a few days ago and ran across someone I had not talked to in several years. Our history was that she used to be a VP for a company and we had produced several promotional marketing events for her until she left that company to move to another state with her husband and family. So, these many years later, here she was on FB. I looked at her picture, read her information and marveled at how much her two children had grown.

Before saying hello, however, I went back to my contacts just to see what I had recorded and there were notes that actually told me the names of the children, her husband and even the family dog. I knew where she earned her MBA and I had noted the projects we did for her. When I sent a note and asked how her son Steve and her daughter Carly were doing, and to be sure to say hello to her husband John, it demonstrated very effectively that I cared enough to make notes and remember. She responded immediately and really appreciated that I had taken the time to acknowledge the most important people in her life.

The Way of The Conscientious Connector is a culmination of better ways to interact with each other for the greater good that can come from it. I do not pretend to claim that my ideas have never been thought of before by anyone else on the planet because that would be untrue. We all learn from others who have come before us and I hope to continue to learn from you, as well, what works and how to continually improve. Universe owns all this information.

A Tribute: What Harvey Mackay Taught Me

One of my greatest teachers is Harvey Mackay, best-selling author of *Swim With The Sharks Without Being Eaten Alive* (Ballantine Books, 1988) and many others. Harvey is a consummate sales guy, great writer and fantastic speaker. He taught the world, and me, to take notes. *'Go see a guy and write down as much as you can remember from that conversation. Keep adding to it because it helps you connect the dots.'*

I love how Harvey says he would go see someone on appointment, capture information and then rush back to his car, pull out an index card and write down everything he could remember about the appointment. Not just from the business side of things, but also the personal side of things.

In fact, he created 'The Mackay 66,' which is a list of 66 things he would strive to find out over the course of his meetings with that person. Though he rarely, if ever, filled out all 66 answers, he recorded a ton of information. He included everything from where the guy attended college to his kids' names. To paraphrase, here is what it might have been like inside Harvey's head as he took notes.

Where did the guy go to college?

The diploma is right behind him on the wall.

What kind of dogs does he like?

There's a picture of him and his wife, two kids and a Golden Retriever on the credenza.

Did he grow up in the area or elsewhere?

The fact that he is wearing cowboy boots might lend a clue.

All of this information is like rich cream added to a cup of coffee. It makes things less business (bitter) and far more interesting (sweet) because unearthing this additional information and recording it for future use widens the number of things you have to talk about next time and provides insights to how you might be able to help one another be more successful.

Whether you are in sales or administration or looking for your next gig, the most important keys to becoming a *Conscientious Connector* are *conscientiously* *listening, observing and recording for later.* Develop skills that will enable you to hear information and use that information to help others on their journey. As you hear the details of their needs, don't assume you will remember them a week from now. Rather, treat those pieces of information as gold. Write them down.

Remember: You want a full picture of things, not just the familiar information that comes from an arm's-length, surface connected approach of, *"Hi, how are you?"* Interviewing people and getting to know them is an art as well as your objective, no matter what their position happens to be in the company they work for.

HOMEWORK

1. This is a fun exercise that you will learn from and is part of what I call 'notice what you're noticing.' It has to do with how you greet people and how people greet you. In this exercise, as you're going about your day or as you're attending a networking event, notice how many times either you or someone you run into starts the conversation with, "Hi, how are you?" While there is nothing wrong with asking that question, notice how many times it really serves as an icebreaker, giving the conversation time to get started. It is commonplace to do this.

2. Next, write down some other ways you can open the conversation, because it's likely everyone else will opt for the easiest, which is the, "Hi, how are you?" question. Instead, a way for you to immediately stand out from the crowd is to develop a better opening. Try, "I don't believe we've met but my name is _____ and I would love to know what you do. Better still, I'd like to know who you are looking to meet." That kind of opening is perfect for getting the other person to go first with information about them. That's your goal. It takes the pressure off them in their otherwise obvious attempt to stick with small talk until reaching a point of conversation they can deal with. If you start out with something different, that also helps them relax into telling you more about themselves right out of the gate. Now you are half way home to understanding how you might be able to help them. They will be much more interested in what you have to say when it is your turn and you will have skipped over the un-comfortableness that pervades most initial conversations.

Practice this method of breaking the ice until you are totally comfortable with several ways to open up a conversation. Always keep your focus on them, not yourself, and always speak in a genuine, authentic and sincere way.

STEP 3

SPOTLIGHT *THEM,* NOT YOU
YOUR REPUTATION AS A CONNECTOR WILL GO UP!

Section One helped you change your approach by giving you permission to shift your paradigm.

Section Two provided you with ample ammunition to understand why everyone you meet has the potential for helping you and, at the same time, offers you an opportunity to help them. Now we're gaining momentum and picking up a broader view of things. I hope this is as exciting to you as it is to me.

Section Three helps you see that by taking the spotlight off yourself and placing it squarely on those you meet, talk to and work with, you can actually accelerate your progress. But it requires, ironically, that you slow down a bit to allow the progress to happen.

I've brought along several examples and interviewed great people who have things they, too, want to share with you.

We will also talk about tough industries. If you think that this isn't as powerful in your industry as it is in others, I've asked a few of my friends from Showbiz to stop by and let you know that the tougher the industry, the better this stuff works. But, as they say, don't take my word for it.

Read on!

NOTES

STEP THREE / CHAPTER SEVEN

ACCELERATE YOUR PROGRESS BY SLOWING DOWN YOUR PROCESS

It's amazing how much more you will accomplish.

We've talked a lot about the benefits of having a consistently growing bank of contacts that continue to feed you referrals and support while you look for ways to return the favor. I think you will agree that to have that kind of reservoir of connections and support is ideal.

Many, however, will react to the title of this chapter with disdain because slowing down any kind of process sure seems like it would slow down the progress one is trying to make. After all, we live in a fast food environment; quick meals, quick access to the Internet, quick loans, quick delivery, quick car maintenance, quick electronic devices and quick downloads. Everyone looks for speedy solutions because we're conditioned to not enjoy waiting, even for a traffic light, if we can avoid it. We seem to celebrate speed and that is a conditioned response that can easily shortchange our experiences.

Nature, on the other hand, cannot be hurried: Till the soil, plant the seed, nurture it and wait for it to spring forth with the harvest we look forward to enjoying. No amount of watching and encouraging that plant to grow faster will expedite the natural process. Hurrying harvests simply doesn't work with nature and nature has been around a lot longer than you and me. Even if you try to hurry it, the end result won't be as sweet.

Can a *Conscientious Connector* be a time-efficient treasure hunter? If you want to speed things up in the world of building a base of best contacts and referral partners, you can accomplish more by slowing things down...a little.

It has to do with momentum. When you slow down the process of gathering good, strategically valuable information and you put that information to good use, you support everyone involved. It might start slow, certainly, but it will quickly begin to gain momentum as you nurture the process. In fact, it will actually *accelerate* your progress and you will marvel at how it all comes together faster than you probably thought possible. Have you ever made a snow ball, then rolled it into a bigger one, then rolled it downhill? The more it travels, the more snow it picks up and the bigger it gets.

Another great example of this is a rubber band. When you pull back on the rubber band, you store up additional energy. When you release it, that energy propels the other direction much faster. The same is true with a bow and arrow. When you slow down long enough to gather a little more great information about someone else, then properly store that information for retrieval later on, this act will, by its very nature, accelerate your progress.

As my friend Norma T. Hollis, author and founder of The Global Authenticity Movement (normahollis.com) will tell you, the key lies in our ability to be *consistently authentic*. When you demonstrate authenticity with every new contact you make and you show genuine interest, people catch on. They want to support you because you are the real deal. When this starts to happen there is a multiplier effect. You begin to gain momentum and the process of finding new connections that are 'you-friendly' actually *accelerates*. It is the coolest possible way to build your base of contacts and, frankly, the only way I know to build sustainable relationships.

Conscientiously Connected Strategic Thinking

Remember, you are now on the lookout for the treasures that embody the people you meet and already know. This process that your strategic thinking has designed, works for you no matter what your job description. It also works for those who are seeking to advance their career. I cannot overemphasize, however, that you must remain authentic. You must continue to demonstrate the value you place on others' information right along with your own needs. It means you must continue to look out for them, too, or this will collapse on you like a house of cards.

My objective is to help you become the most successful treasure hunter of information about other people, in modern times. In order for that to happen, you must become an empathetic listener, for this is all about creating the atmosphere by which relationships can develop and grow.

~~~~~~~~

Keri Tombazian (keritombazian.com) is my friend and a good example of a consummate listener. Along with millions of others, I first fell in love with Keri when she hosted her nightly radio show for years on a very popular smooth jazz station in Los Angeles, KTWV 94.7 The Wave.

I have often referred to Keri as *the best voice on radio*. An incredible voice-over artist you've heard perhaps hundreds of times on national TV and Radio commercials for cars and other products, Keri's job requires her to be an expert at communicating with a target audience only after being a skilled listener. Think about it: When she sits with a client to set up for a commercial, Keri must have the skills that enable her to work with a diverse group of people. She must communicate with clients, agents, agencies, managers, public relations folks and a mixed bag of producers, directors and writers who are all hedging their bets and hanging their lives, fortunes and egos on Keri's ability to deliver the right words, the right tone and the right feeling, all with just her voice. In order to accomplish that, she must listen carefully, ask many questions and allow for numerous opinions. Once that information is collected, dissected and discussed, Keri knows how to make it all work. In the process of working with so many people, Keri tells me she pays attention to each person she meets. She learns about them because one never knows where that connection will lead. She shared with me this story:

"I recently met with a General Manager of a television station for whom I have been voicing promos for eight years. He recounted that when it came time to renew my contract, he asked every single one of his producers if I was worth keeping on. He was thrilled to tell me that, to a person, it was unanimous. I have booked more work via one station manager recommending me to another manager in another state within their network than I have via straight auditioning."

Keri continues…

"Getting to know your buyer is more than just understanding the nuts and bolts of the service they require of you. It's earning a place within their sphere of influence. The last piece of that is regular and authentic gratitude."

~~~~~~~

The Push, The Pull And The Difference

There are two approaches you can take with others. One is what I call the Push and the other, the Pull. Which one do you use most? Let's break it down and discover which approach offers the most opportunities.

To **Push** is to take the approach of most: *Push* your agenda onto others, weed out those who don't fit your desired profile and move through the crowd like a hot knife on butter.

To **Pull** is *The Way of the Conscientious Connector*, which means you recognize everyone's value and you first work to see if you can help him or her before moving the conversation over to you. You *pull* the information from them by encouraging them to tell you what they need and who they are looking to meet. In doing so, you *pull* them into your confidence and you into theirs. That's where good things for both of you can happen, long-term.

That is efficient use of your time. Keep working on your goal to have more people want to refer and support you. Don't be overly concerned with immediate rewards. In fact, don't be afraid to spend time with someone who may *never* become a customer.

Everyone Counts!

Co-Workers - Non-Customers – Customers - Prospects

Let's go deeper with your peers, most of whom, I will assume, are not your customers but are people who have value and who know other connections. When you spend time getting to know them, their needs, their experiences and backgrounds, you open up possibilities for both of you. From the perspective of the *Conscientious Connector,* everything you do for anyone that ends up being recorded in his or her memory will always be a positive reflection on you. Some things you do won't be recorded, because we are all very busy with life. Some specifics of what you did or attempted to do for someone else will be left out, but the overall feeling they get when they hear your name or see you again is priceless and worth your effort, so don't worry so much about whether they remember all the details of what you did for them. Let nature take its course with regard to specifics.

Additional quality connections can be collected in less time than you probably think.

For example, let's say you are like my friend Stephanie who is starting her own Yoga studio. In this example, Stephanie spots an ad in the paper for an upcoming seminar about real estate taxation, a topic Stephanie cares little about. But, because Stephanie has adopted *The Way of The Conscientious Connector,* she recalls that a client of hers works for a mortgage lender and might be interested in knowing about the seminar. Stephanie pulls the information, sends off a note to her client and says hello. The time it takes to pull that information, add a note and put a stamp on the envelope is less time it takes to turn on the lights to her studio. She needs clients but instead of passively waiting for connections to find her Yoga classes, Stephanie proactively does something for someone else that is unrelated to her own profession. Will her mortgage lender client also share what

Stephanie did with others in that company? Quite possibly. That's the multiplier factor that comes with this kind of forethought and action.

Think about it. Stephanie made contact with her client on something unrelated to Yoga entirely. (Thank you again, Harvey Mackay) She sent off information that would help her client in his specific profession. If the guy already knew about the lecture, so what? Stephanie enhanced her professional standing in the eyes and mind of the client. If that client is ever approached by another Yoga teacher to come and check out a different Yoga studio the guy will think twice before switching. In fact, he will likely join the ranks of those who want to refer Stephanie to others.

Efficient? Yeah. In fact, uber-efficient would be the word, if that were a word. Stephanie went first. Kindness was extended. All Stephanie has to do now is keep on keeping on with good service and an ear to the ground for others she can help.

Start with one person and nurture that relationship. Figure out how to be of service to them. The majority of my database is made up of professionals who are not my clients. The majority of your database won't be your clients either. They will be contacts you make in other departments, other companies in other parts of the city or even around the world. There are no limits to how far your influence can reach.

When it comes to identifying who it is you need to be talking to out there, whether you are in sales or not, it will probably surprise you to know that *few of your competitors will go after more than a very tiny portion of the available market and the market they will focus on will be the most crowded.*

Further, if you think about target markets being made up of individuals from every kind of background, experience and expertise, *Conscientious Connectors* look at every person as someone of value.

Thank You, Chet Holmes

The late Chet Holmes, author of *The Ultimate Sales Machine* (Portfolio/Penguin Group 2007) was arguably one of the best sales trainers on the planet, evidenced by over 1,000 clients that included 60 of the biggest companies who paid very large fees for his advice.

Chet was all about helping his clients gain an edge over their competition. To that end, he taught that the buying public is really broken down into five categories, from those who are ready to buy right this minute to those who don't believe they have any intention to buy from you, ever. See if you can spot the metaphorical parallels at work here as I further explain Chet's philosophy.

In terms of sales and who is ready to buy, Chet broke it down into these five categories:

'3-7-30-30-30'

Ready to Buy Now	3%
Open to the Idea	7%
Not Thinking About It	30%
Probably Not Interested	30%
Certain Not Interested	30%

The 3%, ready to buy right now and the 7% who are open to the idea combine for 10% of the market. This combined 10% is therefore referred to as the *low-hanging fruit*. It represents the easiest of the group to convince and therefore, is where most salespeople hang out.

Likewise, it should be no surprise that most surface-connectors are searching for low-hanging fruit when attending a networking event. They will look for the fresh faces, go right up, get a card and keep moving because they figure they have a better chance with someone who doesn't already know them. They are usually correct.

By this analogy, however, Chet Holmes pointed out the much richer opportunities for those who can figure out how to go after and convince the other 90% to consider doing business with you. Chet taught that if you could figure out how to satisfy the needs of the tougher-to-convince market, the remaining 10% would likely fall into place and be easier to pick up as well. His consulting, I am told, started with that premise. Go after the prospects that might be tougher to figure out, but who also offer the greater potential. These prospects are more loyal and they are going to be your customers for life if you play your cards right and take good care of them.

A *Conscientious Connector* sees the low-hanging fruit, too, but also sees the rest of the room for the potential it represents. There are tremendous advantages to tapping into the creative resources that are already in your experience, not just at networking events but wherever you happen to connect with people.

Non-sales professionals should use this same approach as you seek to add key contacts to your database. It is shortsighted to assume that non-sales people cannot contribute to finding more connections for the company. When you think about the atmosphere in your company, do you notice that some folks push their own agenda while others keep to themselves? Of those who you have never really talked to all that much, do you see their potential? Whom do they know? What are their experiences, both in the company and in the former jobs they've enjoyed? Whom do you have in your experience they, too, might want to know?

Accountants went to school to become Accountants just as Purchasing Agents went to school to become Purchasing Agents. They connected with other accounting and purchasing students, but also with *everyone* they met. Friendships and professional associations were formed. Grad school may have been in the mix. Affiliations with others who went to work for different companies represent resources for both of you.

The experiences, connections and contacts that most of us have are disguised to everyone else until we bring them out of the shadows and examine them. That's where relationships are formed.

"As a solopreneur and business owner, relationship is everything. 90% of my business is referrals, so this is pivotal. When I come from a place of giving rather than what I can gain, the experience is far more dimensional, rewarding and enriching. If everyone were to focus on 'what can I do for this person?' or 'Who do I know that can help this person?' most people, if not all, will leave feeling uplifted, supported and energized by the experience."

Nicole Danielle Cavanaugh (nicoledanielledesign.com)

~~~~~~~

The 'Two-Hundred Fifty' Principle

How many people would you say you know? People you would say you know well enough to say hello if you ran into them at the grocery store? Probably more than you realize.

I have great appreciation for Donna Fisher and Sandy Vilas, authors of the great book called *Power Networking* (Bard Press), who tell us researchers say that each one of us have, on average, about 250 people we interact with in our lives. Some have 500, some have 100, but the average is about 250. The list is made up of family members, friends, college buddies, the dentist, the person who delivers your mail and so on. You don't necessarily know them all as well as you know your parents and siblings, but some of them you do know well, and everyone on your list of 250 has another 250 in *their* network.

250 x 250 x 250 x 250

I find it fun to imagine there is a bubble floating above the head of everyone you meet. Let's say you attend a networking event and there are 99 others in the room, all of them with a bubble above their head. As they turn toward you or as they walk around, their bubble follows them, just like the one above your head follows you. As you step closer to someone, perhaps your bubble and her bubble sort of bounce against each other like balloons, each seeking space to float above the two of you. If four or five people are gathered together in

The Way of The Conscientious Connector

a circle and talking to each other, five bubbles float above the group. I think you get the picture.

Now it is time for the fun part - math. Let's assume you have 100 people in your organization. How many potential connections to other people are represented in that group alone?

100 Employees x 250 = 25,000 Potential Connections

That's kind of crazy, don't you think? But it is true. Whomever you talk to and get to know has about 250 other people in their experience, on average. Ten people have a relationship representing 2,500. It doesn't mean you can automatically tap into that vast resource and suddenly have that many customers or people who want to hire you and it doesn't mean if you are a car salesperson that you will now sell every car on your lot in short order, but it should tell you that, with the right approach and the right tools in place, you have a ton of connections to others right in front of you. By concentrating on just your ten best connections, whether they are clients or people you work with, what could happen? Let's keep going, here.

A Radical Idea - Take An Untypical Guest With You

Want to have some real fun and gain an enormous perspective at the same time? Take your VP of Purchasing with you to your next networking event. Seriously! If not Purchasing then Accounting or HR. Take someone with you who knows the company from a different perspective than your own. If you're not in sales but are attending a networking event, bring someone else from the company who is in a different department. Treat them to it. Buy them a sandwich if you must. They will love it and your company will gain insights.

Why? Because it sends a profound message to everyone at the networking event as well as everyone in your company that you are a team player, that your special guest is a team player and that your whole company thinks differently.

Few companies ever let the 'other support people' out to go do this and yet, when you think about it, everyone else in a company matters just as much as you.

Let's say your VP of Accounting is Roberta. You ask her to accompany you to a networking event. You introduce her and she is asked to give her perspective of your company. What do you think Roberta would say? Very likely, she would find herself with the unusual opportunity to brag on her Accounting Division and say great things about the systems she has implemented and the solid support staff she supervises. Think about it: Roberta rarely gets to do that in public with total strangers and, if I were standing there and listening I would be very impressed. There have been only a handful of times I have ever seen a company represent themselves in this way, but each time I did it was refreshing to hear someone other than in sales talk about the company. I felt I was gaining an even better perspective about how solid that company is and I was delighted that other departments came to the event and 'represented'.

~~~~~~~~

There exists enormous opportunities for having your connections work, once you understand all of the avenues available. Multiply your influence by tapping into the accessible resources. Take others in the company with you when you network. Gain information from seasoned people in your company. Find out what they know, whom they know and then find out from them how you can help yourself and the company to be more successful at the same time.

When you walk into any networking event from now on, see beyond the dollar signs on everyone's forehead and appreciate how much we all have in common. As a bone fide *Conscientious Connector*, you will no longer have preconceived notions about who has value and who does not. Everyone becomes someone who might either need your help or provide help to you.

HOMEWORK

1. Pick someone you have never met and test yourself on how much information you can gather and how long it takes.

2. Practice asking questions and gaining information from people and, as you do, notice how they react to being granted your full attention and the benefit of your multiple questions as you interview them. You'll continue to become a master at this.

3. Practice writing down everything you hear them say. Have your notepad ready. Don't try to remember everything, but use your paper and pen and show genuine interest in them by recording their responses. You can use this information later and input it into their profile.

4. Notice how comfortable you become after you ask a few questions and get things rolling. Notice how the other person is regarding you as someone interested in them, which is always a high compliment from anyone.

5. Practice this on others. Get really good at this and you are on your way to being a true *Conscientious Connector.*

6. Journal everything and all your experiences; the good, the bad, the uncomfortable. It will tell you volumes about where you really are now and show you how you can get to where you want to be in this process.

ALWAYS LOOK FOR WAYS TO WIN THE ROOM

It's not about you and never will be.

"People do not buy goods and services. They buy relations, stories and magic."

Seth Godin

~~~~~~~~

Judy Nelson has been with the Long Beach Chamber of Commerce for more years than she cares to remember and is one of the many reasons their program, under the fine direction of Randy Gordon, is so successful. Judy is their untiring VP of Business Councils and has supervised, coordinated, and produced hundreds upon hundreds of events for the Chamber. She and I have enjoyed many a conversation and Judy shares the same perspective and opinion that it is the Chambers' responsibility to provide the 'arena' and it is we, the attendees, who must bring our 'game' and make the most of it.

Unfortunately, when folks decide not to renew their membership in chambers or networking groups, it's usually because they didn't apply the right thinking and actions that would have produced better results and, as a result, they will often try to use the excuse that the organization *didn't do enough for them* or *didn't bring in business*. That's unfortunate, for *The Way of The Conscientious Connector* makes Chambers of Commerce and other networking organizations virtual goldmines for opportunities to grow databases of the right contacts and connections.

A major reason some people fail is because of their approach, which is to show up with the answers to what I call the big three questions: What is your name? What is your company name? What do you do?

The big three are usually covered this way:

(1) *My name is Tom.*

(2) *My company is Tom's Shoes.*

(3) *I sell shoes.*

Let me just tell you that immediate, better results are waiting for you when you adopt a better approach. Are there differentiating facts in this fictional example that could vastly improve Tom's ability to attract contacts and connections? It all has to do with providing the right, compelling information that differentiates Tom's business from everyone else.

For example, does Tom's company-

- Provide people with comfortable, affordable and good-looking footwear they will be proud to wear?

- Offer styles no one else has?

- Deliver shoes?

- Have a website?

- Include package deals and wholesale discounts for multiple purchases over a certain period of time?

- Have other items in his store that compliments shoes such as handbags, scarves, jewelry, etc.?

- Carry more sizes and varieties of shoes than other stores?

- Have any additional training and education that is rare amongst competitors?

- Raise funds for the homeless or provide shoes for them with the purchases we make in his store?

Take a look at this example and apply it to your company. Once you have thought through all the ways you and your company are different than your competitors and you share this information when you introduce yourself, people have a chance to grasp the reasons why they might consider helping you be more successful by thinking of good referrals. First, however, you must give them compelling information for that kind of opportunity to be worthy of their time and effort.

Let me give you more examples.

Betsy Takes Notes

Let's say Betsy is a professional bookkeeper and attends one of Long Beach Chamber's network breakfasts. Will Betsy stand and say she is (1) Betsy, (2) works for ABC Accounting and (3) does bookkeeping? If Betsy listens to the others' remarks and perhaps even takes notes, she might find opportunities to provide others in the room with potential possibilities for more success.

"Hi, I'm Betsy from ABC Accounting firm here in town and I handle the bookkeeping for five firms across several industries. Our company is diverse and we have served this community for over 25 years. In addition, I am on the Board for the local YWCA and devote many of my off hours to helping young women decide what they would like to do for their careers. Because I am involved in many activities, I am sure I have made connections with people you would like to meet. My name is Betsy. Let's talk more afterwards."

~~~~~~~

Let's analyze the many lessons from this example.

First, Betsy didn't bother telling people her last name.

- Last names are only going to be important for people to know when it is time to connect. No one is going to worry about writing down a last name right in the middle of these announcements. Writing down a first name and following up later is sufficient. This takes away any concerns for trying to hear the last name correctly or spell the name correctly while missing the next few remarks that are far more important. Don't worry and don't waste precious time with last names.

Second, Betsy didn't bother to tell you how long she has been working for ABC Accounting.

- 30 seconds goes by quickly. We hear Betsy mention that the company has been in business for over 25 years and she handles five different industries herself, so we quickly learn that she is the real-deal in terms of credentials. Moreover, Betsy gets to another aspect of her existence and her passion and lets us know she cares very much about helping young girls through the YWCA. Perhaps others will find this most interesting, too, and want to learn more about it.

Third, Betsy told us she has developed many connections that might be good for us.

- Betsy shared she knows a lot of key leaders. People who might also be good leads and referrals for others in the room. Remember, when you are seeking what to say when it is your turn, look for ways to talk about others, not yourself. In this example, Betsy is letting the room know that she has connections they might also benefit from. If you heard that, would you seek her out later for more information? Of course you would, and you'd appreciate the offer.

Instead of providing what everyone expects, Betsy is a great example of how you can say a lot in a little amount of time and how, when remarks are focused out toward what you can do for others instead of toward yourself, more dialogue can open up for everyone.

By learning to listen to what others will tell you, whether you are interviewing them one-on-one or you are listening to their remarks when introductions are being made, you can craft your responses to demonstrate your interest in helping others be more successful.

Paul

Let's take a look at an excellent example of two approaches to what is said by a fictional character named Paul. Attending a networking breakfast, Paul Johnson has taken his place at one of the 15 tables and the opening introductions have already started. Paul subconsciously counted how many people would go before it's his turn and now it's 'crunch time.' The microphone is about to be handed to him. As he scoots back his chair and prepares to stand and deliver his 30-second introduction his mind is already speed-testing his remarks. As he rises, he can already feel a hundred sets of eyeballs on him. He comes to a full upright posture and reluctantly brings the microphone to his lips only to pull it away because of feedback. His mind tells him to smile and be friendly and he can feel the palms of his hands tingle from the adrenalin. There are many in the room he already knows but there are many more he has yet to meet. He, like everyone else, wants to make a good first impression.

[Note: The following set of examples demonstrates two introductions Paul can use. The first is typical. The second is revolutionary because there is so much more depth and potential involved for everyone who hears it.]

30-Second Introduction, Take One

"Hi. My name is Paul Johnson and my company is Johnson & Associates. If you are ever in need of a new roof, please call Johnson & Associates at 555-123-4567. I am in the phone book and we are members in good standing with the BBB. Not all roofs are the same, so please give us the opportunity to serve you. We do free evaluations and would love to provide you a competitive quote. Thank you." Paul passes the microphone to the next person and sits down.

One could describe his remarks as clean and clear. Paul gave us information about what he does and what he knows for those who have their own homes. Everyone should be concerned about his or her roofs and he offers a competitive free quote. Paul follows this logical formula because he believes this is all he can do with a short intro. It represents the standard answer to the question of *"what do you do?"*

Could Paul do more with this opportunity in the same amount of time? Let's see.

A Better Way

30-Second Introduction, Take Two

"Hi, my name is Paul Johnson and my company is very good at repairing and replacing roofs. But the more important thing to remember about me is that I know a lot of people you might be looking to meet. After 25 years of serving this community, I have a pretty substantial contact database and so if you are looking to be of service to homeowners in some manner, we should talk about that because I might be able to help you." Paul passes the microphone to the next person and sits down.

As a *Conscientious Connector,* which version would you say is the one that will garner more attention for Paul and his business?

Take One is a clean and basic introduction that most people would like. Paul tells us what he does, how to reach him and why we should. He leaves the door open to a free quote and gently suggests we might want to have him check our roof now rather than later. It is a gentleman's way of not pushing; just being a nice and friendly guy who wants to remind people he has been around a long time and provides an important product and service that people need. And, frankly, there is nothing wrong with this approach, except for the fact that it only talks about how Paul's company can provide a new roof or repairs to an old one. This same message is repeated once a month and Paul hopes people will remember where to find him. I liken this to having a monthly reminder on your computer that tells you about a product you may, someday, be interested in purchasing.

Does Paul want to improve his market share? The old saying that 'if you just sit on the fence without making a decision you can get shot from either side' holds true. If Paul does want to improve his market share, he must do more than just show up. He needs to generate more connections and contacts who have many good reasons to want to help him be more successful and the way Paul can do that is by helping them, first.

Take Two acknowledges others in the room. The basics are still here in terms of how to reach Paul for more information but he doesn't spend a lot of that precious 30 seconds talking about what he does for a living. Instead, he spends the time talking about how he could probably help others in the room be more successful and, in fact, when he takes this approach, there are over three-dozen extensions of other related professions, many of them represented in the room as he speaks.

1. Life Insurance

2. Real Estate

3. Landscaping

4. Termite Control

5. Pool Maintenance

6. Garage Doors

7. Windows

8. Home Furnishings

9. Electricians

10. Painters

11. Plumbers

12. Appliances

13. Garage Makeovers

14. General Contractors

15. Tile

16. Flooring

17. Carpets

18. House Cleaning

19. Awnings

20. Patio Furniture

21. BBQ's

22. Patio Covers

23. Fencing

24. Lighting

25. Medical Practitioners

26. Music Lessons

27. Karaoke Machines

28. Gyms

29. Caterers

30. Family Dentists

31. Restaurants

32. Private schools

33. Dry Cleaning

34. Pools

35. Landscaping and more...

Do you find it interesting that each and every one of these professionals (as well as others I haven't listed) go out every day looking for the same clients Paul services? And, just as we talked about in the last chapter, each of them has an average of 250 in their own experience that might benefit each other. (The Dentist, for example, might also need everyone else listed, just as the Painting Contractor, etc.)

250

This is where my head starts to hurt, but let me do the math: 250 x 35 different-but-related professions represented in this example equals *8,750 connections...* and we're just getting started.

While you ponder the thought of how long it would take to actually connect with over 8,000 people, it is far more important that you understand what *one person at a networking event can accomplish in less than 30 seconds* when you are a *Conscientious Connector.*

Let's review what Paul said as well as how he said it and what we can learn from this.

First, Paul kept the remarks about himself and his company to a minimum.

- If you want to investigate Paul's company, it is easy to do. Ask him for his business card and follow up. Paul didn't lose anything by not giving us a history of the company. He also demonstrated that because he knows that our investigation to learn more about Paul and his company will only yield additional good news, he isn't worried about whether you retained historical information about his company in the brief time he had to speak. As a result, he put everyone else first by doing this!

Second, Paul focused almost all his remarks on (a) the fact that he has a lot of contacts and (b) he *might* be willing to share those connections with others in the room.

- This implies his willingness to do that. It doesn't guarantee he will. He left himself the option of which people he will refer to his valued clients only after he has a certain level of trust with those who approach him. Those who want to jump on Paul's bandwagon should expect Paul to protect his own reputation with his customers in this process and they should also expect

Paul's scrutiny, which is certainly fair.

Third, Paul went first.

- Paul demonstrated how a *Conscientious Connector* thinks and, thereby, demonstrated how this should be done. Paul set a totally different stage than those who only look out for themselves. When others see how effective this is the shift will begin. This is what I call *a standout* approach.

Fourth, Paul set the stage for building camaraderie amongst his peers.

- Those who heard Paul's remarks likely have competitors of their own in the room. Those who see the value of what Paul said will line up to talk to Paul afterwards. As a *Conscientious Connector,* Paul will take it from here and decide whom he wants to add to his list of referral partners for his clients and also gain information on everyone else at the same time.

The Way of The Conscientious Connector is much like a quarterback at the line of scrimmage who reads the defense. You are your own quarterback who must learn to read the room and identify potential opportunities to help others become more successful. You know what is possible; what crazy numbers of connections are represented within networking groups, companies you call upon, people you meet, friends and family who also have tons of people in their experience. Think of yourself as a professional treasure hunter because you truly are surrounded with the potential for building a tremendous team for yourself and others.

Team Thinking

My son Joe owns a success story called Anaheim Hills Tile & Supply (ahtile.com) and he knows he cannot do everything himself. He continues to collect the best experts he can find who know all there is to know about flooring, carpets, bathroom fixtures, tub replacements, kitchen cabinets, painting, drywall and more. It is his 'team of experts' that he counts on to do the jobs right the first time. Sometimes he will also call upon the expertise of his brother-in-law Jason, an excellent finish carpenter who is building his list of qualified and reliable people.

As Joe adds another contractor to the team, everyone knows the level of service and performance each contractor must uphold, not only to their own standards but also to the high standards of the group. Each contractor on the team also knows they can be replaced. It works well because everyone is invested in the group's success, not just the individual companies involved. The winner in this arrangement is Joe's client because Joe knows that anywhere along the line, if someone doesn't do their job well, it is an ultimate reflection on Joe's team and Joe's company even if Joe had nothing to do with the poor performance of a team member.

What kind of 'team' can you build for yourself? In the example above, we see that Paul starts with recognizing how much more he can accomplish when he first looks to see how he can support others. When it is your turn to introduce yourself, start with telling people how you can support *them*.

Use a Drill to Make a Hole - Use a Hammer to Drive a Nail

The more thought-out the answer to these questions the more effective you can be. If you are Anaheim Hills Tile & Supply, do you provide tile or do you *provide your valued clients with affordable ways to make their homes more beautiful and enjoyable while protecting the homeowner's investment?*

- Advertising Specialists help ensure your target market finds you.

- Architects build nice, functional places for you to work and live.

- Bankers take a special interest in being there to help your business grow.

- Carpenters build you structures that are safe, secure and beautiful.

- Dance Instructors bring the joy of dance to you.

- Dentists help your families live healthier, more attractive lives.

- Florists bring the wonder of nature into your office and home.

- Hair Stylists bring out the best in your beauty.

- Insurance Agents help you live a secure life, free from financial worry.

- Lawyers protect your interests while you live your life.

- Life Coaches help you realize your full potential.

- Mechanics ensure your family arrives home safe and sound.

- Painting Contractors provide you beautiful, welcomed environments.

- Psychologists help you have a healthy inside and outside.

- Purchasing Agents provide you diligent oversight of your company's expenditures.

- Real Estate Agents help you find the home of your dreams at the price you can afford.

- Restaurants treat your family like their family and serve unique meals.

- Web Designers create ways for you to capture more audience and market share.

No matter what your occupation or training, when you answer "what do you do?" with more than your job title, you are effectively opening up the potential for a conversation, which means a two-way dialogue rather than a one-way dialogue that is only about you.

In every instance, the emphasis should remain squarely on the benefit your occupation and skill set brings to the other person you are talking to and to the customers, clients and associates you serve. *It's never about you.* It's always about *them.* Even when they ask you to talk about you, keep the emphasis and focus on them in every way you can, because unless they are also *Conscientious Connectors* (and you will be able to easily tell if they are), they will nevertheless naturally want to fit you into a category they can call upon later. Ensure that what they remember about you and the category they place you in is related to how *they* can benefit by knowing you.

When in Doubt, Point to Someone Else

All of us at one time or another can become tongue-tied and lose track of what we should say when it is our turn to stand and deliver information about ourselves to someone else or to a group.

If you are ever in search for what to say when it is your turn, pick someone you know or just met, go over (in your mind) what it is you can do for that person and construct your remarks around them. Put yourself in their shoes. What would they want? Why would they want it? What's in it for them? How would that make them more successful? Happier? Just keep asking until something comes to you.

And, if you *still* struggle with what you can offer that person, you nevertheless have the option of talking not about what your products or services might do for them, *but how you see the opportunity to introduce that person to people you know.* It will still remain something you can do for them, not yourself. Either way, your remarks will serve someone else and that will always separate you from the rest of the room.

When you demonstrate your willingness to help the other person, first, you begin to pull people toward you. They see it. They hear it. They witness the reaction from others you put first and few can deny how much they would like to have that same quiet confidence you demonstrate. Instead of talking about you and selling your company, you stand and deliver sincere caring for others. I can tell you from first-hand experience that *The Way of the Conscientious Connector* ultimately wins loyalty and a following.

Imagine I am at a networking breakfast and it is my turn to stand and introduce myself. I might say something as simple as this:

"When I arrived this morning I had a nice conversation with Bob Phelps, right there (motion to Bob who raises a hand) and I just realized that I have an associate I want to introduce to Bob and I will do that as soon as I return to my office. My name is Dave and I help companies and individuals by promoting them to the right people. Have a great week everyone."

~~~~~~~

Conscientious Connectors 'read the room' and hold in mind the needs of the audience with every statement, example and story. It is not about you; it is about them. The construction of the remarks you make must always have that focus. Otherwise, you will blend into the walls like everyone else who still thinks all they are supposed to do is show up. In the example, above, what do you think the reaction is going to be from the audience? Will they think of me as someone who pitched to them? Who tried to sell them something? The lasting impression I will leave with most of them is that I am a professional who gave up my time with the mic to help someone else and that I am obviously confident enough in my own business success story; I am not in need of pitching my company to anyone. In other words, I am demonstrating the reasons more people would want to know me.

It is no different if you are asked to be a guest speaker at an event. By constructing your talk for the benefit of what you can provide your audience, you stand out from someone who wants to only talk about him or herself. People respond well when there is something in it for them. You can set it up with relative stories about yourself but you must *always* be sure to circle back and tie it in to what your audience will want to hear and embrace. And, by the way, the next time you sit and listen to a guest speaker, take special note as to whether the speaker is focusing his or her remarks on themselves or on information the audience can use. If you start to feel you'd like to find the nearest exit it may be because you feel underappreciated.

Conscientious Connectors speak in terms that *audiences* relate to according to the *audiences'* needs. Whether you are giving a presentation or a 30-second intro, and anything in between, the more you relate your remarks to reflect your concern for others and not just yourself, the more of a standout you will become.

HOMEWORK

1. Write out what you do and what you represent. Are there any other non-competing companies you know of who also sell to your target market? List them.

2. Look at the networking groups you belong to. Are any of the above-mentioned professionals in your group? Have you already introduced them to your target audience?

3. Who do you know that can benefit the group? Have you had that conversation? Explored those possibilities? Perhaps you did if you had to turn in leads and referrals in your networking group. Perhaps not.

4. Write down how you're feeling about turning over these leads and referrals to someone. Are you excited to do that or are you guarded because you are not sure you want to give certain referrals to key people you know? Are there trust issues? This is your reputation on the line, here. Whomever you refer to your valued clients carries a responsibility. Don't apologize for that.

THE TOUGHER THE INDUSTRY
THE GREATER THE NEED

Belong to a tough industry? All the more reason…

A few years ago I sent a personal note to one of my heroes, Zig Ziglar, to thank him for his inspiration, humor and lessons learned from his books and videos about business and about creating relationships. Zig was one-of-a-kind. Knowing that he was aging and starting to slow down on personal appearances, I determined that at the very least I could express to him my appreciation.

About a month later, I was over the moon the day I received a response via a personal note and autographed picture from him. I have his note framed next to the picture. I re-read it from time to time for inspiration. The last sentence says, *"I look forward our paths crossing one day, too, Dave. In the meantime, keep up the good work, have a good forever and I'll definitely see you over the top!"*

That note is dated November 4th, 2008 and Zig transitioned November 28th, four years later. As I read his note and reflect back on all that he taught me, and continues to teach me, I realize now that the book you are holding was inspired by Zig's admonition that so many of us have heard and adopted:

"You can have anything you want if you will just help enough other people get what they want. "

Zig was fun, funny and humble, but he always made his point to the audience and to his students. His storied metaphors about 'priming the pump' complete with a physical pump handle he would bring with him on his speaking tours and training sessions, was legendary and timeless. It demonstrated the idea that once you connect with someone and help them reach their goals, success will come to you, too, if you continue to serve others and never let go of that responsibility.

So, some industries are tougher than others, as we would all agree. Does that mean that the concepts of *The Way of The Conscientious Connector* only work for certain industries and not all of them? How about Show Business?

Showbiz is tough!

I love it when folks challenge me with this question and I think it is only fitting to test it out. Let's pick a really tough industry, an industry where there are people climbing over each other in their individual pursuits, where legendary examples of cutthroat management tactics have been the fodder for any number of great stories: Show Business!

Thousands of actors are out there each day, vying for one or two available jobs, which means the odds are really stacked against them! If they are even invited into the audition, it is still a huge, uphill climb to win over the director. The variable reasons why one actor is chosen over all the others can be innumerable.

And, that's just the beginning. Fairly or unfairly, tales of nepotism, playing favorites, old money, investors who want to control things and the ever-familiar and so-called casting couch, I know of no other industry that has a bigger reputation for unscrupulous activities than Show Business. And I should know because, as I like to say, I married into it.

For example, my wife, Gaye Kruger, was an actress, singer and dancer and now directs on occasion following a great career that spanned 25 years. Her sister DeeDee Rescher is a very talented actress and voice over specialist who continues to star in plays and

TV. She auditions every other week, it seems, for a role in something. Both sisters, as well as their younger sister, Debbie Jean Miller, successful director of preschool programs, were blessed with an actress mother and an award-winning director of photography father. Of course it all started with their grandfather Otto Kruger, who starred on Broadway and in the movies. Everyone agrees that Showbiz is tough. How does one deal with such a tough industry, then? By being a *Conscientious Connector.*

Here's what I mean. My friend Barbara Niven is arguably one of the hardest working actresses in Hollywood. You have probably seen her numerous times in stories presented on the Hallmark Channel. After reading her resume (barbaraniven.com) you will wonder when she has any time left for herself. She is an Actress, Producer, Video/Media Trainer, Speaker, Author and the founder of Dreamer's Network. Just imagine for a moment how many people she has to stay in touch with, how many people she has to work with, report to and audition for on a regular basis. These contacts include writers, producers, directors and associates, plus managers and publicists. I asked Barbara to share her thoughts on the subject:

"My secret for having a 30-year career in this very fickle industry? I'm a *Conscientious Connector* who builds and nourishes great relationships and I concentrate on giving.

"I always tell acting newbies, 'you got booked? Great! Celebrate, but keep it in perspective. It is just one job. As soon as it's over you'll be unemployed again. Repeat business is what gives you a career'.

"How do you become someone that gets booked over and over again? People want to work with team players; people they genuinely like who bring good energy into a project, whom they can count on and whom they know will have their back.

"Being a *Conscientious Connector* in my profession also means helping others make the connections they can rely upon. We all need friends we can trust and as word gets around, people learn they can rely on you. They become loyal fans that recommend you and sing your praises to others. That goes both ways too – I do the same for them.

"Now that I am also a Video Coach and Media Trainer, every one of my students wants to know the right people to work with for branding, marketing, getting their book published, their website established and their email marketing campaign going the right way. I never hesitate to recommend people I can vouch for to others whom I know will take good care of them. That is what a *Conscientious Connector* does. We take care of each other, we watch out for each other and everyone benefits."

~~~~~~~

There's a need for connections in every industry and *the tougher the industry, the greater the need* for people who see the benefits of helping each other reach success. Not only does it feel right, it is logically imperative that we all get behind this idea and bring it into our every day. If you are in an industry that is filled with people who are difficult to deal with (like many of the people in Hollywood), you need connections and you need to know they are connections you can count on.

It is fascinating to me how the very nature of tougher industries easily confirms that the tougher the industry, the greater the need.

HOMEWORK

1. We talked about tough industries. Do you consider your industry to be in that category? Why? Are you looking to get into a tougher than usual industry? Whatever your situation, write down how you feel about your category of business and what are your perceived obstacles.

2. Think about whether you have fully captured all the information on the people you are dealing with and whether you have more you can do in terms of finding out how to help them. These are leverage points; they are the process of taking the spotlight off you and placing it squarely on the people who are providing you a tough atmosphere. The way to counter that is to show them you are more than willing to go to work on their behalf in helping them be more successful. Most people will respond favorably to this kind of attitude. For the tougher industries this kind of approach is rare and that's great news because it will help you become a standout in that regard.

3. Put together a game plan for how you can use your information to get inside the inner circle of influence, the place where you want to be to enjoy more success for yourself.

4. Practice going over everything from the other person's perspective and do this before revealing the help you are about to offer them. Get yourself primed because this could be a game changer for you. Your competition hasn't likely bothered to take things to this higher level of detailed planning and preparation and that is all good news for you.

NOTES

STEP 4

EXPAND! EXPAND! EXPAND!
GROW YOUR TALENT & GROW YOUR EFFECTIVENESS

Let's recap! You are doing great! I hope that by now you are embracing *"The Way"* as your own personal approach to the world. I am sure you will agree that the more *Conscientious Connectors* we can create, the more success stories we can expect.

Section One is about the inherent advantages available when you approach this process from a different perspective and the difference between surface connecting and really going to a deeper level with a much broader audience; why worrying about reciprocation is a waste of your time, energy and emotion.

Section Two opens things up even more by talking about how this broader audience can become more valuable to you from now on, how the wisdom of Walt Disney teaches you that everyone matters and how you will now look at everyone as people who have needs you can assist with and people who also have connections they can share with you.

Section Three further expands this thinking by showing you that you can actually accelerate your progress by slowing down, just a bit, so you can capture more information about other people. We talk about ways to turn any room of professionals into a group of supporters and we challenge whether some industries are tougher than others.

Section Four shares many things to consider when joining organizations; about how important it is to not rely totally on the Internet for connections; about how to really know what motivates people. Get out your Journal and get ready to write!

NOTES

STEP FOUR / CHAPTER TEN

INFLUENCE *SEVERAL* GROUPS

A breakdown of organizations and why you need more than one

Dr. Ivan Misner, founder of the world's largest networking organization (BNI) will tell you the same thing I am about to tell you: *Be a member of more than just one networking organization.*

Why? Because there are advantages to spreading your influence! People come and go. I have many friends who have been members of various networking organizations for years yet they move around to check out new groups. I, too, continue to enjoy the relationships I have made from a variety of organizations I supported and, through them, I have met incredible people and expanded my database of *Conscientious Connectors.*

As the saying goes, the one thing that remains constant is change. People transfer to new jobs, new cities, and new departments/divisions. Their companies merge with other companies. Some may even change careers. Circumstances in our private lives often dictate necessary changes. We face financial challenges. Some folks simply decide to move to a different or better neighborhood.

Things are constantly evolving and if you stay in touch with people even after they, or you, move away, you will continue to build a bigger and better database of connections. People will take you with them. Therefore, it imperative that you become a member of more than one networking organization and you dedicate yourself to staying in touch with members who move on. Continue to 'collect' connections in an authentic way and you will continue to expand your potential for success no matter what you want to accomplish.

I have many friends in BNI, Le Tip and other groups. Many who are members of those groups are also members of at least one Chamber of Commerce. It's a good idea because it exposes you to more people and prospects right away. Important note: Chambers have more members than private groups.

Should Larger, High Profile Companies Also Join? Yes!

An attorney friend of mine (whom I met, ironically, at a smaller chamber network mixer) once told me that his client, a high powered investment group of professionals, would never need training in this way because *"their target market would never be in the room."* Really?

I reminded him that if his client were only interested in showing up to sell and not interested in building solid, long-term relationships with people who would refer them to others, then I would have to agree with him. But, as you know by now, there is a better way. The larger companies that join chambers and participate can do a lot of good for the group as well as for themselves and that is good public relations, if nothing else.

A *Conscientious Connector* who understands the value in being a part of more than one networking group will have a decided advantage over folks who limit themselves to one arena of networking possibilities. Not every organization, however, will let you be a part of more than one group, so let's talk about your options.

Chambers of Commerce

Following an idea that was developed in Europe a century and a half earlier, Benjamin Franklin brought the idea to America that if local merchants could come together and figure out ways to make the farmers coming to town want to stick around a bit longer, all the merchants might benefit. That idea was the foundation for what we would later refer to as the Chamber of Commerce that has served all of us so very well ever since.

But the Chamber of Commerce is there to set the stage, not to bring you the business. As my friend John Wilson always said, *"The Chamber brings the arena but it is* you *who must bring the game."*

I have many friends who work for various Chambers of Commerce and they all say that when membership renewal time rolls around, the most common reason members don't re-up is because *'the chamber didn't bring me enough new business.'*

Seriously? It is not now nor has it ever been the responsibility of the Chamber of Commerce to provide *anyone* business. It provides the setting. It provides the audience. Its truly dedicated organizers stay up at night and dream up additional ways to draw the crowd so that WE can go to work and make the connections we are looking to make. If there isn't enough business coming from your membership in a Chamber is it because you aren't working hard enough, or smart enough, at helping others become more successful.

Could it be because you have a reputation as a surface connector like I used to be and you need to expand your influence in a better way?

A Note To All You Big Companies Out There

There are huge companies in every city that will join a Chamber of Commerce for the 'community relations' benefit it brings them and yet they already know they will never send a representative to any of the events, breakfasts or mixers. Why? Because they only see the membership made up of companies and individuals who will never become their direct customer which is yet another example of 'Surface Connecting 101'.

Here are the facts: No matter the size of a company, it is always going to be made up of people who need dentists, doctors, lawyers, florists, real estate agents, contractors, investment experts, accountants, and restaurants. If a big company thinks all it needs to do is write a big membership check once a year in order to gain good press and attention, it's sadly missing the advantages of being a

Conscientiously Connected Company.

Typically for a Chamber membership, you pay a yearly fee and a fee for some of the events like the breakfasts and for access to all the functions. You can have your information listed in the online directory. You can be a sponsor of an event, a speaker (usually for a fee) and you can be a member in good standing with a certificate handed to you when you do your ribbon cutting and the local paper takes your picture. Many excellent Chambers of Commerce around the country are there to advocate for you.

The difference between Chambers of Commerce and private networking organizations is that there is no limit to how many members of a particular profession can become members. As a result, most Chambers have more than one insurance agent, attorney, real estate agent, bank, chiropractor, financial planner, handyman and other types of local businesses and that's ok, too, because the more people of various types of professions in a Chamber, the better, especially when *Conscientious Connectors* are involved.

Private Networking Groups

As I mentioned earlier, there are private networking groups including BNI, Le Tip, ProVisors and many other very good organizations. These groups provide a more exclusive experience for members. Some folks feel they do better when there is less competition, but there are tradeoffs.

I happen to know that if you are a *Conscientious Connector* you will be fine no matter where you are, but hey, that's something you've heard from me a few times already.

BNI is a great organization and has a list of 50 categories. If your profession qualifies and there is an opening for that spot you can apply for that position. In most cases, you will have to be recommended and interviewed, so reputation for being a top notch professional will help you gain that spot over someone else, which is one of the objectives of going through the interview process and having someone recommend you to the club. It keeps the level of professionalism as high as possible with the theory that every member will carry equal weight in contributing to the group and conduct him or herself in the best professional manner.

A typical *private* networking group like this will have one CPA, one Divorce Attorney, one Real Estate Agent and so on. As long as a member continues to contribute their fees, their time, energy and referrals to the rest of the members, that arrangement can continue for years.

If, on the other hand, the referrals they count each week fall off, the group may want to replace that person with new blood so that the rest of the group continues to thrive. That's the objective and the reason for having the exclusive membership in the first place.

Which leads me to why being a *Conscientious Connector* is so valuable when you are considering joining any networking group.

Consider Other Organizations

Your higher skill level, as a *Conscientious Connector,* will help you see with different eyes. Once you know what you are looking for in a group to join, it will become evident which groups would be best.

Most people who join Chambers of Commerce or private networking organizations have an agenda that includes selling their products and services. They may be a CPA or an Attorney, meaning they don't have *salesperson,* necessarily, as part of their job description, but they are, nevertheless, acting as sales people for their businesses when they show up at networking events.

Are there other organizations where you could *also* do more good for yourself and for others you meet? My answer would be: "*Yes, quite possibly.*" Service organizations are also amazing networking groups. Here are three service organizations with which you may already be familiar. I have pasted information straight from their websites.

Lions Clubs International, *a service membership organization of over 1.4 million members world-wide (as of April 2015), was founded in the United States on June 7, 1917, by Melvin Jones, a Chicago businessman. Jones asked, with regard to his colleagues, "What if these men, who are successful because of their drive, intelligence and ambition, were to put their talents to work improving their communities?" Jones' personal code, "You can't get very far until you start doing something for somebody else," reminds many Lions of the importance of community service.* (www.lionsclubs.org)

As my friend, Sara Blatt Collins will tell you, **Rotary International** *is an international service organization whose stated human rights purpose is to bring together business and professional leaders in order to provide humanitarian services, encourage high ethical standards in all vocations, and to advance goodwill and peace around the world. It is open to all people regardless of race, color, creed, religion, gender, or political* preference. *There are 34,282 member clubs worldwide. 1.2 million individuals called Rotarians have joined these clubs.* **(www.rotary.org)**

Service is at the heart of every **Kiwanis International** *club, no matter where in the world it's located. Kiwanis members stage nearly 150,000 service projects, devote more than 6 million hours of service and raise nearly $100 million every year for communities, families and projects. Key Club members pitch in 12 million hours of service each year, and CKI members another 500,000 hours of service! Aktion Club members donate another 92,000 hours of service every year. Add it all up, and that's more than 18 million hours of service every year!* (www.kiwanis.org)

What you will gain from joining such organizations is a healthy helping of connections to many other professionals in many other industries, something a *Conscientious Connector* will relish.

Wait! There's *More!*

You also have all sorts of other groups and organizations you can be a part of. Are you a CPA? There's an organizational association for CPA's that has local representation. The same is true for everyone from Real Estate to Law to Landscaping to Butterfly and Bird Watcher groups. What lights you up? What are you interested in? What would be an organization that you can join that might afford you a good balance between your profession and your private life? What would be fulfilling?

When you approach organizations as a *Conscientious Connector*, the world is your oyster. You have many different places you can go to help fulfill your own needs, to contribute to and to get great networking opportunities from your involvement, guaranteed.

Check out every opportunity to meet people. Don't limit yourself to just one or two places to become a member. Work on learning how to be a *Conscientious Connector* so that you are the one who brings a new approach to the art of connecting. By just doing this, you will stand out from most everyone else.

You will also broaden your influence by joining different organizations. The connectivity going on does not stop, nor do you want it to. It's more of that same, steady stream of the best connections you are creating each day and that will continue to serve you and those you meet. Always remember, too, you are bringing *them* more connections they would otherwise not have made and that's very cool.

HOMEWORK

1. What group(s) are you considering becoming a part of? If you are looking for an organization that also fills a need inside you, like Rotary, that's a consideration. Will a Chamber of Commerce be a part of your group of networking organizations you join?

2. Make up a list.

3. Plan and visit several groups. The first time you go is typically free and some will allow you to visit twice before they ask you to either join or stay away for a while. Keep in mind there are multiple groups from the same organization. Visiting one in Santa Monica doesn't preclude you from checking out a similar group in Sherman Oaks, for example.

4. After you have visited at least twice, write down what you are looking for, what groups would be ideal for you, whether you know anyone already in a group and what you want out of it. Decide, too, if you can afford it, both financially and with your time commitment.

Enthusiastically join and then immediately ask what committee opportunities are available. Find out who is looking for volunteers, for that is the absolute best way to immerse yourself into the group and become known quickly, which should be your goal. Don't hesitate and don't wait for an invitation; just get in there and start being the best *Conscientious Connector* on the planet.

STEP FOUR / CHAPTER ELEVEN

DON'T LET THE INTERNET DISCONNECT YOU

The Internet, Social Media & The Conscientious Connector

John Mackey, co-founder and co-CEO of Whole Foods Markets, and Raj Sisodia, co-founder and cochairman of Conscious Capitalism, Inc., credit in their great book, *Conscious Capitalism,* (Harvard Business Review Press 2014) the famed British physicist Tim Berners-Lee as the inventor of what would later be termed the Worldwide Web.

Their remarks echo what many others have said, that Berners-Lee *"did more to transform the world than any single individual in the past hundred years, including Churchill, Roosevelt, Gandhi and Einstein. His invention is at least as dramatically culture changing as Guttenberg's printing press was over five hundred years ago. In an extraordinarily short time, the Web has evolved into a shared nervous system that links much of humanity."* (p27)

The Internet is a fabulous tool; an unparalleled communication network that affords us the ability to connect to, learn about and approach others instantaneously. Technological advances of such magnitude also come with their own set of challenges.

Today, we rely on the Internet, digital marketing and social media of all types to pursue customers, gain information, gather referrals and research anyone or anything. We now buy online, sell online, conference call online, research online and can even turn the lights off in our home from halfway around the world, online, for example. Research tells us that more than 800 million updates happen on Facebook every day and users spend almost eight hours per month on that network. I am sure these numbers already need updating.

It was recently reported that in any given minute online, just 60 seconds, over 4,000 people visit Amazon, Apple users download more than 51,000 apps, Twitter users send over 347,000 tweets and Skype users make over 110,000 calls. Further, it has been estimated that the average Internet user in the United States spends 32 hours or more online per month. There can be no question the worldwide web has spawned a shift that has created irreversible cultural changes.

Likewise, at a recent digital forum for entrepreneurs, the following sign was displayed in consideration of how far we have come in a very short time. The observation:

The Digital Disruption Has Already Happened

- World's largest taxi company owns no taxis (Uber)

- Largest accommodation provider owns no real estate (Airbnb)

- Largest phone companies own no telecommunications infrastructure (Skype, WeChat)

- World's most valuable retailer has no inventory (Alibaba)

- Most popular media owner creates no content (FB)

- Fastest growing banks have no actual money (Society One)

- World's largest movie house owns no theatres (Netflix)

- Largest software vendors don't write the apps (Apple, Google)

Just as digital communication makes it possible for banks to transfer 'money' without any real dollar bills being rounded up and placed into a satchel, we now have whole companies who digitally 'own' property, 'house' headquarters and stream movies anywhere in the world without the need for a brick and mortar building. It is that self-perpetuating, age-old question of *"where, exactly, is the Internet?"* for which no one has a satisfactory answer. The one thing that is certain, however, is that the thirst for communicating digitally continues to accelerate, and with it, individual identities are slowly eroding.

Have we become so dependent upon digital capabilities that we have problematically become lazy in how we communicate with other human beings on a one-to-one basis? How many of us would rather type out a quick email to someone than call on the phone or meet with him or her in person? Go anywhere where there are people and count how many of them cannot function while walking or sitting at lunch without being intimate with their smart phones. I have learned, in fact, that for clients and connections of ours who are from younger generations, I stand a much better chance of their receiving my note if I text it. Getting them to pick up the phone or email me back can take days or weeks. Fire off a text, however, and the response is immediate.

If you are relying upon online automation tools to do *all* of your personal follow up, *please suspend that practice for the time it takes to consider this information,* **because the payoff in being more hands-on with your connections can be substantial! ...dr**

Clarifying *Conscientiously Connected* Internet Marketing

I cannot blame anyone for liking the convenience of creating 'evergreen' programs online that run themselves, collect data, accept and verify payments for something then sends out a receipt with the hard product or makes the soft product (download) available. That kind of thinking and the companies who constantly dream up new, more efficient and effective software to accommodate such needs will continue to proliferate the market. There's no turning back now, nor should we expect that or even want that. I, too, subscribe to this. Chances are you found this book through similar online activities and my training was formatted for download as well as for print.

Having said that...

Not everyone buys everything from the Internet nor will they ever. Sure, there will be more ways all the time to use the online exchange of information, but the Internet will never be able to replicate a child's awkward hug or accurately convey the inflection in someone's voice when they first learn they can hear after being deaf all their lives. The Internet cannot demonstrate the power of the love we have for someone else. The human interaction between patient and the doctor who made it all happen requires more than just words. It is about feeling, about humanity, about caring about someone else's success in terms that printed words and pictures will never fully convey. It is about human touch, inflection in one's voice, the personal stuff that goes well beyond opt- in pages limited by this same digital world we live in. Virtual hugs will never replace the real ones.

Connecting with someone online may be all some folks want to accomplish because they are just out there to sell something or to drive traffic. That's ok because the Internet allows us to reach a ton of people at a time.

But also recognize this fact: If the objective is to sell something without any interaction between the parties, it is a wholesale commodity approach, much like surface connecting at a network mixer. It is a one-way street, at the initial stages, and it may or may not ever turn into anything more than that. It is tantamount to being a collector of business cards and it remains to be seen whether there will be any interest in doing more than just selling something to someone.

Bringing value to the other person in more ways than just selling them good training or a product/service is what this book is about.

From the perspective of a *Conscientious Connector*, there can be more to the story that benefits both parties. Think of it as a two-way connection, a two-way street that allows you to also see what you can do for the other guy, too, just as if you were standing there in the middle of a networking event.

This chapter is about the human touch via the Internet and social media. It is about how to use the Internet to influence other professionals in a personal way.

Most people have a website or landing page attached to their business. It's often the first point of reference people check when considering doing business with you and it can be a safe place where they can take a peek at you without you knowing it so they can decide if they want to interact with you. Call it an electronic dating service, if you will. Is it possible for a *Conscientious Connector* to use this set of common circumstances advantageously?

Absolutely. I will show you many ways you can do just that. It will take a little work, but will be well worth the effort.

Always Bring It Back To Personal

For years I was privileged to write a monthly column for *Brilliant Results,* (brilliantpublishing.com) a business magazine dedicated to the Promotional Marketing industry and to the clients we serve. My good friend Maureen Williams, CEO of Brilliant Publishing, pulled experts together from both inside the industry and beyond to share their best advice, best practices, recommendations and insights. My monthly contribution was entitled *It's All Personal* and I shared stories that demonstrated how important it is that we treat our relationships with everyone as personal, not just business. Maureen is now launching several other E-magazines that deal with everything from Home Schooling to other critically important subjects, each one of them personal and very resourceful.

A *Conscientious Connector* looks at the world in that same way: Personal. If there is a slowdown at a company in Canton, Ohio, for example, and someone gets laid off, that slowdown in business affects the rest of us whether or not we know the person or live in that town. We're all connected and we all matter.

When it comes to being on the Internet for the purpose of generating interest in our products or services, why do we think we can skip the personal part of the equation? If we are out there pushing what we sell and someone shows interest, the next step is to ensure they know us, like us and want to do business with us. Is there any difference between the reassurance *you* seek when it is *about you* and the reassurance *they* seek when it is *about them*?

I totally understand the desire to speed things up, to run through potential prospect lists quickly so that you can move your business forward. That's been the methodology for years and more trainers pop up every day that train people how to write better content that leads to better conversion rates and sales. Brendon Burchard (brendon.com) is arguably the best in the world at this kind of training and I am most appreciative of what he continues to teach me, and millions more. But Brendon is first in line to also tell all of us that our purpose should always be to be of service to others, not just for grabbing sales, providing little value and moving on. I appreciate that more than I could ever express.

The goal and the ultimate payoff for all of us lies in creating more success stories for the people we come into contact with. By maintaining that focus, social media affords us cool ways to do just that.

It Is Built Into Our Nature

Psychologists have long studied the value of human touch. Jack Canfield, Wayne Dyer and many other experts have written and spoken extensively about it. Bruce Springsteen even enjoyed a hit song by the same title. We know that touching someone by giving them a hug, paying them a compliment or showing them a kindness, whether it be in physical form or through a conversation or a written complimentary reference about them to someone else, that act has actually been proven to boost the immune systems of both parties as well as anyone who witnessed the act.

In study after study, human touch is undeniably something that each and every one of us is programmed to appreciate from the moment we take our first breath. Studies are now coming out that our youth are struggling with interpersonal relationship-building aspects because they spend most of their time clicking replies on their cellphone and do not practice speaking directly to someone else. It's becoming an epidemic. Personal interaction with other human beings is essential to our collective well being. Becoming a *Conscientious Connector* can help not just you, but also the many others you connect with on a daily basis and it is clear to me that this is sorely needed in our society, both professionally and personally.

If you are not selling a commodity, like cooking knives or jewelry, facial products or DVD's to support public television, and yet your goal in using the Internet is to generate interest in your product or service such as would be the case with insurance salespeople, contractors, home furnishings experts, real estate agents, family law and thousands of other examples, the key phrase here is to 'generate interest.' This should be the *beginning* of your communication with anyone who shows an interest, not the end-all.

Rather than just sell them something, you have the opportunity to grow a relationship with them, find out how you may truly be of service to them and you have the opportunity to connect them with other people they are looking for. An automatic response (auto responder) from your online ad can get that started but it cannot finish the cycle because a personal touch is required. Don't just take my word for it. Let's ask an Internet expert.

Alex, one of my three terrifically talented kids (Joe and Katie are the other two) is an expert at all things digital. He and his team at Big Chief Creative Media (bigchiefcreative.com) create everything from Websites to Internet Marketing campaigns that include social media and search engine optimization. They then report volumes of data back to their clients; information collected non-stop, 24/7, to ensure the right people are seeing the ads, responding to the special offers, reading the content and reacting favorably to their marketing efforts in the best, most predictable way.

With all this knowledge, experience and training collected for over a decade, you might think it a simple matter for Big Chief to continually find more customers for themselves, as well, via social media. The fact is Alex and his team *continually* connects personally with prospects and clients. Alex belongs to several local networking organizations, is a major sponsor for the Little League program in town, has been a coach and manager for his sons' baseball teams and has supported his daughter's soccer activities. On a daily basis, you will find Alex talking one-to-one with prospective clients and looking for people he can help. He's a *Conscientious Connector* and even he knows that the initial effort he makes through the Internet and social media represents *part* of the picture and *only the beginning* of the work that needs to be done. Alex's take on things:

"Our job is to create awareness and drive customers and prospects to our clients. It is our job is to help cut through the 'noise' and make an impact using all of the social media tools at our disposal. We must continually remind their target audience that our client is good at what they do and anxious to be of service. No different for our company, we must use these same tools to create awareness for what we offer. We must work hard to differentiate Big Chief Creative from our competition and go after our target market with our capabilities, history and our track record. Once we have their attention, we know our job is to provide them the personal touches they are looking for, which often times includes helping to write content for them."

Social media, web presence, television, radio, magazines and other media all have one objective: create awareness. You cannot buy toothpaste from a television ad, but you can certainly jump off the couch and find a store that sells it. If your Web presence is working well, you will have people seeking you out. To speed up the process by over-automating your follow-up is something I see too many professionals do in the name of expediency and convenience. That tradeoff can be a high and unnecessary cost.

The *Conscientious Connector* sees with new eyes and hears with new ears, which separates you from all that 'noise' out there. As you approach people in your unique way to see what you can do for them, you will start to take on a different persona. People will investigate your social media platform with new interest. The Internet marketing you do for your business will start to get second and third looks, which is what you want.

Reminder - It's *All* Personal

A good example is The Breakfast Bar, a small restaurant owned by Pam and Josh Beadle here in Long Beach. Open every day for breakfast and lunch, Pam and Josh are restaurant experts and they rely on the Internet to help spread awareness. And, they know that while the Internet presence helps with cognizance, their work really starts as soon as you walk up and ask to be seated. Immediately, the wait staff greets you as they pass by your table. *That's personal.* Several will stop by while you are eating to see if they can get you anything. *That's personal.* Others will be there to thank you for coming as you are heading out the door. *That's personal.*

The same is true for a restaurant I used to take the family to when the kids were little. The food was great, the atmosphere was perfect, but the reason I came back often was because the manager took the time to memorize the first name of all three of my children. *That's personal.*

Leads, Lead Companies & Lists
The *Conscientious Connector* Approach to All Three

Just out of curiosity, how many different methods would you say are out there for capturing information about someone? Typical census reviews that are public record for a neighborhood will tell you who purchased a new house. Information about changing addresses is tracked. Change your phone number, order up cable tv, subscribe to a new local newspaper, change driver's license, send a forwarding address to the post office or a myriad other indicators and you will be caught up in the research that Leads companies go after. Insurance agents, real estate agents, local dentists, chiropractors and others will note you came to their neighborhood, as will pool cleaners, roofers, garage door experts, landscapers, painters, carpet and tile folks and more, all thanks to the diligent work of the Leads company. Telemarketing companies, direct mail companies, local grocery chains, restaurants, lawyers, and dry cleaners also use this information and I'm just getting started.

If you just had a new baby, how do you suppose an offer arrives at your door about a special deal on bottled water and diapers?

Hundreds of thousands of pieces of information about you are being assembled on a daily basis. *Did a telemarketer just call?* Yes, all of this information is compiled, combed through and made available to folks who are specialized in slicing and dicing this information six ways from Sunday. Big data is a thriving industry. In fact, did you know there is something called '*LeadsCon*', a convention dedicated to this entire industry? Go to LeadsCon.com for more information. You might be surprised at just how vast the industry is in terms of all that it does and how many different businesses and organizations use the information that is gathered. It is mind-boggling.

The collection of data that also happens online is yet another avenue for people who are looking to connect with other people but want to accelerate the process. Go to Amazon and show interest in a particular subject in the book section and watch how quickly other, similar titles start showing up on the sidebars of your FB page. You'll see what Search Engine Optimization (SEO) and other methodologies can truly accomplish and it all happens very quietly and without fanfare, yet it contributes to moving more products at retail, just for one big example, and there are many other applications you can learn more about.

I have a confession.

In my on-going research, I must confess I infiltrated an online group dedicated to insurance agents looking for marketing guidance from their peers. I decided that since I was a marketing aficionado and there was no barrier to entry, I could join the group and listen in on their comments and complaints. You will see more opportunities pop up as you continue to evolve into a master *Conscientious Connector*.

For over a year I faithfully read every remark anyone entered into this particular online chat. Many of the comments circled around the use of leads provided by Leads Companies. It was a fascinating project and it taught me a lot about what those hardworking, independent insurance agents have to deal with. It is no different for real estate agents and many others who use the pages of the Internet as well as the leads from Leads companies to look for clients.

Did you know that, for example, if you fill out an enter-to-win form for a drawing to win the new car on display at your local shopping mall, those little pieces of paper are typically sold to a Leads company? A local car dealership might use that information about you and follow-up, as one example, and invite you to come in for a test drive.

One agent said that one of the leads he received indicated that the guy had mentioned on the form he filled out for a sweepstakes he wanted an agent to call right away. The agent did. Four times. On the fifth attempt to leave a message over the course of ten days, the guy who asked for the call finally picked up the phone and asked the agent why he was calling. The agent, of course, said he was calling because the guy had indicated on the form that he wanted an agent to call right away. Only then did the guy own up to the agent that he only said he wanted an agent to call right away because he thought that would up his chances at winning the sweepstakes!

Just be careful when you put your hard earned dollars on the line and expect great referral sources. You'll probably get good leads this way, but I want you to convert them into warm leads even before you make the initial call, if you can.

Social Media Landmines

A cautionary remark:

Whether you are directly involved in sales or not, the Internet offers you an enormous opportunity to enhance your reputation. That could be good news or bad news, depending.

I will assume you have are exceedingly and excessively careful about what you say on Facebook, LinkedIn, Twitter, Email and the rest because you already know you will never be able to retrieve something that reflects negatively on you after you hit the 'send' button. Yes, it may be true that you can delete an entry on FB. Yes, it's also true that you can edit a post on LinkedIn and I have done so. In certain respects, you can even retrieve an Email, although I have serious doubts about that truly returning to you.

In a nutshell, here it is:

I hope you are as paranoid about the Internet as am I.

Don't turn anything loose to the Internet until you are absolutely certain it will only reflect positively on you, even **years** from now. In the time it takes you to send a message, then discover your error, edit it and put it back on the Internet, your original has already circled the globe a few thousand times. It's not coming back. It's not going to be 'un-seen' by people. Like that time you walked in and Grandpa took out his false teeth when you were 7 and it left an indelible mark on your psyche. Game over.

Yes, you may have corrected yourself later, but when you told your keyboard to turn it loose to the World Wide Web, *it went! To infinity and beyond!*

Applied for a job lately?

If you've applied for a job in that past few years you know that they probably won't see you in person, first. Rather, you will have to fill out applications, submit resumes online and then wait. While the Human Resource folks probably love this, it's a depressing reflection to me on how the Internet has made it so easy to compartmentalize this process of matching jobs to people. There is so much more to the makeup of a human being than what shows up on a well-constructed, one-dimensional resume.

If it is true that you will be judged long before you ever have a chance to do a live interview, let's talk about whatever trail of information about you someone can find. Remember that forever is *forever* when it comes to any prospective employer who wants to check you out, thanks to the Internet. Those pictures of you hanging from a chandelier back in your good old, carefree college days are still there. Ok, now that I have made my point, how about some good news.

Good News You Can Use

The good news is that social media can also be used to your advantage if you know what you are doing and if you understand how to use its power. It's like a multiplier effect on super steroids: When you know you can project your remarks and information to a larger audience, you are assured that more people might respond to it the way you hoped. Therefore, it is critically necessary that you say it right and have a plan in place ahead of time for what you will do with the opportunity.

Whether your plan includes conquering the world or just your area of the country, I must suggest a certain protocol I believe is necessary so that you always put your best foot (and reputation) forward.

LinkedIn, FB, Twitter & The Rest

Let's start with a seemingly simple thing like LinkedIn. For many, LinkedIn is considered more to do with business while Facebook is more to do with personal. I am sure Facebook will continue to attempt to change that and more power to them if that is their desire. In the case of LinkedIn, you might be invited by someone to join his or her database of connections. That request may look something like this:

> 'Hi Dave! I would like to add you to my professional connections on LinkedIn.'

There are some stopgaps built into that request, meaning that the 'inviter' is asked to indicate to the LinkedIn people how it is they know the invitee (me) to help safeguard against someone spamming me and, if they do have some information that indicates they know me, it is a simple matter. Perhaps the person who invited me to connect with them read one of my posts or my book, or perhaps we met at a networking event. We may have even worked together in some manner before. There is also the very real possibility the person was referred to me from my *Conscientious Connector Tribe*. Building up a list of connections this way is critically valuable for a lot of Internet marketing and social media reasons and I encourage you to continue to always be looking to expand your database with quality and qualified connections.

When someone asks to connect with you on LinkedIn, do it with the same professionalism you would demonstrate if you met them in person.

Your tendency might be to simply click 'accept' and move on, but think about this for a minute and look at all this opportunity affords you. They saw something in your profile that prompted them to send an invitation. Perhaps it was your good looks, but it may have also been your company, job title, experience or potential for becoming their client. These are all good. Clicking on the 'accept' button and moving on won't, however, gain you any new information about them.

Just as you have opportunities to learn more about someone when you are standing right in front of them, you can learn a lot about someone who approaches you via LinkedIn. You just have to invest a little extra time on it and if you do, all sorts of good things can come from it, including how serious the other person is, or not, in wanting the connection with you.

Let's explore this further with examples.

Scenario A: Someone on LinkedIn Requests to Add You to Their Network

Say I get a request from you on LinkedIn. Thank you! I can accept the invitation with the click of the mouse. If I click accept, we are now inextricably linked together but the only information I have about you is what you have shared on your page. I do not have to settle for that and neither do you.

As a *Conscientious Connector*, I have the option to find out more about you. Let's go deeper.

Opportunities Are Everywhere!

1. I have the opportunity to demonstrate that I am a professional; that I am serious about this exchange of information.

2. I have the opportunity to turn this into a conversation.

    a. To find out more about your background.

    b. To ask why you were interested in me.

    c. To explore whom you might also be looking for that I can help with.

3. I have the opportunity to research that you have in your database that I might also want to meet or know about.

4. I have the opportunity to test you and your true interest in me by how quickly and sincerely you respond to my additional questions and conversation.

Surprisingly, or perhaps not so surprisingly, relatively few people ever take it this far. I often do, however, and my experience in doing so has yielded rich insights about the people who say they want to connect with me. Some do not ever return my inquiry, while others jump in with both feet and engage in answering my questions and asking me a few of their own. Instead of surfing to see what they can find, the professionals I have conversations with actually yield more possibilities for both of us, which is what I believe this whole *Conscientious Connector Movement* can develop into (with your help) for all of us.

Try It Yourself!

A few weeks ago someone actually took the time to read my information before asking to connect with me and I so appreciated the fact they mentioned that they attended the same university:

"Hi Dave. I, too, graduated from Chapman University. I'd like to add you to my contacts."

How difficult or time-consuming was that? By simply mentioning this fact, I had a much better reason for accepting their invitation because we had a commonality, a point of reference. It could have been just as effective had they told me they, too, grew up on a farm or they, too, played sports.

What if someone doesn't go to the trouble to mention commonalities? I do not want to dismiss anyone before I have given myself the chance to learn more about him or her. If someone didn't take the time to research me before inviting me to join their database, I still have the opportunity to demonstrate my professionalism and to search for those talking points, anyway. I'll just go first:

"Hey there, Christine: Thanks so much for asking to connect with me. I really appreciate it and I hope you will tell me more about you, about what you do and whom else you might be looking to connect with. If I may be of assistance, I hope you will let me know and I hope you will visit my website to learn more about me. I will look forward to hearing from you. Best regards, Dave"

What Christine does next will tell me a lot about what type of relationship she wants this to be. Maybe she just wants another human being to add to her list of connections. If that is all she wants, can that be any different than if she surface-connected with me at an event, grabbed my card and disappeared into the crowd?

On the other hand, she may choose to respond back to my inquiry right away and tell me of a particular need our company can help with. She may refer me to someone else or ask me for help in connecting her to someone I might know. Whatever Christine does with this will speak volumes. I'm not looking for a specific response, but I am looking to test the waters to see what to expect from Christine.

Look For Talking Points

When constructing a note to anyone you are interested in adding to your list of connections, your homework assignment as an investigative reporter should be to look for talking points. Through my initial investigation of Christine, if I learn that we share similar interests in certain authors, or we played the same musical instrument, or she used to work at a familiar company, it lends immediate assistance to the process. There is now a more pronounced 'comfort level' commonality. When you give someone more talking points to chew on, everyone relaxes a little sooner and more important dialogue is allowed to flourish. The same is true if you are the one to initiate the request to be connected.

Scenario B: You Request to Add Someone to *Your* Network

The same is true when you are the initiator. Don't just ask to be connected; give the other person reasons to want to help you. Look at their profile first. Find talking points, similar interests, things you can drop into the conversation. It will show that you really are interested in getting to know them. It shows that you are different than someone who just wants another name added to the list:

"Hi Bob: I hope this finds you healthy and having a good year.

Your profile information tells me you used to work at Disneyland. I was there back in the late 60's and my very first job was selling popcorn on Main Street USA. I'd like to add you to my professional contacts on LinkedIn. Thanks very much."

Those who take the time to do this will always stand out from everyone else who doesn't bother, even if you do not get a response back. How? They will see that your level of professionalism is high and if ever your name comes up, that will serve as the reminder of their impression of you.

This is a new concept for many, so don't be surprised if, at first, your attempts to reach out to others this way falls on deaf ears or, more appropriately, people who are more in the frame of mind of a surface connector. In my on-going investigation of this, we need to convert more people into becoming *Conscientious Connectors.* Few people as of this writing fully understand how easy, simple, effective and valuable this idea is, especially when you consider it takes almost no time and costs nothing. It's even less intrusive than going to a networking event and this activity and approach can develop into a treasure trove of great connections, once you understand how to do it in a professional manner. You'll also find out very quickly who is serious about building a database of the right, sustainable connections.

Ok, we are about to talk about Email. If through Social Media or live events you connect with someone who seems to be a potential *Conscientious Connector*, I recommend you take the conversation to your respective private Email address. By doing so, you will immediately make it an even more personal relationship.

How To Use Email To Your Advantage

I believe Email can be just as much a 'vast wasteland' as television, the Internet and social media. It can overwhelm. It can be downright dangerous to your database and therefore your livelihood, thanks to hackers who have nothing better to do. Like anything else, however, there are people who have figured out how to use Email in a way that doesn't take over their lives.

One of the most respected trainers on the planet is Brendon Burchard, whom I have followed for several years and who helped inspire me to write *The Way of The Conscientious Connector*. Brendon is the bestselling author of *The Motivation Manifesto, The Charge, Life's Golden Ticket,* and *The Millionaire Messenger* (www.brendon.com). He writes his own marketing content, his own training content, produces and headlines his own Expert's Academy and his High Performance Academy and still finds time to take several yearly vacations. Brendon does private coaching and has shared the stage with luminaries that include Anthony Robbins, The Dalai Lama, Jack Canfield, Les Brown and so many more. He is a highly successful and motivated teacher and a gift to the rest of us. And, he's clearly a very busy man.

So, you would think he has at least one eye on his emails at all times, yes? Hardly. In fact, he will tell you that part of his daily routine is *to not look at his Email for at least the first two hours every morning.* I offer this 'food for thought' for you, me and the rest of us who may think that unless we check our email every 30 seconds we will miss something earth-shattering.

~~~~~~~

The *Conscientious Connector* loves any opportunity to help others be more successful. There are numerous avenues through which this can be accomplished and Email is one. It may sound like more work to devote extra time and thought to how you use Email, but I will tell you that when utilized in its finest form, it can be a very useful tool.

Email Handoffs - *The Conscientious Connector* Way

When you refer someone via Email, how do you do it? Far too often, I see opportunities go flying right by because people think that just providing a name and phone number, or Email address is sufficient. It's not sufficient because there is so much more to a person. But, because we love to take shortcuts, the farthest people go is typically, *"Hey Bob, contact this guy. His name is Bill. Here's his Email."* Really?

Key Points & Commonalities

Let's take a couple of characters from the first chapter to illustrate what is possible, but instead of introducing John to Dennis in person, I am providing a referral via Email. How would I structure that to best benefit everyone involved?

Let me set it up this way: I meet John at a networking event and later decided to introduce John to Dennis via email because Dennis wasn't in attendance that morning. John is a Handyman, he loves working with Realtors and he is a member of another nearby Chamber of Commerce. Dennis happens to be a local Realtor and a member of the same Chamber of Commerce as me. All I have to do is drop in a few pieces of information about John in my email and Dennis will be able to take it from there. Both parties can do research on each other if they choose. This gives both of them a chance to 'hit the ground running' when developing a relationship. Remember, I am just providing talking points.

In reality, it's possible that after Dennis receives my information about John and does his own due diligence, Dennis isn't interested in using John's skills as a Handyman. Only Dennis will know what he wants to do, here. The one thing I know for sure is this: Both of them will have a much better initial conversation because I gave them good information. That is what *Conscientious Connectors* do. Secondly, I know that just taking a moment to set this up right will shine a very positive light on me from both Dennis and John, which certainly makes it worth it for me to do this.

In the Email Correspondence Sample below, there are four key pieces of information in the body of my remarks. They are written as a template for you to use if you want. As you do this more often, you will find your style and discover how to craft the perfect message.

EMAIL CORRESPONDENCE SAMPLE

Subject Line: John, meet Dennis

Hello Dennis Murphy. Hello John Oliver.

Dennis, I had the pleasure of meeting John this morning at the Chamber Breakfast. John is a second-generation Handyman and loves working with Realtors. He said he is a member of another nearby Chamber, knows a lot of people and would love to meet you. I have included phone numbers for both of you below and now you have each other's Email addresses. Please connect with one another and see where it goes from here.

I hope it all works out. Take care. We'll talk again soon.

Dave Ribble

StandOut Marketing Strategies

~~~~~~~

Here are a few of the immediate benefits to setting up an Email handoff this way:

1. It gives both parties talking points. When they do talk over the phone, the first minute or so will be in reference to a third party, in this example, Dave Ribble, who set this opportunity up for both of them. They don't have to start the conversation by talking about themselves.

2. It puts a nice *Conscientiously Connected* spotlight on me. Few people go to this much trouble, which isn't really trouble at all, as you will learn quickly, but it is clearly a positive gesture for both people who might tell others what I did for them.

3. It puts both parties on notice that I am a professional and therefore a certain respect and regard for me enhances my image across the board.

4. It reinforces my respect for both parties, which is just as important.

5. It assumes a certain responsibility now from both parties to follow up because the next time I talk to either of them, they have to assume I will be asking about this and that I will want to hear what happened.

6. My status was just enhanced, too, to a whole new set of contacts from Bob's membership in another Chamber. Where that goes from here will be interesting.

7. I made sure to include the first and the last name of each person so that they could begin to memorize each other's full name.

8. Further, if John decides to invite Dennis to come to one of his own Chamber events, John may also decide to invite me, too, which is quite normal in the life of a *Conscientious Connector.*

Think of it: The first four sentences in my brief Email produced eight immediate benefits that will very likely lead to more and better connections from both John and Dennis. Quite possibly, it will lead to life-long relationships between two other professionals who have at least another 250 people in their experience... and we're just getting started.

I could have added more talking points in my initial Email to both parties. Sometimes I will. For example, I might throw in something more personal, such as, *"Oh, and John tells me he also went to your same University,"* or, *"John, be sure and ask Dennis about his twin daughters trying out for the Tokyo Olympics,"* etc.

Talking points, remember? Anything you can add to a *Conscientious Connector* special Email Handoff that helps expedite the potential for two people to better know each other is a plus for everyone involved, including *you.*

"It's amazing what doors can open if you reach out to people with a smile, friendly attitude and a desire to make a positive impact." Sir Richard Branson

HOMEWORK

1. Take a close look at just one day's worth of social media activity on your computer, from emails to FB, Twitter, LinkedIn and the rest, or a week's worth. Look for any referrals you may have awarded someone.

2. If you have instances where you referred someone to someone else, go back and read your words. How extensive were your remarks? Could you have spent perhaps just three more minutes on it and added rich information that you didn't bother with? Can you see how adding a little more information, initially, could be life changing for everyone involved?

3. Practice this. Go to a fake email content section and re-write it to that person without actually filling in the email address at the top. All you want to do is see how you could have added to this email that would have enhanced it while enhancing you in the process.

    a. Is there more you could have told both parties about each other? Probably. If not, ok. But, if there were additional pieces to the puzzle you could have added, like where they went to school or that one of them was a former baseball player, or loves golf, or is a person you met in grade school, these are all talking points that will help the conversation along.

    b. In this process of adding rich content you will be telling each person involved they matter and that you are a 'noticer.' Easy to do.

STEP FOUR / CHAPTER TWELVE

ALWAYS KNOW WHAT MOTIVATES PEOPLE

The information is there. Let them tell you.

What lights a person up? A *Conscientious Connector* wonders about such things. Some folks are motivated by fame and fortune. Others are motivated by necessity. Some are motivated by the desire to avoid something from happening, like losing one's house to foreclosure or losing one's job to poor performance. In the simplest analogy, *Motivation* starts with a desire and quickly moves to a decision of action or inaction, as in a desire for something to either happen or not happen.

This chapter is about learning what motivates others, whether that is about your customer or prospect or someone you happen to work with but don't know much about. In the process of finding out more about someone else, you often will discover new insights about what motivates you. The importance of this purposeful activity is that when you understand what motivates someone, you can usually figure out how to help *him or her*. As you build your connection database and the referrals start to accelerate, the notes you record for recall later will multiply quickly, so be prepared!

Motivator Mike & Football

My childhood pal, Mike Presnall was at least a foot taller, it seemed, and outweighed me by 50 pounds, probably from birth. I loved baseball and basketball. Mike loved those sports, too, but he really loved tackle football. So when it was my turn to come to his house to hang out, I always knew Mike would want to go out to the huge grassy area adjacent to his parent's house because it was a perfect, makeshift football field. We would get on opposite ends of the yard and Mike would throw the ball as high in the air as he could and start running directly towards me. My job was to catch the ball before he got to me and then dodge his incoming frame without being killed in the process. If I did manage to get to the ball before he got to me, the race was on.

The difference in our respective sizes, coupled with the fact that Mike loved to hit things with his body, provided me plenty of motivation. If Mike caught me he would fall on me so hard I would leave an outline in the grass like a chalked crime scene. Mike would laugh as he peeled me back up from the ground so that I could refill my lungs, spit the grass from my teeth, *count* my teeth to ensure they were still there and wait for my heart to start again. It only took a few of those experiences to find new speed and agility as a broken field runner. I was motivated.

The fear of pain can be a *huge* motivator. But there are tons of other reasons why people are motivated and you can't possibly know what those are until you learn more about them. People need to trust you before they decide to let you into their inner sanctum. Sure, as a *Conscientious Connector* you know you will want to support them after you understand how you can do that, but first you must ask questions and allow them to tell you what they will. Otherwise, you won't stand a chance at understanding what motivates them. Ask questions and listen.

Have you noticed the more people talk, the more they tell you things? Have you also noticed that you cannot speak and listen at the same time? Alfred Brendel, classical musician and poet, once observed that the word 'listen' and the word 'silent' have the same letters. Listening is more than a skill; it is an art.

The more you understand others, like those you work for and with, the better the chances that you will discover what lights them up, what motivates them, what their challenges are and how you might be in a position to help them be more successful. You will not know any of this about your co-workers or about people you deal with on the outside of your business until you ask. And asking isn't something that comes easy for some.

One day I was discussing this with my friend, Chellie Campbell, author of *The Wealthy Spirit, Zero to Zillionaire* and *From Worry To Wealthy-A Woman's Guide To Success Without The Stress* (Sourcebooks, 2015-Chellie.com). Chellie gave me great advice on the subject of gathering information about someone and it is something I use to this day. Here is what she shared with me:

"Dave, it's easy to learn more about someone. If you want to gain as much information as possible from someone, ask him or her a question. As soon as they answer that question, ask another. As soon as they answer that question, ask another and keep doing this until there is nothing left for you to ask them."

Perhaps you think this too simple, but I will tell you that in my experience most people would gain a ton of information about other people if they followed Chellie's simple exercise. Remember, as a *Conscientious Connector,* your objective is always to learn more about the other person, not listen to yourself talk. When you are being authentically interested in someone else and you want to learn about them, ask them a question and follow that up with another, then another, then another. Don't stop to offer your opinion or confirm anything or tell your own story. Your time to talk about you will come later. Just keep asking question after question and listen to what comes from this interview. And, don't think for a minute you are being pushy or obnoxious because you will soon learn that people love to talk about themselves.

Here is an example of how it might go when interviewing. Pay attention to the sequencing and how one question follows the next:

1. **"Where do you work?"** (Be silent. Listen.)

2. **"What do you do for them?"** (Be silent. Listen.)

3. **"How long have you been in that line of work?"** (Be silent. Listen.)

4. **"What do you like about that work?"** (Be silent. Listen.)

5. **"Did you take training for that?"** (Be silent. Listen.)

6. **"What part of the training did you like the most?** (Be silent. Listen.)

Each question leads to a subsequent question and each time you do that more information is revealed. The more information revealed, the closer you get to what motivates them. Why do they like their job? Why do they like the coaching they do with kids after leaving work for the day? Why are they going back to college for additional classes? Why is that important to them? What are their aspirations? Where do they plan on being in their career five years from now? There are so many questions to ask and, as you do, those answers will automatically lead to more questions you can ask.

The story I like to tell is that, as an experiment, I secretly went through this process with someone just to see how far I could take it and, at the end of it, I had asked over 30 questions. We then finished talking and said our goodbyes. A few days later I learned from a mutual acquaintance that the guy I interviewed said, *"That Dave Ribble is a heck of a conversationalist!"*

The truth of the matter? The other guy did all the talking. He felt really good about being able to talk about his business, his family and all the rest. Yes, I have developed into an excellent interviewer, as will you, but the fact remains that people love to talk about themselves but do not often get the chance. My advice: Get them talking about themselves in an authentic, caring way and watch what comes of it.

As a practicing *Conscientious Connector*, the information you are going after on a deeper level is next to impossible to obtain if you don't take the time to truly get to know someone, at least a little, and certainly beyond the surface connectivity of a 'Hi. How are you?' approach to everyone. By following this simple formula, you can learn more about someone in five minutes than the next person might learn in five years; not just what motivates him or her, but how you might contribute to their success in whatever way(s) that means.

A Very Motivating Experience For Me

Nestled in the Colorado Rockies at the intersection of Interstate 70 and State Highway 9 sits beautiful Breckenridge, a product of the

1859 Pike's Peak Gold Rush. People from all over the world came to strike it rich back then. Miners discovered gold, silver, lead and other precious metals. As is well documented, the many who fared well were sorely outnumbered by those who did not.

Metaphorically speaking, Breckenridge represents for me a fitting place of personal discovery as well. Many years ago over a series of four days I attended a special workshop called *The Power of Creativity Seminar* sponsored by the Promotional Products Association International and headed up by my very capable friend, Natalie Townes.

44 representatives from supplier and distributor companies around the country descended on this beautiful old mining town to learn more about ourselves, about how to relate better to others and how to motivate ourselves to grow through the 'power of creativity' that is in all of us. I couldn't have known at the time the profound affect this experience would have on me that I am, clearly, still talking about now as evidenced by this chapter of my book.

Natalie and her team assembled experts in many disciplines, including a psychologist who had us take DISC personality evaluations and turn them in many weeks in advance so he could get to know us and then talk about our tendencies and how they relate to selling and working with others. Everything about this particular week was at once enlightening and revealing for me.

I remember in one particular instance the psychologist called me up and explained to the class he was sending two other guys and me out of the room to do some creative brainstorming. We were to go off into a little adjacent room away from everyone else and take a set of crayons and big pieces of paper with us. The psychologist followed us in the room and told us to work together to come up with an ideal scenario to the question: "If money were no object, what kind of lifestyle would we have and where would we live?" The psychologist then left us and went back to the classroom with the rest of the group.

When time was up, the three of us returned and the first thing the psychologist asked was which one of us would present our information to the class. I said that would be 'me.' The second I said that, the entire group started to laugh. I didn't learn until later that the psychologist had predicted that's how it would go, based on the way our personality profiles turned out. He knew I would want to be the spokesperson. In fact, he predicted I would also be the scribe who wrote on the paper and coached the other two participants.

This is why asking questions of someone, the right questions, can reveal so much. Most people actually love to talk about themselves. Watch any interview of someone on television and if the interviewer asks the interviewee about the interviewee's kids, a smile will usually replace the current expression. Talking about something that is a source of pride almost always guarantees a smile because that is something near and dear. It probably is part of what motivates that person to show up for work and stay late to finish something that needs to be finished.

Committees & Motivation

Motivation can also either show up or be absent within the makeup of the individuals in a group or on a committee. To demonstrate this fact, 12 of us agreed to go outside and take on the "River of Death" element challenge. It took a lot of talking to accomplish the challenge.

Two identical platforms built of solid wood stood about 24 inches off the ground with reinforced posts and, once you were up there, it was just high enough to give us a sense of having an imaginary river flowing around the square 'island' we stood upon. On the platform we all occupied were also three heavy boards that were about two inches thick and 6 feet in length.

The second platform was about eight feet away, which meant none of the three six-foot boards would reach it. Our job was to figure out how to safely move all 12 of us from one platform to the other without losing anyone to the 'River of Doom' that imaginarily flowed below us.

Once everyone understood the objective and challenge, it was as if the 12 of us were all sequestered inside a room, like a committee, and as a result, dividing lines emerged immediately.

Five + Four +Three

Five of us believed we would figure it out and began immediately tossing around ideas. The next four were pretty skeptical that there was a way to do it but didn't want to let anyone down, so they took a 'let's wait and see what develops' posture. And the last group, the group of three, crossed their arms, stepped to the rear of the platform and enjoyed themselves in idle conversation about *'how lovely Breckenridge was this time of year.'* They immediately wrote off the idea of success altogether and seemingly waited for the rest of us to come to our senses.

Did we come up with a way to meet the challenge and get everyone across to the other platform safely? You bet. The last group, the ones who were sure it couldn't be done, were the first ones across. The second group, the ones who were skeptical but didn't want anyone to know, went next. As for the 'believers,' as I call them, we went last.

So, let's talk for a minute about motivation and what prompted the individual decisions and reactions that came up for all 12 of us.

Group One - The Conquerors

Those who immediately went to work on how to achieve the 'impossible' were motivated. They were made up of people who had achieved the impossible before, as well as some who had decided that today would be the day they would throw caution to the wind and give themselves permission to go for it, even though they had no idea how it would be accomplished. Their motivation might have been a simple desire to be on a winning team that wasn't afraid to try, for a change.

Group Two - The Skeptics

Those who folded their arms and took a wait-and-see posture might very well have been motivated by the possibility of success, but they were equally motivated by not wanting to look stupid if we failed. As a result, they opted to wait and see what happened before jumping in.

Group Three - The Naysayers

This is the group of three who took one look at the challenge, figured there was no possible way to do it and left to go talk amongst themselves while the rest of us tried something that was, in their estimation, futile. There was no interest in contributing suggestions. It was a foregone conclusion that this would be a waste of time and energy, so they sought out a nice place to wait for the rest of us to finally realize how smart they were. The only motivation for them was to not look stupid in front of strangers.

What motivates one person versus another is a huge question that is often not easy to answer. People that you've worked with for years have stories you may not have ever heard. They have situations they've had to overcome, triumphs, and tragedies. They've been through experiences. They've won and lost. And they put their pants on one leg at a time, just like you and me, which means we all have more in common than we oftentimes remember. We all have experiences that formed our motivation to do something or to avoid doing something. When you can figure out what motivates someone, whether positively or negatively, it will help you know how to *Conscientiously Connect* with them for the greater good.

As I have since learned through training from my friends Sheila and Marcus Gillette of AskTheo.com, all of us have, to varying degrees, things in our past that influence our behavior and affect our motivation. Perhaps, for example, someone had something traumatic happen that was never dealt with or even recognized and, years later, a situation or something that someone says suddenly triggers a bad memory, a negative reaction or, in many cases, a limiting belief that keeps them from moving forward. I am indebted to The Theo Group for the many things I have learned and continue to learn that have helped me understand how much this can affect a person's life, their job, their relationship with others and their motivation. Better that I would have had this training back then, because I was about to meet Tammy from Idaho.

The Ropes Course

The third day the Outward Bound people walked us even further down the gravel road to another outdoor activity and more challenges.

This time it was the platform obstacle course they termed a hybrid Ropes Course, consisting of 12 different challenges or 'elements' that were built out over a sloped grassy hillside. A permanent fixture, it consisted of several huge vertical and horizontal telephone poles that connected to wooden platforms with cables running above our heads for each of the challenges we could try to negotiate. At the lowest point we were easily 40 feet off the ground and it went up from there, providing each of us a true sense of danger if we were to lose our balance and fall. The harnesses attached to the overhead cable would, of course, prevent us from falling more than a couple of feet, but it nevertheless sent adrenalin flowing and hearts skipping beats each time we took on a new 'element'.

Challenges in life come in various forms. You may be perfectly ok with climbing a ladder while others may break out in hives at the very thought of doing such a thing. No one should ever be thought of as less than equal to the rest of us just because we have challenges in doing certain things.

Tammy, whom I had only met two days earlier, walked along with me and the rest of us toward where our group would soon turn left and go over a small hill. Quite excited to tell me about her experiences in helping us move the 12 people safely to the other platform the day before, she talked glowingly about her experience. But as we turned off the road and climbed up and over the hill to the entrance to the 12-elements challenge, we all saw for the first time how massive it truly is. Someone from Outward Bound motioned us toward a small suspension bridge that served as the entryway; one we would all have to traverse to reach the first of the element challenges.

As we got closer, Tammy stopped walking and, mid-sentence, became silent. She stared at the bridge that other people were easily traversing and she froze. Others walked around us and headed for the platform but Tammy continued to stand erect. I searched her face and I could see tears welling up. I waited. She finally spoke to me.

"Uh.... oh boy, Dave, I think you should go ahead without me on this one," she said nervously, continuing to stare. I motioned behind me for others to go ahead of us. We stepped off to the side and I gently asked her to tell me what was going on. She took a deep breath, then glanced up before looking again at the entryway.

"It's the suspension bridge, Dave. I have always been deathly afraid of suspension bridges, ever since that time in Hawaii. I don't know what happened, but..." her voice drifted off. I encouraged her to continue. She gave me a half smile.

"I just know I may have to pass on this one today. You go ahead. I have to think about this."

I tried to make light of her anxiousness. "Let's go across together," I said. "Let's tackle this just like we tackled getting all those people across to the other platform yesterday. You and me, kid," I joked.

"Nah. I don't want you to miss your turn. You go ahead and I will see you when you're done." And, with that, she motioned for me to go on as she folded her arms, turned from me and took a few steps away, looking down. I got in line and, as I finally arrived across the bridge I looked back. Tammy was now sitting down by the bridge's entrance and had wrapped her arms around one of the posts the bridge was anchored to, staring at the hillside below.

I began to ready myself for the element challenges. I stepped into the harness and put on my helmet. There was no one right way to complete each element and we were told that the Outward Bound people were not allowed to offer any suggestions. It was entirely up to the individual to handle each challenge in our own way and without assistance of any kind.

The large, smooth log before me had been placed horizontally between the first and second platforms and measured about ten feet in length with nothing around it but air. The first challenge: Traverse it without falling off. Above my head ran two steel cables and there was just enough slack in my harness to allow me to move freely and gain the sensation of not having any protection whatsoever.

After reconfirming the steel karabiner was securely snapped into place I started my journey across to the platform on the other side. It was at once exhilarating and scary as hell and I searched for balance and strength to make it all the way. I took my time, step-by-step, which tested my patience to get it done and over with. By the time I arrived at the other side, I was already convinced this was a wonderful place to test oneself.

By the time I finished my 12 elements my shirt was soaked with sweat, the good kind of sweat that comes from releasing fear and doubt and feeling good about what had transpired. I returned to the first platform, anxious to see how Tammy was doing and if she had, indeed, started going through the series of challenges yet.

I found Tammy sitting down on the first platform, tears of joy streaming down her face. The assistant sitting next to her shared that although it had taken almost 15 minutes, Tammy had worked up the courage to cross the suspension bridge to that platform, *on her hands and knees*. I knelt down to her.

"Congratulations!" I exclaimed. "You did it, Tammy! You made it across the bridge. You figured out how you needed to get it done and you got it done!"

We hugged and more tears rolled down her face. I said, "Ok, let's go tackle the 12 elements! I'll go with you. We'll do it together!"

She raised her hand to stop me. Then she smiled, wiping away more tears.

"Dave, if this were the last day of the seminar, if they told me that it was time to pack up and head on out of here, I would be going home as one fired up and changed person. I don't need to do any more today. I'm fine. I'm really fine," she said with confidence.

I half-tried again but she was firm in her resolve and so I stopped. We walked back across the bridge where many in the group waited to give her hugs and to congratulate her, and then we all headed back over to the gravel road that would take us to the hotel for dinner.

Suddenly, I realized I had not seen my friend Michael Kogutt for a while and stopped. Michael and I had started the elements together but then I lost track of him. I looked back down the road and, here he came, grinning from ear to ear. Michael said that after everyone else had finished, he asked if there were any more challenges to take on and one of the guides told him that doing an element without the benefit of sight was also quite an experience. Michael then went back a second time to the tallest element and traversed it, blindfolded!

As the group walked, people laughed and many shared stories of the trepidation all of us had experienced to one degree or another while traversing the elements. The enormous pride in our individual accomplishments was palpable. The expressions on each face told individual stories of fears being overcome, of challenges being met, of a sense of pride and renewed beliefs in what we were capable of.

And I wondered about Tammy, for there was clearly more to her story. Tammy had been so outgoing just the day before but today she had run directly into a substantial issue that had overtaken her and locked her up. Why did that bridge represent such trauma and difficulty for her? Why did getting across it, on her hands and knees if need be, represent such a significant breakthrough? I wondered if I would ever know. That night, most of what I wrote in my journal had to do with Tammy.

The next morning at breakfast, Natalie greeted us in the informal setting and asked if anyone wanted to say anything about the events and experiences thus far from the Seminar. Across the room and behind me I saw Tammy's hand go up first. Natalie encouraged her to stand where she was and talk but Tammy wanted to come up to the front and address everyone from there.

"Yesterday," she began, with tears again welling up, "most of you saw me freeze up when we reached the suspension bridge. Some of you had to walk around me while I sat there. Dave and others tried to encourage me and I appreciate each and every one of you. You were there for me."

Tammy looked down at the floor as Natalie walked over and quietly asked her if she was ok. Tammy thanked her and said she was fine but needed to do this. Natalie retreated and sat down in a nearby chair as Tammy continued.

"For some of you, walking across that bridge was just a way to get to where you wanted to go next. It was simple. It represented a sort of 'means to an end' for you I guess, because once you got over to the first platform, you could start your 12 elements and get through them, kind of like getting from here to there to go to work or crossing a bridge to pick your kids up from school. It was routine for you, but not for me."

Natalie looked over at me, her expression searching for what was going on. I shrugged my shoulders. I didn't know, either.

"Most of you don't know me," Tammy went on. "I come from a very small town in Idaho. I'm a single mom raising three kids and splitting custody with my now ex-husband who cheated on me after 22 years of marriage."

Tammy looked around the room with a half-smile and some of us nodded, acknowledging that we, too, had been there and experienced similar circumstances.

"About a year and a half ago, after not working at all for most of my marriage, I had to go back to work. I got a job in Customer Service for a supplier in our industry right there in my hometown. I had to start at the bottom, of course, because I didn't have a lot of the skills, but they offered me the entry job and I worked my way up to Customer Service Manager."

Tammy fumbled with the tissue, wiping her eyes with nervous fingers.

"About a month or so ago the owner came into my office one day and sat down across from me. I thought I must have done something wrong," she mused. "You know, for him to be paying me a visit to my office like that. It's usually the other way around. I've known John most of my life. We went to the same small high school and John graduated a couple of classes ahead of me.

"Well, this particular morning he walked in with this piece of paper in his hand and he was *smiling*. John's a pretty quiet, buttoned up guy so I was curious as to what he was up to.

"It turned out to be the paperwork about something called *The Power of Creativity Seminar* in Breckenridge, Colorado. He told me that he had signed up for it but realized he couldn't take the time off to attend this himself so he said he wanted me to go in his place.

"All of a sudden, John sits up in the chair, hands me the flyer and he tells me he has already arranged with my mom to watch the kids. He said he would oversee Customer Service while I was gone and then he handed me the plane tickets! My mom had known about this all along but John had sworn her to secrecy.

"I remember how John got a little choked up. He told me that he wanted to do this for me because of the past couple of years I had gone through with the divorce and everything. He told me I was going and that he expected a full report when I returned and that was that. I was going to Breckenridge, Colorado and my boss was paying for everything. Holy crap!"

We cheered and laughed and started to applaud. Tammy smiled, took a deep breath and held up her hands to quiet us down so she could get through the next part.

"You guys have to understand: This was the first time I have been out of the state of Idaho since our honeymoon in Hawaii. This was only the second time I was ever on a commercial airplane in my life and the first time I have ever attended anything like this, ever. I mean, I always stayed home. I was the housewife. Divorcing my high school sweetheart wasn't even," she stopped and searched for words again, then continued.

"Divorcing the quarterback of the high school football team? Who does that? It's all supposed to be 'happily ever after', right? The truth is, it's been tough. Getting a divorce and starting over was the furthest...." she paused, "starting over like this was something I never thought I would have to ever go through."

Many of us wanted to rush to her but Tammy wasn't done. We glanced away, swallowed hard and let her continue.

"So, Dave and all the rest of you who were so encouraging, thank you for that. I really appreciate it. But I wanted to just explain the lessons I learned about myself yesterday. That suspension bridge represented for me a bad memory. My husband insisted we had to stand out on a suspension bridge in Hawaii when we got married for the photographer. It was a beautiful setting, of course, but I hated it. I had to stand there for the photos and I couldn't wait to get off that thing.

"I didn't realize until yesterday that something as simple as a suspension bridge was holding me hostage. I was afraid to cross it, like I was afraid of a lot of things. But, the more I thought about it the more I realized I didn't want it to control me any longer, just like

I didn't want my husband to control my future.

"The bridge is just a bridge, but I figured out that crossing it was a choice and as hard as it was for me, I crossed that bridge to the new and improved Tammy. I decided this was my life going forward. Instead of that bridge scaring me away, instead of that wobbly 'uncertainty' that kept me tied down to what I had become, I was going to choose to be someone who can take on anything!"

The room exploded with cheers and applause. Tammy grinned from ear to ear.

"This is my new life", she exclaimed, pointing her finger to the sky and then repeatedly touching her chest. "*This* is the Tammy that goes home tomorrow a new person. I love each and every one of you. Thank you for helping me create a new chapter to my life."

~~~~~~~

When you become a *Conscientious Connector*, stories like Tammy's will come up for you more often all the time because they only show up around people like you who can be trusted to not abuse the honor and privilege of receiving the information that someone entrusts with you. You will be more empathetic, more forgiving, more willing to understand the many different possible reasons for certain behavior.

Get to know your associates by keeping a keen, open eye on the fact that all of us have experiences, fears, dreams, goals and circumstances we have had to deal with in the past and circumstances we are dealing with in the present. Start there, with the full appreciation for the fact that information coming to you will only come at the speed in which trust is apparent.

Enjoy the experience. And, before you dismiss anyone as not having things that motivate them, look again. There may be positive reasons or negative ones, but more times than not, motivation is there in some form or fashion. Learn from each person you get to know.

One More Thing...

As we have talked about throughout this book, the people with whom you work can be great resources for you and you can be a great resource for them. Just like you, they bring with them unique experiences from former employers. They have different backgrounds and attended different schools. They were involved in the same or different sports, played the same or different musical instruments, grew up in the same or different areas of the city or state or country and they certainly married into different families and had different kids than yours.

Their commonality with you stems most often from the work you share. They may work in the same company as you or they may serve you and your company in some other manner. You speak a similar 'language.' There is a familiarity that can serve as a head start to getting to know them better and that's a foundation from which to build upon.

About the only thing better than becoming a *Conscientious Connector* is getting to work with other *Conscientious Connectors.* Is it possible to create whole communities of companies who think and work this way? Would that be a giant up leveling of possibilities for everyone involved? You bet. Hold on to your hat, for you might find yourself in the wonderful position to positively affect many. This is also a critically valuable way to approach supervising someone else. Find out what lights them up. Record it. Work toward helping them enjoy that. Support their dreams and desires, even if that means one day they leave you. Give them reasons to tell others how cool it was to have you as their leader.

HOMEWORK

1. Become a collector of information. Notice what you're noticing. You are on the lookout for information about anyone you meet, what motivates him or her, what their interests include and how you might help them. You are geared up with a new attitude about others. You understand your new system and you are already enjoying being a 'connector' and building a database of people who are looking for ways to help you as you help them. Look around at all those people with whom you work and associate. Your empathy level has probably started to increase. You are more cognizant than ever that people are just people, like you and me, and they have their own challenges, hopes, dreams, obstacles, fears, and doubts.

2. Begin adding that personal information to their contact profile, so that you can start to explore how you can help them. Maybe they want to take a Tai Chi class, like I did for years, and are looking for recommendations. Become a new resource of information for them. The extra effort you invest in this process will pay off in smiles and good feelings and appreciation, guaranteed. Look for those opportunities. Every time you are able to pass along information like this, do it. Take the time and do it. Remember, you are building your reputation as someone who cares, who notices, who does something to help. This will start to become your new modus operandi. It is the new you that demonstrates your positive regard for everyone else.

3. Journal your newfound info and keep it up. Write down your thoughts about all this and look for ways to reinforce, practice and get really good at this. Don't worry about reciprocation. You will continue to enhance and improve your skills and those new skills will continue to reward you, regardless. Keep going. Your actions will inspire others to live this same way, and that, my friend, is the much bigger payoff we all want and need.

STEP 5

INVITE EVERYONE TO THE PARTY

INCLUSION IS KEY - BRING IT ALL HOME

At this point, it should be clear to you that no matter what your occupation there are many ways for you to expand your influence and continue to add the right people to your database; people who *want* to see you successful. It's not about chasing people just long enough to get what you want or need from them. Demonstrate your desire to help them be successful, first, then watch what can happen.

Section Five is about creating success stories wherever life takes you and the art of connecting that is just that: Deeper thinking, finesse, forethought and follow-through in a professional way with an eye on long-term relationship building. The challenge is that not everyone understands this...yet. With your help, however, I know we can move this into overdrive, especially as more people experience the good that can come from this mindset.

Don't miss the bonuses coming up that include 26 things to think about as you go out into the world each day. Also, many recommended ways to make your job search more effective and how to turn cold calls into warm calls in a matter of seconds.

We're beginning to bring everything into full focus now. You're about to embark on a life-changing approach to connecting that will tap all your resources, not just a limited few.

I am grateful that I can help and extremely proud of you for dedicating yourself to really learning this and to helping me move the needle on how we relate to one another going forward. Your leadership will be felt for the greater good you bring to each day. That is a blessing.

NOTES

STEP FIVE / CHAPTER 13

SCALE YOUR SALES FORCE

Without adding anyone.

Zig Ziglar said, "I have always said that everyone is in sales. Maybe you don't hold the title of salesperson, but if your business requires you to deal with people, you, my friend are in sales."

Would you agree with Zig? Dealing with people is certainly something most everyone in a company does from their respective positions, but is *sales* everyone's responsibility? Well, I can tell you this: When everyone in a company is trained in the art of being a *Conscientious Connector*, magic can happen across the spectrum.

1. *The value of an entire company involved this way will far outweigh whatever positive influence sales people generate by themselves.*

2. *Every person in a company should know how to proactively promote their company to the outside world and be encouraged to do so, no matter what their position or responsibility.*

3. *To proactively promote that company goes well beyond just saying something nice to a colleague; it goes to the heart of creating a Conscientiously Connected company.*

College Football & Your Company

If you've ever watched Notre Dame University take the field at a home football game you know it can take several minutes just to get the entire squad from tunnel to sideline so the game can begin. Some colleges will bring as many as 100 players even though only eleven of their players can be out there at a time.

Think of it: At any given moment, just eleven players, about 10% of the team carry the fate of the entire organization. The other 90% of the squad, the coaches, parents, teachers, bus drivers and everyone else associated with that school are looking for the win they all came together to collect, but, because of the rules of the game, just 11 can be out there.

Now, look at a typical company, perhaps one like yours. When you add up the various jobs associated within, a similar ratio is often the case: About 10% are considered responsible for sales and the other 90% are considered 'other'. They are there in support but aren't really expected to know how to close sales. They are more like 'specialists' and they are designated to do certain jobs, but not sales.

How much better would Notre Dame do if they had everyone on the team in the game at the same time?

Ridiculous question? 100 players against 11 would certainly be better odds, wouldn't you agree? So my question to you is, who says you have to go into the marketplace with just 10% of your team? The other 90% are not considered in 'sales', but that hardly means they are any less important or significant or, for that matter, any less *potently essential and potentially effective* to the success of that company. Why not inspire and train them in every way you can so that they are in the game, too?

<u>Write this down:</u> Wherever and whenever there is an opportunity for human interaction, therein exists the opportunity to create positive influence, no matter who in the company is involved or from which department.

Borrowing from what ol' Zig was telling us, there is a sales component whenever two people are talking to each other. The other 90% of your work force can have tremendous influence on your marketplace if your people know how to talk about the company and know how to help other people in a *Conscientious Connector* way. There are golden opportunities here and missing them because you have a workforce that is not on the same page is costing your company, perhaps dearly. It doesn't have to be that way.

Once a *Conscientious Connector Culture* is adopted, embraced and encouraged, new avenues of possibility for growth and expansion will start to show up everywhere it is encouraged to flourish. It won't take long for that to happen.

Scaling your sales force this way is like giving special assignments to everyone who isn't directly involved in sales but who can wield enormous influence on behalf of the company. All it takes is a committed paradigm shift and some training so that the 'ninety-per-centers' can more-effectively promote the company, too, on going.

~~~~~~~

Take a look at the company you work for because this can represent a *revolutionary difference* between where the company is now and where this new mindset and practice can take it. For far too long there has been this separation of the team that has cost companies dearly.

This shift can help solidify your entire workforce and provide better backup for your salespeople while sending an important message to the marketplace that *this* is the company everyone wants to work for and with.

Note that this culture reaches well beyond the employee's job description and it should, because employees want to contribute more and will when we give them avenues and some direction. Rewards for this kind of extra attention to the success of any company should be part of this shift, as well.

You may want to consider incorporating this culture into your Mission Statement and into the expectations you place on everyone involved. It should serve to remind everyone of whom you are, what you represent and how you choose to do business. It should be a part of ongoing training as employees move up in the company and more people are brought on.

Support for the Sales Force

Let's first talk about how having this support for your sales force will help them. I come from the world of sales, so I can tell you that while it may look like your salespeople have it easy, most don't. They're out on the road for long periods of time, often living out of a suitcase and away from their family and they make a living from being on the front line; that wonderful place where all the rejection takes place. Anyone in sales has experienced victory and defeat and the pressure from management to hit the numbers can be daunting.

So, if you are in sales and you happen to be representing a company who has a reputation for being a really good company, it paves the way and takes some of the pressure off. You will always want your company's good reputation to precede your salesperson.

This is why reputation is everything. Here are a couple of examples.

Example: Disney. Let's say you are a parent and are about to choose a movie for your four-year-old to watch. You have a choice of two features and you have never watched either one. You look at both movies and note that one of them is a Disney movie and the other is from another source you have never heard of. Which one will you choose? The Disney reputation for quality would be stronger because you trust their brand based on your personal experiences. You probably grew up with Disney characters, enjoyed the people you met who work at Disney theme parks and you probably experienced Disney movies, yourself. The reputation Disney has for quality family entertainment is second to none. Your company can enjoy just as good a reputation in your own industry if people have experienced your employees being proud of who they work for. This solid reputation means everything, and the more people from your company who prove and reprove this each day adds to the many reasons people will choose your company to work with over your competitor companies.

Another example: IBM. Back in the 60's if you worked for IBM you worked for the most popular tech company on the planet. All their salesperson had to do when calling on a prospect was to mention those three letters and the appointment was confirmed because the reputation was in place.

Support from everybody else

IBM's reputation didn't come from just the IBM sales force; it was built by the quality of the products and services, certainly, but perpetuated by the people who talked about the company. That feeling was pervasive and the more the employees talked the faster IBM's reputation grew.

When enough people in your company talk this way at every opportunity, they create an assumption. It is this 'positioning' in the marketplace that should be taken ultra seriously because it is like jet fuel when it takes off. It sends a message out to the world that your company *must* be exceptional because everyone says so, which, in turn, suggests your products, services, your attention to the needs of your customers and the quality of your personnel throughout the company....*must also be exceptional.*

If they hear it from multiple sources, your prospects will make this assumption all day long until proven otherwise. I call that the grand slam of positive influence and that is what your company can achieve. Word gets around quickly.

Let me give you a few examples and break it down even further, so that you can see how departments who have nothing to do with sales can nevertheless have profound influence on the outside world.

Accounting

Typically, accounting folks talk to customers in order to get invoices paid on time, situations handled and reports generated. Most often they talk to customers directly or to their accounting 'counterparts' who are responsible for issuing checks and other accounting matters.

So, let's review a few things about those accounting folks before we go further. Do they meet the basic tests?

- They are people like you and me

- They have challenges, dreams, desires and frustrations every day like you and me

- They would love for their day to be a great day and they would like to avoid any further frustrations from the people they have to call in order to get an invoice paid or a problem handled.

- They would love even more if someone would listen to their needs and come back to them with solutions they can use to make their life a happier life, both personally as well as professionally

When you institute a *Conscientious Connector Culture*, the same culture that the salespeople use and utilize, greater accomplishments throughout your company accelerate.

Accounting folks with permission to be more personable, to ask more questions, to find out what they can do to help their counterpart changes everything.

What is a much better relationship worth to both companies these days? In relatively short order, both your company and those your accounting people call can develop better relationships with each other, which can, in turn, be the catalyst to much more. Accounting people who explore this notion, who start to get to know their counterparts this way and who are encouraged to do so, talk to others within and beyond their own company walls.

Can you imagine accounting folks having just as much fun doing this as sales? Why not? Then, watch the relationships with your customers continue to expand. When this happens and those relationships continue to solidify, advantageous avenues for both companies continue to expand, as well. Perhaps, for example, your accounting person can win over their counterpart to ordering more products from you than your competitors, simply because your company is easier to work with, more personable and more understanding. They won't always know why they favor your company, but a lot of it will have to do with your *Culture*.

Purchasing

Likewise, purchasing people talk to supplier partners each day to order products, equipment and the like. The job of purchasing is to spend money wisely and to get the most from every dollar. Just like accounting people, do they meet the same basic test as we described, above? Of course they do.

Because the personal relationship between your purchasing personnel and your supplier partners is allowed to flourish, what soon happens is both parties start figuring out how they can work more closely together. It's just something that naturally happens. Everyone wants to get along, to enjoy their job, to help the company that writes their check and to have a good day, every day possible. If the supplier partner volunteers to see where else they can save your company money, will that be because of your *Culture* that encourages such a relationship? You bet. People love to partner up. Purchasing departments that 'team' with their supplier counterparts will often see a significant monetary and service advantage over their competition.

Customer Service (CS)

It should come as no surprise that *The Way of The Conscientious Connector* works for every department, division and discipline in any company. Let's take a moment to talk about customer service. CS typically handles those who call in or come in who are already customers. They might have a question or need clarification about something, they may be calling to complain or even want their money back due to a defect. Or, they simply want the product replaced.

Keep in mind that one person saying something negative about your product or service will wipe out ten who are positive, so let's take this as seriously as it needs to be taken.

You can win the customers' loyalty or lose it by the way you handle the situation. And, from the perspective of a *Conscientious Connector Culture,* this opportunity is an opportunity to shine and to win over a loyal customer.

Whenever people go to the trouble to complain about something, assume they are not pleased. They have been inconvenienced and taking the time to call and complain means, from their perspective, that your company is now taking time away from the customer's day. They are frustrated. Many of them have had bad experiences with other companies in the past, which means they are probably already anticipating a similar experience with your person.

But, if that customer service person is well versed in the *Conscientious Connector Culture,* this negative situation can oftentimes be turned into a positive opportunity and place your company squarely on the road to gaining this customer as a raving fan. You could, in fact, end up with someone who wants to say nice things about you to everyone they talk to. The best form of advertising and influence in the marketplace is word-of-mouth such as this, and it also happens to be the *cheapest.* When someone says great things about your company, *voluntarily,* that's about as good as it gets.

Here's one example: Let's say the product your customer purchased from you cost them $100. It needs to be replaced. For you to replace that product it will cost you $25 plus shipping costs for the shipment of the new product and for the shipping necessary to get the defective product back, because you want it back. You don't want your defective product to remain with your customer because you don't want it to be a reminder of this bad experience.

You have authorized CS to offer either:

1.   A full refund or a replacement of the product.

2.   An added bonus item that is worth another $45 that costs you $15.

Your net cost for that $100 product is just $25. So, you can afford to replace it and pay for the shipping and still be ahead. This may be all you need to do and you'll still clear $50 or $60 net after you take good care of your customer.

Or, your CS senses they need to add another incentive to the mix to *make sure* that customer remains satisfied and, hopefully, will become a raving fan. So, you go to #2, above, and you offer a Bonus item that is worth $45 but costs you just $15 plus the shipping.

Now, your total net cost might be $40 plus another $20 in shipping charges, which means you will still clear $40 after all is said and done. Your customer feels great about the fact that they will (a) get a replacement product, (b) get another $40 gift item they will like for free and (c) they will also be offered to be placed on your company's VIP list, let's say, as a Very Important Person, and they will receive your newsletter or special offers more often than the general public, for example, or receive discounts on future purchases. This can be a very clever way to figure out how to penetrate accounts and to also gain *foundational loyalty* that can grow from here.

Your customer will feel like they won a small victory. They will look at it as a win because they will receive a brand new item and they will receive, essentially, $140 worth of product from you for $100, so they are already $40 ahead of the game.

Remember, your net cost for all of this is $25 plus $15, which means that from the $100 you received in the first place, you are still $60 ahead of the game, regardless, and have money to spend. And, for that small investment of your time and a little coordination of shipping, you have 'purchased' the loyalty of a customer who will tell this story to his/her friends for who knows how long into the future.

Happy customers talk about good experiences. It only takes one bad remark out of 10 to ruin a company's reputation in the marketplace. So, while you may think I am done with this example of Customer Service, I have more to say on the subject.

If, during the course of learning from the customer who called in what the problem is, your CS person is also encouraged to talk to that customer in a *Conscientiously Connected* way and ask them about their business or about their life in general, that customer may start talking about other needs they have. Perhaps they need other products or services that your company provides and you can go there with the conversation. But quite often, the customer might talk about other needs they have that your company cannot help them with, but your CS knows where to send them for more information.

Does that seem like it will take up too much time and require too much energy for you to have your CS people look into that for them? I can tell you that the times any CS person in our industry took the time to help me with that kind of dilemma, I never, ever forgot it and I remained more loyal to her company than her competition. I, too, became a raving fan and told others about it! Why? Because she treated me as someone who mattered.

~~~~~~~

Let's change the culture within whole companies. No matter where you happen to 'live' within a company's organizational chart, you have an inherent capability to add favor and good fortune to your company's bottom line if you and the rest of the people there all know best practices in how to talk up the company to the outside world.

Always be gathering info...

As a Territory Rep for Rand McNally back in the day, I always enjoyed having our EVP of Creative, John Manning, ride along with me to see distributors. John would fly in and meet me at whatever the closest airport was in my nine-state territory and off we would go for a few days so that he could help me help my distributors understand how to sell our products to their customers.

It was like magic for John, too, because he thoroughly enjoyed meeting my distributor salespeople, asking them questions, finding out what products we needed to create and what the customer base was asking for.

For the distributors, it was a great opportunity for John to regale us with stories about his forty-two years in the print industry and to tell us about some of the custom print projects he supervised such as Road Atlas Travel Guides for Harley Davidson Motorcycles.

John's visit to the field also reinforced appreciation. John was able to ask questions and take answers back to home office that helped us improve our service to those distributors. And the other thing that John was extremely good at was asking questions of the distributors and then doing whatever he could, personally, to help them, because he knew, instinctively, that they would never forget that an Executive Vice President of the world's foremost maker of maps walked into their office one morning, thousands of miles from Chicago, and offered to help them in any way possible.

~~~~~~~

It is my firm belief that non-sales personnel carry just as much an important responsibility and capability for the company this way as salespeople. They talk to people every day and the better equipped and trained they are at knowing what to say and how to lend a hand, the greater their influence. When everyone is on the same page because the *Conscientious Culture* is in place, great things happen.

I believe we're missing opportunities left and right and when we finally do get on the same page with how to relate to one another across the board we'll start to make success stories happen everywhere we turn, and for those we assist as well as ourselves.

When every employee knows how to project the best positive light on the company, more opportunities will come to that company and, quite often, those will show up in places the salespeople wouldn't know existed; from the other non-sales people talking to their counterparts.

More often than you might imagine, it is the non-sales personnel who make more things happen for a company and that is important for you to remember and understand. One example of this is what can happen when a new, inventive resource for more business makes its presence known. Let me tell you a story.

The Day the Pros Came to Town

You would have thought Divine Intervention had bestowed great blessings on our Chamber of Commerce. Jeff, Chris, Kecia and John had all worked together for Tony Robbins and were trained by him earlier in their careers. One morning these four strangers came rolling into what is now the West Valley-Warner Center Chamber of Commerce (formerly Woodland Hills Chamber) breakfast meeting and introduced the brand new networking group they were forming. That they weren't wearing superhero capes is still surprising to me because of what they represented that many of us were, in retrospect, hungry for.

This particular membership group promised to be different than any other while also serving to compliment the Chamber and other networking organizations. The added components they promised included specialized speaking and presentation skills training, great speakers, special events, VIP memberships and a lot more. For most of us who had nowhere else to go to get this training, it was like offering water to a thirsty man. It was wonderful news. The promise of the opportunity to be trained in the way of Tony Robbins was like a golden ticket. I remember that over sixty of us who were there that morning, circled back later that afternoon to hear more and many signed up.

The audience that yearned for this information and support consisted mostly of small business owners: Real estate brokers, insurance agents, mechanics, florists, restaurant owners, painting contractors, accountants, lawyers, pool cleaners, massage therapists, credit card processors and many more types and varieties of small to medium sized businesses. In fact, of those who circled back and showed up to learn more about this new organization, very few actually carried the title of 'Sales' on their business card.

Rather, the vast majority of people I have interviewed in dozens of professions like these rarely consider themselves professional salespeople. Instead, they consider themselves specialists at what they do but do not like to network. Most consider networking as a necessary evil and know they must network if they expect to expand their businesses. If they could be more comfortable, however…

So, when my friends came to town that morning and promised all of us training to help us get better at something many of us felt we had never really learned how to do well, we jumped at the opportunity. If we could, once and for all, feel more comfortable about knowing what to say and how to say it, if we gained confidence from practicing with the pros this training would serve us for a lifetime and would certainly be worth it. Whether it was to stand and deliver a 20-minute presentation or a 30-second introduction, it was clearly obvious people needed and wanted this training; something that was not lost on me these many years later.

I tell you this story because when you and I and a few million more start to change this paradigm and turn the world into very capable *Conscientious Connectors* who are trained in how to relate to other people at an obviously higher level frequency, when we turn more toward helping each other instead of turning any more inward, *we will move the needle on the economy and improve lives.* No longer will we rely just on what 10% of the workforce can generate for more business. No longer will we assume that if you are not in sales then you cannot contribute or help out the bottom line. We know better than that.

There are a lot of people who would love to be better at knowing how to promote their company and cause positive influence. We all love to contribute. The idea of helping everyone to be better at this, not just those in sales, and by enlisting and engaging everyone in the process, this represents a silent sales force that can instrumentally and positively affect everything.

The Boardroom

This new networking group I spoke about gained immediate momentum and the meetings and events were well attended. We all loved being a part of this. Many I met in this process became my lifelong friends and most became connections to many others. Eventually, the group disbanded and my friends went on to successful careers in other professions, but during our heyday, great accomplishments happened and substantial growth in individual abilities occurred. People came out of their shells, found their voices and thrived.

One of the most interesting ideas that came about during that time was something we called The Boardroom. I became very involved in not only participating but also leading many of these special meetings. This story, as well, demonstrates the very real need by most of us for better skills in presenting and in finding one's own voice. Many in the membership clamored for better training in how to communicate what they do and to articulate why people should hire them, refer them, buy from them and want to help them. The need continues to this day and I hope to contribute to an instrumentally valuable new way of thinking about all of this.

The Boardroom was borne out of a series of 'What If?' questions and designed after dissecting all the other networking groups, memberships and programs out there. We asked ourselves a lot of questions about what was good and what else could also work, and then narrowed it down to these:

1. **What could be designed that would compliment what other networking meetings and groups already do?**

2. **What could we add or change to make it unique and valuable to everyone who attends?**

3. **How could this be expanded to other cities and towns and regions in a duplicable way so that people could**

attend it again and again?

In the ideal, here are the basics for the Boardroom as we called it.

- You had to apply for a position at the Boardroom. Karen Ellsesser handled the electronic calendar, so if you wanted to book yourself in for a Boardroom that was to be held a certain day and time you had to go through Karen, who checked and confirmed no conflicts, no challenges. We often had several Boardrooms scheduled in different surrounding towns at varying times, so if you knew you were going to be in the area of one of them, you could check with Karen. I will forever be in debt to Karen for the hard work she put in for this

- The Boardroom was free, although parking might be a charge, and it would be held at a conference room or bank-type boardroom setting

- The Boardroom was limited to a facilitator and ten non-competing professionals and professional attire was expected

- No food or drink was offered or served during the one hour together

- Everyone would get a full five minutes to stand and tell us about themselves and about who they were looking for, but no pitching

- Everyone else was expected to take copious notes and to ask questions if necessary so that when everyone left, they could remember what was said and how to help the others

- Business cards were not passed out until the end of your five minutes

- Boardrooms started precisely on time, regardless, and ended exactly sixty minutes later, regardless.

- The facilitator spent the first five minutes welcoming everyone and explaining again the rules of engagement

- The facilitator also got the last five minutes to introduce him or herself to everyone, too

That was the gist of the Boardroom setting. Professional, yet small enough to be a personal hour with others that never failed to reveal more information about people. It was magical for me, because here is what would invariably happen: As people introduced themselves I encouraged them to tell the rest of us about themselves. I discouraged them from going right into their sales pitches and it was interesting to watch some of them struggle with this, because it wasn't anything they were used to doing this way. I also encouraged everyone else to open his or her notebooks and listen.

Without exception, when people stood to talk, their demeanor changed. They were not used to this. They were used to hit-and-run networking, surface connecting, talking louder than normal to be heard over the din of a networking event. Most found themselves relaxing into this and, by the time their five minutes were up, they were shocked at how fast their time to speak had gone by.

Some had to pause to think about what they wanted to say, at least in the beginning, because five minutes seemed to them to be an eternity to speak in front of 10 other strangers. As they searched their minds for what to say, I would sometimes prompt them by telling them to tell us where they grew up.

As each person told us more personal information, clues about how to help that person began to surface. One might share that she grew up in a certain state that another member of that Boardroom also shared, or he attended a certain college or learned to play banjo and toured with a group. Another talked about her kids or being raised by a single parent and she wanted to spend time talking about the Foundation she supported or his ties to a certain philanthropic endeavor.

No matter what they talked about, they talked about things that were near and dear to their hearts. As long as I could, I kept them from leaning back to only talking about their business, because I knew from experience that at the end of the day, people would rather tell you about their personal lives.

And, inevitably, as these little tidbits of personal information began to surface and as additional information was revealed, the others sitting at the Boardroom started to shuffle in their seat because they were beginning to realize there were parallels to *their* stories that were forming. Connections were surfacing. Opportunities were floating to the top.

All it took was for those folks to stop and listen and for each person at the table to open up so that everyone else could take notes and search for how to help them.

To be sure, at some Boardrooms the connections to others weren't immediately evident, but I could always find connections for them because I had practiced this. I took notes on everyone there. Sometimes, in fact, if I had time to review the roster prior to convening that actual Boardroom, I could develop potential connections for people even *ahead of time*. Think about that.

Suffice to say, something good happened at every Boardroom I have ever facilitated and is one of the foundational experiences in my life that prompted the writing of this book. When you spend five full minutes uninterrupted and you listen to someone tell you their story, it allows you to pick up on particulars you would otherwise never hear in a 30 second 'here's-my-business-card-hi-how-are-you' exchange so prevalent at networking events.

The better we are at understanding this and the better we get at using the tools that uncover this rich information, the greater number of success stories we will create. We just need to stop long enough to hear how we can help.

My Boardroom stories demonstrate the ongoing thirst people have for connecting with others. All anyone wants is to be heard, acknowledged and respected for what they do, whom they represent and what they have to offer the world. Companies who encourage *everyone* to contribute and then provide them that space and those tools to do so are way ahead of those who believe that compartmentalization is a good idea.

CFO to CEO: **"What happens if we invest in developing our people and they leave us?"**

CEO to CFO: **"What happens if we don't and they stay?"**

One more very important point I need to make about *Scaling Your Sales Force* is about the highly charged word: **Empowerment**.

For example, the promotional marketing industry we belong to is made up of thousands of supplier partners and distributor companies who have independent salespeople who go out and sell promotional products to end users. My wife runs our small boutique independent distributorship called StandOut Marketing Strategies and we are blessed with an ever-growing list of exceptional clients we serve on a daily basis with marketing and promotional ideas, special event expertise and over thirty years of experience. Our client base is varied, evidenced by the fact that the expertise and seasoned experience we offer will work for every industry.

In order for us to provide the best possible service to our clients, we must have the best possible relationships with our supplier partners. It is they who can make or break our relationship with our customer. This two-way street is very narrow and the fact of the matter is that supplier partners take hundreds of orders a day from distributors like us and there are, with each order, myriad chances for something to go wrong: Inventory issues, imprint issues, packaging issues, breakage, production backups, credit issues, logistics and a whole lot more that are part and parcel to each and every order.

The supplier partners we choose to work with are not only the ones with the best quality products but are the ones who provide us the most proactive assistance to the ever-changing landscape as orders are placed and problems arise. Therefore, it is even more important that we work with people who are *empowered* to make quick decisions and to move mountains for us if need be. People in our industry who are empowered to make adjustments to timetables, or imprint methods, or to provide us better pricing because of our relationship and history with them are the ones we cling to, support, love, send birthday cards to and anything else we can do to maintain that relationship.

> **"If you hire people just because they can do a job, they'll work for your money. But if you hire people who believe what you believe, they'll work for you with blood, sweat, and tears."**
> Simon Sinek, *Start With Why*

My friend Mel Ellis talks about it. Over twenty-five years ago Mel purchased a supplier company that was not doing well at all and this became a place where he could test his business acumen and see what he could do to turn things around. The first order, he told me, was to get everyone on the same page about how each and every part of the business could improve and where the focus should remain. "We applied this to every aspect of our business: **Serve The Customer**. We spoke about serving the customer so many times and in so many different ways that those words came to be internalized in our bones:

'This is who we are. This is what we do.' "

This is what a *Conscientiously Connected Culture* can create. Mel told me that when he arrived the company had lost its focus. People were coming to work already watching the clock for when they could go home. Management was sending out resumes for other positions. Pride in the quality of the products, in the service, their reputation in the industry; it just wasn't there anymore and Mel's instincts told him that in order for the company to bounce back, everyone had to feel they owned the outcome, together.

Twenty-five years later, a much larger supplier partner came knocking and bought the now profitable company outright. What they bought was a success story that continues to grow, but it took Mel and his amazing group years to turn things around. Everyone had to be empowered. Everyone had a voice in the company again and the pride of service and attention to every detail started showing up.

When Gaye or I called Mel's company for quotes, you could actually tell over the phone that things were turning for the better. Mel continued to seek the advice of the Distributors his company served through focus groups. He continued asking how they could better serve the Distributors, whether through better Customer Service or better packaging or better delivery times. Slowly, at first, but surely, business eventually came back.

The company improved their products and services by listening to their marketplace and by them empowering their people. Everyone in the company took responsibility to do the right thing by the Distributor and to continue to ask questions about how to improve. If something needed to be done, Mel's people knew he had their back on decisions that had to be made. If something had to be done over again, there was little to think about. That's empowerment.

Empower your people. Continue to teach them and train them on how to get all of us out here to want to bring our business to your company instead of going elsewhere. Teach them *The Way of The Conscientious Connector* and you will make every encounter with the outside world a more friendly, uplifting experience for us; a place where things go right instead of a place where we are told you cannot make adjustments or help us with our needs.

I promise you we will gravitate toward companies who will take it upon themselves to move up a production schedule to meet a new or adjusted deadline to a project. We will *run* toward people who ask us about our vacation or our family or how we are doing with the new puppy.

It's personal, just like life. Blaine Bartlett and David Meltzer explain it this way from their book, *Compassionate Capitalism* (Best SellerPublishing.org, Pasadena 2016): "…Nothing we encounter is separate and isolated from the whole. We live in and on a closed system that is fully dependent on the viability of each constituent part."

When you add *The Way of The Conscientious Connector* training to what employees already know about their direct responsibilities, their place in your business and the culture of your company, you effectively add more salespeople without adding one more person to the payroll.

By providing empowerment like this, it also sends a loud and clear message to your people that they are an important part of the future of your enterprise. People want to count for something bigger. They want to feel really good about where they spend an inordinate amount of their lifetime away from their family and friends. They want it to mean more than just a paycheck, because it does.

Empower them.

HOMEWORK

Remember that 90% of any company's workforce, with few exceptions, is made up of non-sales personnel. They are the people in purchasing, accounting, warehouse, customer service, administration and so on. Just as we learned in earlier chapters, each and every one of these folks can also have a positive influence on sales and the bottom line of the company if you encourage and empower them.

Look at your list of everyone who works for you or with you and explore the idea of getting to really know him or her better. Ask yourself what opportunities come up in those various departments each day that could positively influence sales outcomes. Are those folks empowered to talk to their associates on the outside in ways that could cause positive influence? Or are they limited? Are they trained on how to promote the company or encouraged to not do that? Perhaps you have encouraged them but they have never received training on the things they can do and say. Perhaps the atmosphere doesn't allow for it, for fear of the threat that they might look better than their superiors. Often, superiors feel threatened by positive input from those who report to them, so everyone needs to rest assured that no one will be threatened and everyone will be empowered and encouraged.

Pull in non-sales focus groups and have that conversation. Dig deep for whether they are (a) empowered properly, (b) trained properly, (c) without fear of repercussion from superiors, (d) able to be rewarded in some fair way for helping and contributing.

Remember this: The non-sales people want to contribute information and be recognized for it; not just expected to do so. There is a huge difference you must understand and appreciate.

STEP FIVE / CHAPTER FOURTEEN

FLEX YOUR MUSCLES

Build success stories one person at a time

"The things you want are always possible; it is just that the way to get them is not always apparent. The only real obstacle in your path to a fulfilling life is you, and that can be a considerable obstacle because you carry the baggage of insecurities and past experience."

Les Brown

Norman Lear's favorite way of explaining how he sees the world was to say that he was "just another version of you", which is to say that every person on the planet has challenges, hopes, dreams, desires and fears and we all struggle to figure out our approach to them. I'm just another version of all of you, etc.

You were borne from perfection. The creative Source that created you also created everything else around you. You came from perfection. *We all start out from perfection.*

So, take heart in the fact that at least you started out that way before you were heavily influenced by loving and well-meaning but often misguided parents, siblings, relatives, friends, clergy, teachers, bosses, spouses, kids, coaches and everyone else who has ever offered you their ideas about how life is to be lived. Know that you are just a different version of *them* and every circumstance you experience or obstacle that comes along is not much different than everyone else's. We just have our own versions of similar challenges.

Be aware, as well, that not everyone you meet will be interested in supporting your efforts or referring other people to you. Some folks will always want to surface connect just long enough to get what they need for themselves and move on. They will complain about anything to keep the spotlight off their own actions, or lack thereof, and onto other reasons why they aren't as successful as they could be. The other day I entered our elevator to go to my floor and greeted a workman who was headed to do some repair work on another condo. I innocently mentioned in passing something like, "heading out to make a buck?" as a sort of hello without any weight placed on it. His reply was, "yeah, I'm off to go earn more money so they can give it to people on welfare."

He was evidently so unhappy with his own life and circumstance he was willing to say that to a total stranger. Maybe some 'welfare kid' struck him out in an important baseball game in his younger days or, more likely, his parents drilled into him that he should resent ever helping anyone else but himself.

It was sad, really, because his blanket statement about anyone on welfare turned me off to having much empathy for him. If you have ever been in financial straits, and I have, you know circumstances beyond one's control are often involved, such as health related issues. As my Dad taught me at a young age, no matter what challenges come along for a person, you can always find someone else who has it tougher.

The business of becoming a *Conscientious Connector* requires a consistent empathetic interest in and caring about others, so if you have that, you are well on your way to making this work for you. If you are just coming around to this idea, work your *Conscientious Connector muscles* and you'll discover how good you feel and how much better you become at adding the right people to your database.

> *"When opportunity knocks, don't forget it is 'work' that answers the door."* Brendon Burchard

Putting together a database of the right, most rewarding and sustainable connections possible for business, career and life is going to take *work*.

But, here is the good news. The *work* I am talking about becomes second nature. It becomes your mindset whenever you are talking to anyone in person or over the phone or even via email and social media. It will surprise you at how you will learn to generate positive influence in every direction and you will marvel at how well your actions are received. Some may show disbelief that you could be this kind, empathetic and conscientious but after they know you are not going to waver, you will find yourself surrounded by people who want to help you, too.

When you, as a *Conscientious Connector*, meet someone in whatever way you do that, whether it is in person, through email or social media, a phone call, etc. your first reaction will be to want to know more about him or her. You will be curious and willing to take a little more time with them because you know what can happen when you do.

Your reputation as someone who has shown him or her respect this way, by demonstrating that their presence is just as important as your own, will become your silent calling card. It will build your reputation almost involuntarily because that's what happens anytime you slow down and truly listen to someone.

We all want to be heard.

Good things come to those who are *Conscientious Listeners*. Here's what I mean:

When you were a kid and you had something happen that you needed to tell your parents about, you ran to them and interrupted whatever they were doing so you could have their undivided attention. That's what kids do. They go to their safe place where they know they will have parents who have empathetic and caring ears to hear what they are desperate to talk about. Good parents make those opportunities for communication with their children paramount to anything else going on at that moment.

We adults are no different. We all want to be heard. We want to be recognized as someone who matters, who counts, who can contribute, who has value and who has a divine right to be here on the planet just like everyone else.

All too often, however, we feel stifled by others who bark orders at us all day, get us caught up in bureaucratic straightjackets, chew us out for making mistakes, pressure us to make more sales or finish reports or get other unforeseen tasks completed before we are allowed to head home to other responsibilities. And, if we do not act like we are a team player in those situations, it plays havoc with our chances for raises, promotions, and can sometimes even get us placed on the short list for who gets laid off. It may not be fair, but it is reality.

Months of living in this scenario turn into years and the folks I am talking about don't even realize they are living it every day. Without them even knowing it is happening, they slowly close up like turtles and live their life as safely as they can to keep their job, not ruffle feathers and make sure they bring home the paycheck. Of course, whether they ever choose to leave that circumstance for something better is entirely their journey and not yours. You are not responsible for taking them out of that scenario, but you are, more often than not, in position to be a bright spot in their day.

When an empathetic listener like you happens to come along, who treats them with respect and concern, and shows a genuine, authentic interest in hearing what they want to talk about and share, those folks are going to naturally gravitate toward you. Your instinctive caring and their desire to be heard and respected will collide, all for the right reasons. It happened because your new mindset showed empathy for what you knew they were probably going through.

I was inauthentic earlier in my career and when I finally understood how much more I could learn about people from an empathetic viewpoint, everything changed for the better.

Inquire about someone's health. Ask about the new baby and be willing to sit through whatever they want to tell you about how beautiful their new child is. Ask about the vacation. It takes much less time than you think to show your respect.

Then, add these notes to what you already have about that person in your contact database, for these are golden talking points for next time.

> *"Hey, Sally. Dave Ribble here. Need to talk to John if he is in, but before you do that, tell me how the twins are doing and didn't you and your hubby take a weekend in Vegas?"*
>
> *"Wow, Dave, thanks for asking. The twins are growing like weeds. Bill and I had a great time in Las Vegas and I won $400 at the slots. Sweet!"*
>
> *"Fantastic, Sally. Don't spend it all in one place!"*
>
> *"I won't. Hey, Dave, let me let John know you are on the phone. I am sure he will want to say hello. He has a couple of other calls waiting, but I will see if he has a couple of minutes for you, first."*

Talking points, remember?

By my recording previous conversations and by continuing to add to that, I know Sally has twins, they are both boys, they are five years old, her husband is a police officer and I know they had been planning a Las Vegas getaway that finally came true last weekend.

Will that get me more business with her boss, John? That remains to be seen. But, I like to think that Sally might mention to him what a nice guy I am for remembering personal things like that. I like to think that bringing up her family and her trip out of town helped me get ahead of two other people waiting to talk to John.

It would not have likely happened, however, had I taken the attitude that Sally is just a gatekeeper who doesn't count, doesn't matter and therefore can't have any positive contribution. Whenever I have a gatekeeper I stop right there and begin my *Conscientious Connector process* to see what I can learn about Sally and then record it. I may list her separately as a contact or I may list her information on John's contact page, but I continue to add anything I can each time we have another conversation. Then, when I am ready to call John, I am already looking forward to catching up with Sally, first.

Listening is an art and when it is done well, it is like a lightning rod for what is possible; you just never know when some information you have might help someone else. You just have to hear the need and that takes effort. You won't always hit a home run by providing them the right people to talk to or the information you can direct them toward, but every once in a while your willingness to help will be met by good information you can share with them. That's homerun time and it sure is fun.

~~~~~~~

Exercise your *Conscientious Connector Muscle Memory*

If you know the game of golf, you know that muscle memory is talked about a lot in golf. My friend Rick Sessinghaus is a former pro golfer and now teaches golf as well as peak performance using golf as one of his many metaphorical examples (ricksessinhaus.com). Rick tells me that muscle memory in golf plays a key role because you swing every club basically the same way each and every time until you get to the point where your body does that same swing over and over again without your even thinking about it. Your muscles come to understand how to work together in harmony to recreate that same swing you have done a thousand times before. Certain muscles that are involved in executing that swing become stronger and it is as if your entire body is synchronized to that perfectly timed release.

Once you figure out the direction you want to ball to fly and you pick the club, get in your stance, measure the right distance from the ball and relax, your body settles in and you execute *your* swing. You forget about everything else in the world and pull the trigger, and your body takes it from there.

Conscientious Connectors practice a similar approach to how they view the world. As you become stronger in your commitment to this, you will see every person you meet as having the potential for becoming a good connection. You will start to see more opportunities all the time to have a positive influence on other people and people will start to gravitate toward wanting to talk to you, hear from you, help you out when they can and recommend you to others. It won't be something they do in order to square the deal and balance out the reciprocity issue, either. It will be something they want to do for you because they feel good about doing so, regardless.

Your new mindset, this natural, evolving relationship to others you work with, meet, talk to over the phone, send emails to or converse with over social media takes on an ever-increasingly valuable way of life for you that you want to never end.

You wake up knowing that each day is precious and that you matter. The people you come into contact with gain a sense about you as kinder, different than most. You go to work knowing you will give it your best and you will contribute good ideas regardless of what your job description might be. You talk to customers and prospects from a different perspective. You see each coworker as someone of value to the company, to themselves and to you and it means you find yourself empathetically listening to each person who wants to share information with you. It just keeps flowing, like a river, as long as you do not cut it off or impede the flow.

Beware the perils of 'corporate shorthand'

Have you ever experienced a sales person reading from a script? At our Promotional Marketing company we constantly look for the latest trends and what new tools, products and services can be used to help our clients stand out from their competition.

Recently, a Virtual Reality company pitched us on how they can create custom content one would watch via a headset. The content can be anything we want and video can be shot from a 360-degree camera, or the content can be graphically created as well. We arranged for an online demo.

He called. We loaded the temporary software onto our computer, punched up the volume on the audio feed and listened to him for the better part of twenty minutes as he regaled us about all the great and wonderful things his company has done over the last several years in this medium.

The information was outstanding, the graphics were superb and the presentation came over the Internet without a hitch. The problem was that after about ten minutes, he still had so much information he had to show us and talk about that we were ready to cancel the rest of the show and go get coffee. We thought better of it than to dare to ask him a question or ask him to go back to something for further clarification.

Corporate Shorthand is my term for the hurry up attitude in sales and elsewhere. Hurry through the demo and hurry through talking directly to people to find out what their true needs are. This fast food, instant breakfast mindset means we all lose in the long run because people get tired of being pushed.

You will stand out from everyone else when you learn to speak and listen at the same pace as the person you are interviewing or talking to. It has to do with how quickly and easily the information is absorbed and comprehended. Even if you are just saying hello and asking how they are doing, let them set the pace and they will tell you in their own unique way the answers to your questions.

This simple act builds trust. It says you understand and that you respect their uniqueness. When you truly 'hear' them in the conversation this way, you will be lofted to the highest of ranking in their mind; you will be seen as someone who listens to them and really cares about them.

And the opposite is also true: If you try to hurry through you will also be remembered as someone who didn't want to take the time for them. Corporate Shorthand is not a friend to long-term building of relationships.

This works in every situation.

Flex your *Conscientious Connector Muscles* in all directions your life takes you. From the needs of your profession to the needs of your personal life, the more you flex your connector muscles and use these new tools, the better the likelihood you will surround yourself with people who offer good advice, contacts and support.

Let me reiterate just a few similar situations I eluded to in the Introduction to remind you of how many different areas of your life this mindset and practice will serve you.

Are you...?

✓ **Applying for a job**

What research can you do on the company you are applying to work for? What can you discover about the people you would be reporting to? What can you learn about the people who would interview you? What can you research about whom the company sells to, or the products and services they offer? Who can you call upon who will provide you a great testimonial? **Do your homework!**

✓ **Looking to gain an edge in sales over your competition?**

What research can you do not only on what your competition offers? Not just the standard fare of information everyone already knows, but information about various other bonus services, special packaging, better shipping arrangements, better shipping rates? **Get organized! List it out!**

✓ **A Student who will soon finish your college education but without connections to entry-level opportunities?**

What research can you do to identify and then campaign to interview mentors to help you understand the street-level, real-world aspects of that profession? **Fire up your research! Get interviews!**

✓ **Seeking advancement or promotion in your company?**

What additional research can you do to find additional good ideas your company can use that you can give them, above and beyond your current job description? **Turn up the heat! Show them you're worthy of the new opportunity. Create it!**

✓ **Looking to buy a car or condo or house or membership in something and worried about making a mistake?**

The more people you can rely upon to help you safeguard your decision, the better. Who can you contact? Who do you know you can trust to give you their honest opinion of the thing you are considering? **Build your database of the right people, and then nurture those relationships so you have people who will provide you backup!**

✓ **A business or personal coach struggling to gain new clients?**

Whom can you call upon to provide you referrals as well as testimonials to your character? If you do not have anyone that comes to mind, ask yourself why. Relationships start with your being relatable and relevant. **Get started building out your list! Collect good people. Flex those connector muscles the** *Conscientious Connector way.*

Do you see how this practice of collecting key contacts that want to help and contribute to your success can make so many things possible for you? Everyone has challenges, but you and I are not islands; the more people who are involved in positively affecting our future, the better.

It may sound too logical, too simple, to elementary for you to believe at the moment, but this mindset is just that: Straightforward with the only surprise being just how much more effective you will be when you begin to practice it.

Getting help in smoothing out the bumpy roads of life is always a good idea and if you have respectfully demonstrated your authentic and sincere regard for those folks who can help you, you will never run out of good advice and recommendations. This mindset of a *Conscientious Connector* is natural to that scenario.

The back cover of this book refers to salespeople, first, but also refers to everyone else, too. It describes what it is like for a *Conscientious Connector* when everything I am talking about is on automatic pilot.

The same kind of atmosphere can be created by anyone, including people who do not sell for a living. Let's take one more look at what I wrote on the back cover:

Just imagine…

Systematically, your sales pipeline of new opportunities continues to be replenished. The phone rings with yet another referral or quality connection. Non-sales personnel experience the same thing; it is perpetual, and seems to want to accelerate because you have created a foundation, a system.

It is your personal flowing river of connections, contacts, referral partners and supercharged associates, all feeding you new opportunities even when it seems to others there are none.

When you have reached this level, everyone is more willing to help you because you have already demonstrated that you care just as much about the success of others. Your listening skills improve immensely. Reciprocation is no longer your first concern.

You are the consummate treasure hunter. You understand the greater good that emanates from this mindset and you enjoy connecting people that might otherwise never meet. Yes, all this is possible.

> No matter what your profession, education, dreams and desires, *The Way of The Conscientious Connector* will always serve you. Always.

Does this sound great to you? Would you like to have this in your life? Does this sound too good to be true?

Whichever way you answer the questions will tell you (and me) a lot about where you are in terms of a paradigm shift.

What you think about comes about.

If you believe that you are in a go-nowhere job and all you can do is work and go home because you will never have a great career, what you think about will continue to show up in your life. If you think you are never going to get the raise you want, you'll probably wait a long time to get that raise.

This is how Universe works. What you devote your time to and give thought to and tell yourself you will accomplish is what will show up. If you doubt that you will be successful, you will be proven correct.

Dr. Ivan Misner, the Founder of BNI-Business Networking International said, *"Achieving greatness in any endeavor begins with mastering the fundamentals."* When we take the focus off ourselves and fundamentally focus on others, listen to others, look out for others and truly hear others, we start to formulate ways to bring new information to others and create success stories from which we all benefit. This new focus never fails to bring good things to those involved because it has no choice. We just have to be willing to dedicate ourselves to it.

~~~~~~~

This book is the culmination of critically important pieces to our story I intend to share with everyone I can. My goal is to introduce this approach to at least one million professionals who will pass it along to millions more. Thank you in advance for helping me, because when we do introduce this approach to as many as we can, folks will join up and be a part of this better way to work together.

The Way of The Conscientious Connector is more than just one guy's take on how to capture market share or extend Brand and Image. This has the potential to permeate whole companies and industries for the greater good and that should be a natural goal for all of us.

"Argue for your limitations and sure enough they're yours."

Richard Bach

The *Conscientious Connector* sees every person you meet in the same positive light until proven otherwise. Let's build on this approach and change the world. Instead of only including sales people this, let's teach everyone. Instead of considering creativity and innovative thinking as something only reserved for certain professions, divisions and departments, let's ensure that everyone in every capacity has the tools needed that will help companies build a loyal following.

What if you and I and millions of others were to adopt this new approach and create an economic environment that demonstrates our 'knowing'; that we all have a stake in the continued success of everyone else, not just ourselves. How would that feel to you?

I hope you will subscribe to this greater, bolder vision that dares to say we will move the needle on our economy, improve our own health and happiness potential and improve the health and happiness of others when we adopt this process as our new paradigm.

HOMEWORK

1.   Go back through all of your contacts and see what information you have and what you can add to each profile. If you are coming up short, you need to apply your new *Conscientious Connector* approach and start gathering talking points, which is a lot different than collecting information just for personal gain. Pick out five such contacts and call them. They must be in your contact database for some reason. If you cannot remember why you put them there, perhaps they are just contacts you loaded from a business card but you have never taken the time to truly understand who they are, what they do, what you might do to help them and support them. Maybe you thought they might one day become a customer or a contact you could use for a referral. Maybe you loaded them in simply because you wanted to get back to them at a future date to follow up, but you never did.

Spend five minutes with each one over the phone and ask them how they are doing, what they need, what their biggest challenges are and start to see what you can do to connect them with a solution or someone they can gain advice from.

   a.   Write into your contact data sheet this information. Ask more questions and see what they will tell you. Just as it is when you meet in person, doing the same thing over the phone can reap the same rich information you need.

   b.   Do not assume that the information you collect will be less than useful. Many times, a little tidbit about one person is the key to the needs of someone else you talk to and when you deliver that information, you become their hero.

   c.   Note that they appreciate your taking time to call them and to ask them questions about how you can help.

2. Take a look at your contact management system. Whether you are on a PC or a Mac, and whether you are in sales or not, you have before you a tool in your contact database management system that I promise you is being underutilized. Did you know that, for example, the Outlook for Mac contact software allows you to load in all sorts of additional notes and key phrases you can then call up later? Do you already know that you can have your Tasks set up so that you do not miss calling someone back *precisely* at the exact time you said you would? One of my favorite things to do is to use this system to call someone back at an obscure time, like "9:09 am" or "11:11am" or "4:44 pm". I can actually trigger my system that way and the reminder will pop up on my computer with a five-minute warning. Try that!

3. Note also that you can load in information this way and then in the Search window in Contacts you can plug in certain criteria and have all your contacts that have that criteria mentioned pop up on your screen. Perhaps I want to see how many people I have in my database who attended my alma mater, Chapman University. I simply plug in 'Chapman University' and the database gives me all those people. Now, I can call any of those folks and one of my talking points can be *"Hey, perhaps you know a friend of mine who also attended Chapman, Charlie Johnson?"*

When you load in this information in a manner that is *retrievable,* you are golden going forward.

Journal your feelings as you find out how much more effective this will make you, for as you read your words later, it will make you want to do it even more.

BONUS SECTION

OK, LET'S GET TO SOME BONUS MATERIAL YOU WILL LOVE & USE!

26 WAYS TO BECOME A STANDOUT©

DAVE RIBBLE

The best advice you will ever receive: A practicum to learn and rehearse that will help you in most every connecting and networking opportunity.

1. Going to hear a speaker? Check with the Host.

If there is going to be a speaker at an event you're attending, know ahead of time the name of the speaker, who they represent and what they will be talking about. You can obtain this information by calling the chamber office or hosting organization a week or two ahead of time. Do your research.

Find information about what they do, their background, education, where they went to school, how long they have been doing what they do, etc. Arm yourself with good information and anticipate a conversation with the speaker. Most chambers and networking groups can only afford to give someone 20 minutes to speak and sometimes only half that, so it will probably either be a demonstration, a talk or a PowerPoint presentation. Unless the speaker is a pro, the talk will be mostly about selling their product or service and much less about the benefits provided to others.

Figure out the people you know who might wish to be introduced to that speaker and invite them to join you for the talk. Connect the dots ahead of time. It could prove to be a conscientiously good idea that helps many others.

2. Get your head in the game. Shine your shoes. Seriously.

This seemingly obvious recommendation might make you laugh but I will tell you that when you spend time shining your shoes (or iron your blouse, etc.) before the event, it psyches you up and helps you get your 'game face' on. It makes you think about what you want to happen when you get there. It ensures you will be at your best. So shine the tops, bottoms, backs and fronts. Iron that blouse. Look your best from head to toe, without exception. You are your best bet and you are a walking advertisement for being the best at what you do, if you are prepared for it. Be the best at what you do and in how you show up. If it isn't shining shoes, pick something else you care about that says to the world you are a true professional.

Not everyone will bother to hold to this high a standard, but you can and you should. Some might argue that if you look 'too successful' it might prevent people from investing their time and money in you. Others have said that you should dress according to the audience. I suggest you be the best-dressed person in the room, professionally, every time you go out. If you are, then people will believe you are successful because of how you present yourself. They will remember you in those terms. That's the ideal reaction.

If you are not sure you are dressing in the most flattering colors and textures, and, before you spend a ton of money on clothes that do not help you look your best, go to a reasonably priced clothing store and get help. The true professionals who work day in and day out in clothing stores study what looks best on tall people, short people, round people, people with fair skin, people with long hair and short hair and everything in between. If you are nice to them, they will go out of their way to help you make decisions because they are looking for repeat customers. Spend some time with this and give yourself the benefit of having a coach in your corner about how to dress to impress. You cannot beat the price for consulting when someone is willing to stand there and tell you what you need to hear, for free. I've done it dozens of times and I am here to tell you that it is as good advice as someone who charges a ton of money for the same information. At the very least, try my idea before you spend any money on a private consultant. After you are extremely successful and have tons of money, you can take it from there and make different decisions if you so choose.

3. Be 30 minutes ahead of the official start time. Always.

If the program says it will start at **7:30am**, be there, out of your car, into the building with your payment for the breakfast handled and your name badge securely in place and you in the room by **7:00am**, if not before. If it is a mixer and you have to stand outside at the entrance for 30 minutes before they open the gates, do it, because you will have first dibs on whomever else shows up early. That, my friend, is what I call perfect timing, because it gives you one on one time before the maddening crowd shows up to interrupt you. Yes! Arrive at least 30 minutes ahead of the start time to give yourself a head start in "reading the room," which means to know who is there and who is new. Ideally, you will position yourself near the entrance where people walk in so you know who arrived. This will also allow them to see *you*. Let everyone else disappear further into the room if they choose; you need to remain visible with a welcoming smile on your face and an approachable distance from them. Remember, as a *Conscientious Connector,* you are on-purpose when you do this. Have your business cards ready and in your pocket, not in your hand. Your tie should be straight and perfect, your business suit pressed, your blouse ironed and you should always demonstrate good posture because it always attracts positive attention. This is first-impression time. Make it count.

4. Your name badge: Simple is always better.

Unless you are on the Board of Directors or carry a certain title, very likely you will use a temporary stick-on name badge and a helper will write your name on it and hand it to you. If they do not mind, have them simply write on yours your first name, as big as possible.

I strongly suggest you try to just go with your first name, only. If they insist that you also have the name of your company on the name badge, try to pick one or two words to describe what industry you are associated with, like "Financial Planner" or "RE Agent" or "Estate Atty" in nice, clean lettering.

(Note: If your handwriting ability is better than the person who is writing out the badge for you, *borrow the pen and do this yourself*. Don't leave anything to chance that you can otherwise control, here.)

The less information you have on the badge, the less confusing your badge will be to the one trying to read it. Keep it simple. Less is more in the case of name badges. Some folks think you should make your industry type the largest lettering so people can more easily spot what you do, the theory being it's easier for everyone to spot the key industries people are looking for. I think that is a limiting idea and I do not subscribe to it because a *Conscientious Connector* sees value in everyone in the room. I want people to find you and engage in conversation with you to find out who you are and what you do, regardless. Don't give anyone an excuse to not engage in a conversation with you. If that means to just list your first name and nothing else, go ahead. If it means your name plus a one or two word "hook" that would spark someone to ask you to explain, great. The badge should be written to help you start a conversation, not to get in the way of one. Use your best instincts.

As for where to place the name badge, most people tend to place the thing over their heart on the left side like we did in school for the Pledge of Allegiance. It is much easier to shake your hand and read the name badge when it is trailing up the right side of your body. People shake hands with their right. Place the name badge on your right side, always.

Ladies, if you do not wish to place your name badge on the right or on the blouse you are wearing, try placing it somewhere that is not any lower than it absolutely has to be, because it is awkward when the rest of us have to look down from your eyes in order to read your name badge and it can be embarrassingly awkward, frankly, if you have placed your name badge on your belt or on your slacks. Please make it the least awkward you can. Vanity is certainly appreciated, but remember, you are there to make it as easy as possible to connect with the right people. If we can't read your badge, we might not stop to talk.

5. Please, no selling today.

Don't go to a networking event with the objective of making a sale today. This is not the place for that. It is a place to understand more about the people who show up and how you might help them connect to people they want to meet. (If you find yourself walking in with an *I-must-make-a-sale-today-or-I-will-lose-my-job* kind of panic, consider rethinking whether you are a good candidate for the type of business you are in, all things considered.) Getting to know someone enough to determine how you can work *with* them and *for* them in a conscientious way will require your full listening and comprehension skills. If you are panicked and afraid you might lose your job if you don't snag a new customer, it has been my experience that it won't go well, in the long run, to show up with desperation in your eyes. Regroup and try another day when you are not so unbalanced and worried.

6. Don't blend in. Instead, stand out.

Resist the temptation to come in and stand with and/or sit with your buddies. When you do that, you no longer stand out from everyone else. Intended or not, you are undoubtedly making it difficult for anyone to approach you. (If you have ever walked into a crowd of people who are already very friendly with each other but you don't know them yet, you probably remember what it feels like to be the odd one out.) Your job is to make it as comfortable for someone to approach you as possible, not build impenetrable walls around you.

Also, be aware of the potential for being measured by whom you are standing with rather than being measured on your own merits. If the person you are about to meet for the first time already has a negative feeling about someone you are standing next to, fair or unfair, deserved on underserved, that same negativity might become associated with you, too, and you'll not even know why. If you ever had 'cliques' in high school, you know the scenario. The grownup version of this, Business networking, isn't any different. Try to stay away from appearing to be a part of a clique.

7. Connect people to other people and watch the response.

A reputation as someone who connects people to other people is a wonderful reputation to have. That's the stuff that gets you talked about, appreciated and respected. It is gold compared to running through the room with your business cards trying to meet everyone and collect their information as quickly as possible, (that kind of behavior screams that you are only looking out for yourself). Consider introducing people to others as the icebreaker, because doing this will instantaneously provide you with a great first impression, every time. Remember, if you don't seem to be desperate for business or connections, that's an attractive quality to display. You are centered; you know who you are and you know the good that will come to you later in some form or fashion.

8. Business cards are sacred. Treat them with respect.

Every business card you hand out and every business card that is handed to you contains information you need, so treat each one with the importance it deserves. Asian cultures consider one's business card of utmost importance. As a result, business cards are presented using two hands and a slight bow of the head as a sign of respect. You may already be familiar with this custom. You do not have to do this in the States, of course, but always show the proper respect when you hand your card to someone and receive theirs. I like to think of it this way: When someone hands you their business card, they are effectively handing you their lifeline to potential business. They are handing you their 'hope' that you will be a good connection for them in some manner.

Likewise, listening to the other person and then recording that information for review and study later is an art form. Trying to write on the back of someone's business card might be a popular way of doing things, but in order to have that work well, the back of the card must be blank and also easy to write on. Most cards these days are imprinted and coated on both sides, leaving you to hope you will remember the conversation hours later after you have also met 20 or 30 other people at an event, which is not good.

Kirby Hasseman, CEO of Hasseman Marketing in Coshocton, Ohio (hassemanmarketing.com) is a consummate professional. He is a frequent guest speaker at promotional marketing events and when Kirby hands you his business card, one side has a great picture of him and the other side has his information. But there is also a place reserved for three lines of notes. Kirby makes it very easy for you to remember how to reach him.

If you don't have that kind of option on your business cards, use a notepad. Taking notes about someone or a conversation you had is always going to be a sign of respect. A notepad provides plenty of room to get it all down and, in the final analysis, getting it all down should be your objective, because you will not remember all those details later.

Remember, when someone hands you their card, they're handing you <u>hope</u>. Just like you, those folks have kids to feed, mortgages to pay and car payments to make. Always treat that gesture with the respect it deserves and with the respect you believe you deserve in return for what you are trying to accomplish. It's that important.

9. Always take notes! Always.

Just like getting it all down when someone hands you their card and explains what they do and who they are looking for, always take notes about the event, the speaker and anything else that will help you gain the most from being there. Assume that you have very little memory in your memory bank and that you must write down everything you can, because, frankly, with this attitude you will write down more detail than you would have ever remembered on your own. Trust that to be true. Get yourself a notebook and bring it with you to every function. Have a backup in your car and another backup notebook in your briefcase. You might even want to invest in a digital tape recorder so that you can safely make yourself notes before driving your car or after you reach your destination. Great connections and critically important talking points will arrive at the oddest moments and you need to be able to record them for later review. Your notes are your lifeline. Your notes never forget something you found to be important. Get whatever information you have down. Date it. Read it again later and then decide where you need to put it for posterity and easy retrieval. It starts with taking notes.

10. If *you* are the guest speaker, be there early.

If you are the Guest Speaker, take this opportunity very seriously, because you will want to be asked to do it again and you want everything to get handled right the first time. Things typically go wrong at times, so leave nothing to chance. Arrive early enough to allow time to prepare, check the sound system, ensure you have water at the podium, check the lighting to ensure your lit properly if that is an option, check the projector, the screen, and the noise factor and your notes, even if you are in a small room at some restaurant and there are only a dozen people expected to show up. Arrive early enough, in fact, that if there are no problems with traffic or your car or road closures or a tornado that happens to touch down, you will have even more extra time to prepare.

How much time will you need to distribute your flyers to each chair, perhaps arrange for a table or two for your books to be displayed and your business cards distributed on a table or tables? How about the microphone? Check for fresh batteries if it is a wireless. Perhaps you need caffeine. Meet the Host of the event to ensure everything is ok and that the Host understands what you would like to be said about you when introduced. How much time will all that take up? Do you need an extra 30 minutes? 45 minutes? An hour?

If I am Guest Speaker, I will arrive an hour ahead of anyone who isn't part of the staff in charge of the event, sometimes more. I have lived the life of someone who had no controls over any of it and have suffered the consequences, so now I give myself plenty of time for those unexpected emergencies. When everything is all set and working properly, I can then prepare to give my talk, I can relax and have fun with the opportunity to enrich others' lives through my words and information.

11. Turn off your phone.

Believe it or not, some professionals I know will try to justify that if their phone goes off during a networking event or when a speaker is speaking that it is a sign of a very successful and important person. What real impression it makes when that happens, however, is quite the opposite. It says that this so-called professional is either unable to delegate responsibility to someone else back at the office for two hours, or they cannot afford to hire someone to do that.

Turn off your phone before you walk in. Just do it. If vibrate is the best you can fathom, do that. Honestly, in the course of two hours that early in the morning, 98% of the people I have ever shared a networking meeting with have never needed to take a phone call or make one, nor have I, because we all set an appointment with ourselves for this time period. (When was the last time you sat in your customer's office and took a phone call from some other customer?) Concentrate and stay focused on getting all you can from this event, for yourself and your company. Do it. Be the example you wish to demonstrate to others. The entire group will benefit.

12. Be prepared for your introduction.

You don't always control how much time is available to introduce yourself, so be rehearsed and ready to deliver something very short, something medium short and something longer. It's not that tough to do if you already know what you will say. If you only get five seconds, however, I suggest you stand, grab the microphone, smile your best smile and say loudly and clearly into the microphone, louder than you think you should:

"Hi - My name is _____. *I help people (*what you do to help them*).*

I look forward to speaking to each of you in the future. Thank you."

Just say your first name. Don't confuse 150 people with a last name just yet. Half of them are either not listening at all because they are instead psyching up for when it is their turn or they are the other half who won't remember your last name until they've heard it at least five times, anyway. Don't spend your precious few seconds on a last name. Save it for when you meet with them one-to-one.

The second fill-in-the-blank, after stating your first name, has to do with what you provide as an advantage to someone. If you sell Life Insurance, say you *'protect families'*. If you are a Mechanic, say you *'protect families on the road'*. If you are a restaurant owner, say you *'help families benefit from tasty, great nutrition'*. That's it. Make them want to know more about you. It's all you can do and it's all you should do with such a limited amount of time with the microphone. Don't overdo it. People who try to take more time just irritate those who stayed within the requested five-second guidelines and didn't cheat.

Going over the time limit casts a negative reflection on what kind of professional you are. If you have just five seconds, make it count, with focus on how you can help others. That's enough.

If you have ten seconds or more to speak, be prepared with your *first name and more* about how you can help others. The same rules apply. Always remember you are speaking to WIIFM (What's In It For Me) people.

13. Lead with praise at every opportunity.

There will be circumstances in your experience where you will have a little more time to talk into the microphone. It might be that you are receiving some sort of recognition for being a sponsor of something and they've given you a couple of minutes to talk about yourself. If you haven't experienced that kind of scenario, there will be a tendency to rush through who you are, what you do and then say something about being a sponsor. However, one very good idea is before you say anything about yourself, first pause for a couple of seconds as you look around the room. This ensures that everyone is paying proper respect to you by being quiet and attentive and when you do this you will be surprised at how quickly the room settles down. When you then speak to the room, it is best to first say something nice about someone else. You might thank the Host or the other sponsors or you might simply say something nice about the person who just introduced you. Acknowledge that person. Say something professionally flattering about them, about how hard they work or how much we all appreciate all they do for us, etc. These moments are precious moments because they are opportunities for you to shine as someone who cares about other people. Lead with a compliment or praise for someone else.

Taking this opportunity to say some nice things about someone else will tell the audience that you put others first, and that is a high compliment they will remember about you. *"Many thanks to our Host,*

Helen, for doing such a great job for all of us this morning. Helen, thank you again!" Note that by saying it this way, you include saying thank you to Helen on behalf of everyone in the entire room, not just from yourself, which helps establish you in a leadership role. This is a powerful way to show you are in control of things and very comfortable in that role. If you simply have little or no time with the microphone, praising the Host and Speaker and others rather than yourself actually will draw more attention to you, because it is a selfless act that can pay dividends in boosting your reputation. If there is enough time, ask the group for a round of applause for Helen, too, etc.

14. Go to the bathroom, anyway.

If you can get there early enough to go to the bathroom ahead of time, do it. Not only will you be more comfortable but you will also give yourself a chance to straighten out your tie and fix the collar on your blouse. If you don't check yourself ahead of time and the first impression you make to someone you are just meeting includes a flipped collar, you will be remembered that way; as someone who didn't take the time. It is that all-important first impression, so act like you are about to go before the cameras and thereby guarantee yourself at least the opportunity to put your best possible 'you' out there. Another reason to go early is so that you avoid being a distraction to the program or the speaker later on when your bladder has said you must now leave the room or else! Don't be a negative distraction. It's like showing up with dirty shoes; it makes others wonder how serious you are as a professional.

15. Do not overfill your plate.

If it is a buffet line, try to stay with a few pieces of fruit and juice and if you can, avoid the heavier meats, potatoes, etc. The reason for this is that certain fruits generally can be eaten without concern for anything stuck in your teeth. Fruits and juices are healthier for you anyway and will send good energy to your brain. Heavy meats, carbs and coffee will make your stomach growl, which means it could not only be uncomfortable for you but uncomfortable for those around you who have to listen.

Don't arrive hungry that morning. Rather, eat something before you leave the house so that you don't have to worry about it. After you have arrived at the event and are seated at a table, your time prior to being quiet for the speaker should be to talk to and listen to others, not shove food in your mouth. Not everyone reading this will think this is important, which means, once again, you will stand out even more and for all the right reasons.

You may be thinking right now about the $15 or $20 you spent for the breakfast and how you believe you should always get your money's worth. I could not agree more with you: You spent the $20 to be in the room! I suggest the more important thing here is for you to limit your intake of food while at the event. If you feel that you must get your money's worth for the food you paid for, you're not approaching this opportunity with the right objective in mind. From the standpoint of a *Conscientious Connector*, you should care more about what connections you might make today. The $20 you spend to find the right connections will be worth a lot more to you.

And, just for the record, I haven't even mentioned the fact that if you have a plate in one hand and you are holding a juice drink or coffee in the other, how are you going to take notes, exchange business cards or, for that matter, shake hands with someone?

16. Stay put.

Once you are seated at your table, stay there. If no one is serving coffee and you have to get up to get more, hold off while the speaker is speaking. If you must have tea, bring your own and just ask for a cup of hot water but after you are seated, stay there. If you have to have a certain type of sweetener or a non-dairy type of creamer, the same thing applies. If you are someone who needs four or five cups of coffee every morning before you can function, have four of them at home before you leave so that you are sufficiently wired by the time you get there. And, uh, don't forget to check your breath if you choose this option, for obvious reasons.

Let me say once again: *While the speaker is speaking, show your respect and* **do not get up.** *Set your best example and stick to it. Others will see you and follow your lead.*

17. Track the speaker.

As the speaker is speaking, jot down the date of this event. Listen for anything from the speaker that reveals clues as to who the speaker might be interested in meeting. Perhaps you can be instrumental in helping the Speaker for your event get booked for another. Every Speaker is looking for more opportunities and if you are the one to help her or him, I can guarantee that you will not be forgotten. You shouldn't scan your contacts while the person is speaking, obviously, but you should already be wondering whom you know who might be valuable to introduce.

If you happen, however, to think of someone to introduce the Speaker to by the time the talk is concluded and you go up to congratulate the Speaker on a nice job, be sure to mention the person you have in mind to the Speaker so that the Speaker knows you are trying to help and so the Speaker associates the opportunity you presented with the fact that you are the person who is bringing that opportunity to them. This may sound redundant, but the more you demonstrate you are clearly trying to help the Speaker this way, the better. You might ask the Speaker for permission to introduce your associate to the Speaker, which is showing utmost respect for the Speaker and which demonstrates you as a consummate professional in that regard.

If someone happens to try to talk to you while the Speaker is speaking, ignore him or her the best you can and honor the Speaker, instead. It sends a loud and clear message about how professionals in the audience should behave and demonstrates how you will want to be treated when it is your turn to be the Speaker.

Try to mention the key points you found interesting from the Speaker's presentation when you talk with her/him afterwards. This is the perfect complement to anyone who is a Speaker and you will, again, be remembered for it. If the Speaker's subject matter didn't excite you or provide you with good information, it never hurts to just say it was great to meet the Speaker and that you wish her/him well.

18. Use the microphone every time it is offered.

There are some out there, especially men, who believe they have booming voices and so they will say they don't want to use a microphone. Don't be one of them. How many stand-up comedians, singers and performers go onstage to entertain you without a microphone or several microphones attached to their person? How many 'booming voice' singers risk not being heard by everyone in the audience? None. If there is a microphone available, use it! Do not take the risk that someone in that room didn't clearly hear what you said.

Project! World famous voice coach to the stars and professionals everywhere, Roger Love, tells his students to project ten to 20 feet out from where you are standing every time. Why? Because when you project that far out, you earn the attention of the people you are speaking to. Anything less than that and you are going to be ignored, or, worse, thought of as someone not confident in what you have to say. Get their attention and use the microphone in a way that helps you sound good and ensure they hear every word. If you are not willing to do this as I have described, what is the point of standing up and talking?

You also need to practice what you will say until you get to the point where you can say it out loud anywhere, anytime and always deliver it perfectly. As Vince Lombardi, John Wooden, Jack Nicklaus and so many others are credited for saying, *"Practice doesn't make perfect. Only perfect practice makes perfect."* Practice what you will say. Make it relevant to the audience and get over being scared or frightened. You'd be surprised how many people do not have any interest, whatsoever, in seeing you screw this up. They *want* you to successfully explain who you are so they can place your information into the proper compartment inside their head. They *want* to be excited for you, interested in you. Give them your information the way you want your information to be filed in their memory bank, their contact notes and their future conversations, and make sure they hear you right the first time.

19. Door prizes should be gifts that keep on giving.

If you are inclined to offer a door prize to be given to some lucky winner from a drawing, choose a gift that will continue to reflect well on you and your business. It is easy to buy a basket of lotions or a bottle of wine the night before, put a bow on it and bring it to the breakfast, but those are items that leave no memory of you after they are taken home or back to someone's office and consumed. They are also the same things everyone else does and I want you to stand out from the crowd.

Consider something that is of value that will last, such as a Journal that can be enjoyed for months or even years that has your company logo on the front and a personal note permanently inscribed inside. Our industry offers the option of putting a custom cover or a tipped-in custom page inside a book that has already been published. You have to buy their minimum quantity, of course, but it is ever so impressive to hand a best seller to someone and it has your personal note written on the inside cover. If not that, the customized journal is always a good bet. Put your business card inside the journal as your simple tagline, for example. Consistency in your message and how you show up is critically valuable and these are just a few of many ways to make your gift personal and always remembered by the recipient. It also demonstrates to the world that you put more thought into it than the average person ever will and that speaks volumes to your professional approach in everything you do.

20. Resist 'hit & run' tactics.

A true *Conscientious Connector* doesn't believe it is a waste of time to talk to people who will never be your target market. There are some who will tell you not to spend any time with non-targets, but I am here to remind you that everyone matters, everyone knows other people and everyone can be instrumentally valuable to you and you, to them. The only way you will know this is to spend time getting to know them, and the only way you will make that information float to the surface is by asking them questions and then listening to their responses. As we said many times throughout the book, the only way you will know if you can help someone be more successful is to ask; to have a conversation and explore the possibilities.

Don't burn a bridge you have yet to even cross, either. Be a good listener. Gather what you can. Keep the information flowing to you. If a surface connector comes flying by who isn't willing to stand there and get to know you, too, this process will quickly point them out.

21. Be consistent with who you are.

Michael is a good friend and excellent personal injury attorney. He specializes in ensuring that people who have legitimate insurance claims from accidents get their money. Michael handles car accidents, workman's compensation issues and the like. His simple and straightforward message to anyone who knows him can be summed up in just three words: Accidents, Accidents, Accidents. Michael has been a member of the Westside Referrals Le Tip group longer than anyone and when he stands and takes his turn to introduce himself to anyone who has not yet met him at a networking breakfast, they hear the entire room repeat those same three words because they have been doing that for him for years. As a matter of fact, most of the members do not list Michael under his name in their contacts but they instead simply list Michael under the word 'Accidents' so that if they are in an accident they look him up that way, at the top of their contacts list, instead of trying to remember his name.

It's this consistency you must also strive for. Whatever you say you do for a living, be consistent with your message and see if you can come up with a word or two that triggers in the rest of us a memory of you when we hear the words or the phrase you mention during introductions. Lock it in, whatever you want us to remember. Continue to reinforce it every chance you get. People want consistency in their world. They need it and thrive on it. Give them consistency about how you bring added value to *their* lives, not your own.

22. Be the last to leave.

If you are there for the greater good and for the benefit of others then you are, by my definition, a true *Conscientious Connector*. After showing up ahead of everyone else, staying for the duration and being one of the last to leave, you send a silent but serious message that you are there for the greater good. If you say you are there for the greater good and then duck out early, well, then you see what kind of impression that makes, too. Choose wisely. An extra 15 minutes out of your schedule might be all you need to have a private conversation with someone that leads to good things. You never know. By getting their early and then being one of the last to leave, you are clearly placing importance on this and people will remember that and describe you to others from a favorable opinion of you. If you are truly serious about being known as someone who is there for the greater good, get on a committee that is associated with the event you are attending, because it demonstrates you are committed to something bigger than yourself.

23. Consider yourself 'always on camera'.

Until relatively recently we didn't live in a world where cameras were on phone devices and, clearly, those days are over. It is something to remember no matter where you are or what you're up to at the moment. Even before you get out of your car to go to an event, there is a likelihood you are being videotaped, either from a security camera or by someone who, for a variety of reasons, has decided to videotape you. It is just the way the world is these days.

Have you ever exited your car tucking your shirt into your pants or adjusting your skirt? It is most often necessary, largely due to the fact that you have had to drive with a seatbelt restraint and you want to straighten out your clothing. There is nothing wrong with that and I recommend you always check yourself after getting out of your car. Just assume that cameras are rolling. Treat each and every event that you attend with proper respect for who might be watching and recording your every move, either in their minds or on camera or both. Don't provide embarrassing footage if you can avoid it. You may never be confronted with anything you object to, but if you have checked social media lately, there is no lack of people with cameras who thrive on hiding behind a camera, shooting unflattering footage and then exposing that footage to the rest of the world. They don't know or care about who they are hurting, so if you keep this in mind and give them nothing that can trouble you later, you will be fine.

Likewise, your statements and your demeanor are going to be scrutinized, good and bad, so you need to always project your very best behavior and choose your words carefully. If you feel like swearing, check yourself. If you feel like telling a derogatory story, check yourself. If you feel like it doesn't matter that you showed up with slacks that are wrinkled, think about the last time you saw someone else do that and how you told yourself you would not let that happen to you.

Everything you do every day leaves an impression. It may not be fair, especially if you have people out there who would like to see you fail, usually for the purpose of building up their own lack of self esteem. Don't give them the opportunity to catch you in a compromising situation. You may not like to be this buttoned up, but just remind yourself that when you decide to go off the 'being-professional-at-all-times' bandwagon there most certainly will be consequences either now or later and it isn't worth it. Be your best when you are in public.

And, just because you happen to be in your car, don't assume people aren't paying attention to you there, as well. You know you are being observed when someone comes up and says, "Hey Dave, I saw you buying ice cream the other night at 31 Flavors. I was driving by and recognized your car and, by golly, there you were!" As soon as someone says that, I immediately think back to that moment and ask myself what I was wearing, if I was grubby or dressed professionally and whether my hair was combed.

Instagrams are instantaneous photos of you. Twitter feeds are instantaneous as well. Facebook Live is LIVE. Video is rolling all the time. The same is true for Go Pro cameras and drones in the sky. From security experts to amateur photo geeks and storeowners, everyone has cameras rolling.

24. Put things in order, immediately.

My friend and fabulous networker, Kecia Wimmer Lyons, told me that as soon as she leaves a networking event she goes to her car, pulls out a small little baggie, drops the business cards and notes in and closes it up. She marks the baggie with her permanent marker she keeps in the car, noting the name of the event, the date and anything else she wants to list for later review. Instead of coming back to the office with all sorts of scattered notes and cards, she can drop that collected information into a drawer to be looked at and poured over later and everything is right there, intact. I highly recommend you follow Kecia's game plan or figure out your own system and start using it right now. Every note you make is a potential talking point for later conversations with that person or someone else you want to refer them to. The more notes you take, the more talking points you get to use and the more accurate you become in how to support the people you meet.

25. Be enthusiastically curious.

You matter. Your success will lead to others being successful, too. That is about as powerful a role as you could ask for and you need to understand that you matter, you are important and that you hold the keys to your future in your hands. When you are meeting people, whether at a networking function or any of a dozen other places, adopt a genuine curiosity about who other people are, what they do for a living, and what their challenges are. If you can get that information you can often change their lives for the better. That's powerful! It will require doing the things mentioned above, of course, but those are the tools and tactics; this is all about what's in your heart and what information you can glean from others you meet.

Be curious. Let them know you want to help them if they will tell you about themselves. If you are authentic in your interest in learning more about them, it has been my experience that they will tell you a lot if you know how to ask the right questions. As for whether they will want to know about you, too, don't be surprised or even disappointed if they do not seem, at first, to be interested in you as much as they are interested in telling you about themselves. That's just how most folks are, and if you are asking good questions, you will see the floodgates of information come rolling out. There will be time later on for you to determine whether they want to know more about you. Let that go for now. Good things will come from an authentic, genuine conversation you have with someone. It always does.

26. Enlist and engage others.

One great way to help all of us be more successful is to enlist and engage the people you meet and convince them that they, too, can become *Conscientious Connectors*. We can all continue to expand our common teamwork, so that this movement continues to grow. Just imagine the positive influence that you will become where you work and in the people with whom you associate! Make this your mission and you will never be sorry, for it will expand your thinking and your actions and, once expanded, it will never return to where it is right now. Your world will open up, more all the time, as you practice enlisting and engaging others in this bigger quest.

> **We can learn to see each other and see ourselves in each other and recognize that human beings are more alike than we are unalike.**
>
> *Maya Angelou*

HOMEWORK

1. As you scanned the 26 various things you can do, learn or adopt, what are the ones you want to work on first, second and so on? If you write them down, you'll be telling your subconscious you want to focus on getting better at those things. Whatever you think about comes about.

2. Add to the list anything else you have recognized in yourself that you want to improve. Same process; same results. Just think about how much better you will be at this and how you will become a true StandOut to everyone you meet.

3. You may decide there are certain aspects for which you need coaching. Every pro golfer has a coach because coaches see things and notice things the golfer cannot. Think about getting a coach.

NOTES

BONUS TWO

JOB SEARCHES & PROMOTION OPPORTUNITIES

Apply what you have learned here to better your chances.

The world is rapidly evolving. Some things we thought would stay the same forever, changed. It is difficult for me to fathom what advances and new inventions we have witnessed just in the last couple of decades. In an ever increasingly complex environment, folks are asking me how *The Way of The Conscientious Connector* can help. Let's talk about that.

Whether you are looking for a job or competing with others for a promotion, you are *competing with others*, which means it is your job to figure out how to show you are more valuable for that position than anyone else applying for it. In order to provide ample proof that you are the one who should be rewarded, you have before you the opportunity to show how your value extends beyond your personal skills and experience. The first step is to learn how to add sustainable and supportive connections to your resume that will serve a prospective employer, as well as yourself, quite possibly for the rest of your life.

Let me ask you, as it applies to this thinking:

- *If you work in a company and are applying for a promotion but do not have sustainable and supportive connections to others who could possibly help the company you work for, can you develop them?*

- *If you are applying for a job with a new company, can you do research and identify connections from your resources that might be of value to that prospective employer?*

Especially when the kids were little, I found myself applying for many and varied jobs and positions, which meant I had to do my work and be clever about it. I had to research the company, research the position and try to obtain as much information as was available so that I could write my resume to fit the position I was applying for. This was before computers and the Internet, so I spent a lot of time in the library, trying to understand the company, its competitors and how I could bring value. It was always about bringing more value than others to that position.

I didn't fabricate information, of course, but I did highlight my experience and my connections to others I felt would relate and be valuable to the company I was trying to work for. It was great training ground for what would later become my advice on this subject.

The same applies for when I am pitching our company or looking to be selected as a keynote speaker or to be hired for corporate training. I need to demonstrate to a prospective client why our company, our skills and experience and our unique perspective make us the company they should hire. If I can demonstrate how we bring more direct value to the client than others being considered, our chances are much better to win that opportunity.

The point is this: The playing field isn't always level. But even if the odds do not seem to be in your favor, you have skills as well as research you can do. If you have been diligently collecting solid connections in *The Way of The Conscientious Connector* while doing your research on the business you are applying to work for, you are learning how to add value; value you can use to your advantage.

Conversely, I have also interviewed people applying for a job with us and, to be sure, I have always looked for the added value those applicants possessed that would be advantageous to us. I can teach just about anyone to do a specific job over time, but I am much more interested in the various ways they will add value to our business. That's the chocolate syrup and cherry on top.

Always Bring Value

There's no question that the process of applying for a job or interviewing people can be brutal. That's because it is very difficult for that process to be a totally honest process. Applicants try to say the right things they think you want to hear. The other side of that equation is that the prospective company is looking for hidden gems of added value that aren't always readily apparent in interviews. I call that a brutal process.

My advice for you is this: Figure out as many ways as you possibly can to add value, always, whether it is for the job you have now or the one you aspire to go after. Keep looking and keep asking yourself 'How Do I Add Value?' as I introduce you to Aggie.

~~~~~~~

Aggie Medrano is arguably the best Customer Service expert we ever worked with in our industry. First, it has always been Aggie's personality to look for ways to add value to the job she is given and the position of responsibility she takes on. Her boss, Bob, recognized early on in Aggie's career that if he empowered her to make her own decisions when it came to rush orders, moving production schedules to fit a specific need, figuring out a discount for a glitch, even requiring overtime or special shipping to meet a deadline, Bob knew it was more important to save the order and maintain their customer's loyalty than to risk losing that customer. When Aggie first started, she didn't have all those skills, experience and knowledge, but, from Day 1, she instinctively went after every ounce of new information she could learn. She quickly became our go-to person, without exception.

Interestingly, when Aggie first began working there, her commute was about 20 miles. Years later, Bob decided to move the entire operation closer to his home, which meant, for Aggie, that her new commute would be over 50 miles one way each day. For a mom with teenage kids at home and a husband whose commute was even further, the hour and a half drive began to take its toll.

One day I had to drive out to the factory to pick up a few

samples. When Aggie personally came downstairs to hand me the box, I innocently mentioned to her that Gaye and I had decided to look for an assistant, and, if she knew of anyone, to let me know.

Aggie knew we lived about 20 miles away from her front door and, as she later shared, we were also one of her favorite distributors. I had no idea at the time she was looking for a change that would change her life as well as ours. I should have heard her wheels turning.

Aggie motioned for me to take the box of samples and said, "Let's go outside for a minute," as she held open the front door for me. When we got to my car she asked me who I was looking for and the qualifications we required. I thought about that for a minute and replied, "Ideally, Aggie, I would describe the person we're looking for as someone who knows this industry, knows how things work, is great over the phone and in helping us be organized, someone that," I stopped to collect my thoughts and looked at her. "I guess I would have to say we would want...you. But there's no one like you. And besides, I can't afford you."

I pulled open the back hatch to my car and placed the box of samples inside. She looked at me with a smile then looked off into the distance before training her eyes on mine once again. I waited and then she said, "Well, what makes you think you can't afford me?" I looked at her and laughed a cautious laugh.

I said, "Aggie, you're the best in this business, so don't mess with me because my heart can't take it."

She laughed again and said, "Well, you just never know, do you?"

~~~~~~~

It wasn't long before Aggie did come to work for us and neither Bob nor any of our competitor distributors around town could blame us for wanting to bring Aggie onto the team. She was excited with the shorter commute and she told us later that, after working on the supplier side for 17 years, she had decided she wanted to work on the distributor side for a while and that maybe the timing was right when I stopped by for those samples. It was fortuitous for us, to say the least, and we've remained close friends ever since.

Aggie continued to deliver that same work ethic and amazing customer service as we had come to love as when she worked for the supplier. It wasn't long before Gaye and I both experienced what it was like for our clients to ask for Aggie, not either of us, when they called.

I teased her about that, too, because if I answered the phone and Aggie wasn't available to talk to them, the clients often asked me to take a message and have *Aggie* call them later. I couldn't blame them.

~~~~~~

I tell you this story because I want you to understand just how much power over your own future you have that you may be overlooking. Aggie served her supplier employer very well for many years and the way she did that was to know so much about that business that she became almost indispensable. She continually improved her customer skills. She continually did research for us on various products we could offer our clients. She mainstreamed our accounting and set up systems we desperately needed. In other words, she continually looked for more ways to add value to our business, which, in turn, added more value to her own resume for any prospective employer.

There are numerous lessons for all of us in this story.

1. Don't focus solely on your job description. Do your very best at your job, but also look for more ways to be valuable to your current employer as well as anyone you might want to work for, next. Always be looking for ways to bring more value.

2. Don't hesitate. Don't think you are wasting any of your time by putting in the extra thought and effort. It is far

easier to figure out more ways to contribute to the success of the company you work for than it is to find a new job and start over.

3.   Always, always, always be learning new skills.

You will very likely have several jobs in your lifetime. You will find yourself needing to connect with others for a variety of reasons. You just never know where this kind of training will come in handy.

If you are looking for a job in a particular profession that you already have experience with, you already know certain things about the industry. You are likely scanning all of the resources and talking to recruiters and sprucing up your resume. I am sure you are working hard at that and I hope you find the perfect job for yourself, whatever that may be.

If, on the other hand, you're feeling a little fragmented and are running into walls because you're not getting call backs or opportunities to advance your career, let's spend a little time on this and I'll offer you some suggestions taken from a *Conscientious Connector* perspective. You may already approach your job search in a similar manner, but it doesn't hurt to think about the following.

The Conscientious Connector Playbook

Over the years, I've helped a number of friends and acquaintances with suggestions on what they could do as they searched for their next career move. Some were looking for a promotion. Others were looking for a job after being laid off and a third group were students coming out of college with very little on their resume but hoping to get that proverbial first foot in the door.

I realize now that I was in the process of creating the *Conscientious Connector Philosophy* that is the basis of everything I write and talk about. This is coming from my many years in the field; calling upon clients and prospects, meeting people for the first time at networking events and the cold calling skills I developed to keep my jobs. Everything associated within Marketing, Advertising, Sales and Public Relations brought me more insights and understanding that eventually culminated in the consulting business we now have, *StandOut Marketing Strategies.*

From this perspective, here are the two things you need to do when searching for your next gig:

a) Look at any job opportunity, and the research you do, through the eyes of a *Conscientious Connector.* How can you demonstrate that you can add value? Is it through additional skills you are learning? Is it through more connections the company can benefit from?

b) Take that information and formulate a game plan that will allow you to become a standout in the eyes of those making hiring decisions.

The Age of Digital Discontent

Have you experienced digital discontent? Resumes and other communication with would-be employers are digital. *"All resumes must be submitted electronically with these guidelines or they will be rejected,"* is the commonality now.

I am sure the folks in Human Resources love this accelerated process and I am equally sure they are not interested in receiving your resume and job application on paper any more than they are interested in talking to you until they are ready to interview you.

My Internet guru, Alex, tells me that resume building is now a fine art. Applicants are coached in how to use 'keyword strategy' in the same vein that his company helps clients with SEO for their websites. The objective is the same: Help one person stand out from everyone else. It's the way the game is played these days and I defer you to Alex and other experts in terms of how to place keywords within your resume.

Follow the process and the reasoning for it: After the HR person scans each application, looking for key points and key words that tie in best to the available position and responsibilities, those applicants are moved to a new stack and only those who are deemed very good candidates for the position are included. Once that is determined, applicants who are still looking and hoping for an interview are notified, digitally, and appointments are set up.

Welcome to the 21st century. Is this what you have experienced? Have we managed to take away the humanistic side of this process to the point where your sum total of value to a company is within the confines of what shows up on an electronic, flat screen monitor? I am afraid so. Like it or fight it, the truth of the matter is that this is how applying for most jobs takes place.

Linda Is Looking

Let's pretend you are like my friend, Linda, who has a background in Accounting and is currently looking for her next job. We talked the other day and Linda told me she was going after an Accounts Receivable position with a small firm, but was a bit down because she had been on many interviews already and had not received call backs. It is easy to let that depress anyone; our egos are involved in the process and we all tend to take things personally at times, especially when we are concentrating so hard because we need the job for the money and benefits. Linda was a bit perplexed and started to worry.

The Conscientious Connector Becomes a StandOut Marketing Strategist

Here is where I am coming from for anyone preparing to be interviewed. It is a similar process to how we approach any new promotional marketing project for our clients. In marketing, we want to know what objective the client has for being involved in a project. It's the first thing any professional Marketing, Advertising, Promotional Marketing or Public Relations expert should ask, every time: *"What are you trying to accomplish?"*

If a company wants to make a big splash at a convention, for example, we will want to know what it is they want to see happen. Recently, our company produced an event in Los Angeles that had to do with helping our client make a big splash in the eyes of their targeted market. The event was held at the Spin Lounge at the Standard Hotel downtown and the original objective was to get 60 people to show up. Even though there were over 20 convention-related parties all around town that night, our event garnered over 200 people. See the video that was shot by our good friend and fabulous videographer, Tonje Nordgaard (vimeo.com/107781688). You will see very happy people who attended a special event that made our client ecstatic. They wanted 60. They got over 200 and rave reviews. Their target market now knew who they were and came the next day to their booth to learn more about them. Mission accomplished.

The Value-Added Attraction Factor

The point is this: Whether you set out to attract prospective customers to your trade show booth or you are looking to gain employment from a company you have won the opportunity to interview with, the basics are the same: (1) take stock of where you are right now, (2) consider what the company is looking for and decide what additional information you will need in order to be successful, then (3) gather those resources, learn them, practice them and be prepared like an Eagle Scout candidate going for that last merit badge. Just by having that kind of attitude you will stand out from everyone else.

This information also helped Linda prepare. Look at everything from the perspective of what you believe the company wants out of this union. Remember, while it is about you, it is about how you fit in with them, not the other way around.

Break it down into simple terms:

A. You want to land the job because you want to

    a. Earn the money.

    b. Gain the benefits.

    c. Belong to the company.

    d. Meet new people.

    e. Start or advance your career.

    f. Do the things you like to do for a living.

And…

B. The company wants to hire the right person to

    g. Gain the most from that person's skills.

    h. Gain the most from that person's education.

    i. Gain the most from that person's experience.

    j. Gain the most from that person's dedication.

    k. Gain the most from that person's loyalty.

    l. Gain the most from that person's honesty.

    m. Gain the most from that person's connections.

    n. Gain the most from that person's willingness to work for that amount of money.

As you look at the difference in positioning from **A** to **B,** do you see how you want certain things and the company focus is different? Your focus needs to be on *them.*

You already know the reasons you want to work there. You will undoubtedly be asked that very question in your interview and most of us would likely answer the question with a series of ready-made responses, like *"I have always wanted to work for a successful company like (this one),"* or *"I've always heard great things about this company from others,"* or *"I am looking for a career because I believe in what your company stands for."*

Now look back at B. The position you are applying for really represents a part of the puzzle for the company that needs to be plugged in so that the company can move itself forward. If you are Linda and the company recently either promoted someone who was doing Accounts Payable to a higher level of responsibility or that person left for some reason, the void needs to be filled. The person in Human Resources was assigned the duties of putting the job opening on a website and recruiters saw that and started to send their client's apps and resumes in, hoping to land one of their clients the job.

The applicant (Linda) is now up against dozens, hundreds, perhaps thousands of other qualified people who want that job. My question to you is this: If this were you, how would you go about setting yourself apart from everyone else who is going in for an interview?

As a *Conscientious Connector* you may very well look at this opportunity differently than you did before. Instead of listing all the reasons you want this job, as in "A" section that we pointed to earlier, if you look at "B" you might want to look again at what it is the company wants from whomever wins the position.

The company wants performance. The company wants someone who will fill the position, add to it, bring other skills to the company and more often than not, the company wants our friend Linda to be someone who will not only do her job exceptionally well, but whom also desires a life-long career with that company so that the company can utilize her in many capacities over the years.

As a strategist, I want everything Linda says to be information that favors the company first and foremost. I want her to pay close attention to how she can take what she knows, what she has learned, what she has researched and what she has formulated as the foundation and think about all of it from the company's perspective, not her own.

No one in my lifetime demonstrated these principles about how to apply for a job or gain a promotion better than my brother. Rip enjoyed a successful 30-plus year career in City Government, specifically for Parks & Recreation. Each time he decided to interview for a better position, he did an amazing amount of research. He studied all he could find about that city: The officials, their long term plans for the city and any obstacles to those goals. He studied the political climate and statistics about the demographic and psychographic makeup of the place he wanted to take his career to next. He even researched comparative information about other cities. He then put together that information into talking points, so that if a certain question came up, he could weave his due diligence into the response he gave them, both on the written as well as oral exams and the interviews. Quite often, Rip knew more about the subject matter at hand than the person interviewing him, and, to my knowledge my brother won most every new position he ever decided to apply for.

That's dedicated attention to detail. I want you to think like this, too. And, should you do this work and still not get the job you applied for, I firmly believe *a better one awaits you*. Dedicated research, planning and development of a game plan when applying for a job is never wasted effort because you always learn from the work you put in. The more you work at it, the more valuable you will become, to your self as well as any prospective employer.

~~~~~~~

Christina Joy Ryan Rodriguez was Director of Students for Charter College's Long Beach campus when we first met. The Marketing Department had invited me to speak to their students and at that time Christina was well into finishing up her Doctorate in Education. Although Charter College folded, displacing many students and faculty, Golden West College named Christina their Dean of Enrollment and she and I have remained good friends and kept in touch ever since. Christina possesses a voracious appetite for studying everything that relates to how we can improve education in this country as well as around the world. She continues to teach me, as well, from her academic perspective, the many sobering facts about our collective future as it relates to education and the coming generations.

Not long ago we watched the largest private tech school in the country, ITT Tech, go out of business, culminating in thousands of employees dismissed and tens of thousands of students displaced who then had to figure out how to finish their education elsewhere. What happened? Did private, for-profit education fail to deliver? Should we rely on private education to ensure our future is bright? Are checks and balances in place when it comes to for-profit educational institutions?

According to some news reports, part of the challenge was that the student loans stopped being guaranteed, which not only affected ITT Tech but most every other for-profit college and university in the country.

Whether education is delivered by private or public means, we need for our people to be educated and flexible in what jobs they are qualified and educated to do. Certain industries that were prominent early in the 20th century are no longer in the mainstream. Travel to Auburn, Maine and count how many huge shoe manufacturing plants stand empty or are being converted into mixed use buildings. History tells us, for example, that in 1917, one factory in Auburn was producing 75 percent of the world's supply of white canvas shoes. By 1961 the largest manufacturers in Auburn had closed their doors.

Things change. People who only know how to do certain things will need to learn new skills. It's not a bad thing to learn new skills. The needs of the environment are up against the needs of third and fourth generation coal miners, for example. Super efficient computer-driven robots that never take a day off are replacing the manufacturing jobs that call for repetitive motion. I watched a demonstration the other day of a construction robotic system that lays bricks and builds walls with very little assistance needed from a human being. The repetitive jobs that were commonplace are being replaced by automation in every way imaginable. We knew this was coming, but did we prepare for it? Some folks have dropped out of the labor market altogether because they continue to look for the same job they had before and refuse to learn new skills.

Changes in the job market are inevitable. Innovation is encouraged and with that, new job descriptions are being written up every day. Computers play a role in most everything, from how you apply for a job now to how you do that job after you land it. Will we meet the demands of this century and beyond if all we do is try to slow down or even reverse the future? I don't think so.

Having said all that, certain things are still certain. When you follow *The Way of The Conscientious Connector* you will realize you need to develop better connections to the right people if you want to compete for the jobs being developed. If you want to stand out from everyone else who is applying for those jobs or, if you come to the conclusion that you will need to get more education, remember that, either way, you will be better off the more you can build a database of the right connections. Remember, too, that you will do that by seeing how you can help others in that process, first.

Education is key to everything and part of that education must include teaching skills that will help students, and mature workers alike, connect with others at a level that helps everyone involved. This is critically important for returning Veterans, too.

We see these skills as an opportunity to move the needle on careers, the economy and life itself, forward. People will continue to want to do business with people they know, like and trust and the same is true for who gets hired and who gets passed up for a job opportunity. The better your database of sustainable, loyal connections and the better you develop added value you can offer in this process, on-going, the greater your chances of moving your career and your life in the direction you desire.

HOMEWORK

If, indeed, you are out there looking for your next career move or perhaps even your first job, you're probably basing a lot of what you go after on the two most common criteria: Money and benefits. That's usually what everyone looks for, first. The third criterion is about whether you will actually *like* and or *want* the job you're applying for.

At one time when the kids were little, I had three jobs. I worked at a church all day, worked at a department store on the weekends, and seven days a week I arose at 3:30 am to go and pick up the newspapers that I delivered in the hills above Anaheim. I would return home by 6am most mornings, go back to sleep for about an hour before showering and getting ready for the day. Others had it tougher and I was thankful for the checks I needed to pay the rent and feed three little ones. Another time I actually applied for a job cleaning an office at night. Yes, even the toilets. The owner looked at my resume and had a difficult time granting my wish to be hired because he couldn't afford to pay very much. He actually apologized to me, but he gave me the job because I wanted it and my family needed it.

1. List out your history on a piece of paper; the places you've worked and the rest of the routine information people ask for.

2. Consider looking at what jobs you have had and compare them to the job you are applying for to see if there are any similarities, first and foremost, but then look at the job application as an opportunity to list, or at least mention, what you learned from your previous employment that would directly and positively affect how much of a great employee you would be in this new position.

3. It has been my experience that people who are looking to hire someone aren't as interested in your skills as they are in your willingness to learn to do things their way. They are looking for someone who is truly excited to come to work and who has the

propensity for building a career with that organization. When you think of yourself as someone who owns a company, isn't it fair to say that you would want people who work for you to never want to leave? When you put yourself in their shoes it becomes more of an obvious trait you will want to demonstrate.

4. Do your research on the company and get to know as much as you can about that company; what their situation is, whether they are expanding, about their competition, about their history and the key profiles of the people you would report to. Basically, anything and everything you can find out about that company before you go in for an interview or write up a cover letter. It matters little to me the level of the job you are going after; this work is necessary at every level if you truly want to land the position and even if your plan is to advance rapidly to something more challenging. You still need the job at hand to get there, so use every tool at your disposal and leave nothing out. You are on a treasure hunt and the treasure is getting the job you want that you will, indeed, devote part of every day of your life to. If you are going to go for it, then really go for it.

~~~~~~~

Tom Ziglar, the son of the great Zig Ziglar has followed in his father's footsteps and carries on the family business through training programs, blog posts and many other avenues that continually lift us up and teach us in the same vein as his father.

As you are writing up your resume and searching for how to be an effective employee or candidate, remember this little story Tom recently posted that his dad authored:

"I have asked thousands of business owners and leaders the following question, and not one of them has ever had this happen. Just think - you could be the first one to do this.

"Here it is. Go to your boss and say, 'I have been doing some research about our industry and I found a great seminar that will help me develop my skills and knowledge so that I can help our company do better. Is it ok if I take time off

without pay and pay my own way to attend this event?'

"Chances are, your boss will end up on the floor, flopping around like a fish suddenly jerked out of water! That, alone, will make the whole thing worth it.

"By the way, if they say no, you cannot do that, start looking for a new job immediately."

~~~~~~~

If you work for someone and you are vying for a raise or a promotion, create more reasons for that company to want to keep you with them and not go to a competitor. Like the old saying goes: "Your raise/promotion becomes effective when *you* do."

You have to provide reasons for justifying what you are asking for. Just because you think you deserve the job or the raise doesn't cut it. It is much easier to ask for something if you have made it abundantly important to the company not to lose you to a competitor. It could be that you have learned more about other ways to contribute to the bottom line or it could be that you brought in new customers or you saved the company money or any number of other ways you have figured out how to add value. Keep providing more reasons for them to want to keep you. You cannot lose with that kind of attitude and application to your job, no matter what that job is.

It is easy to feel sorry for yourself when you are working somewhere and the job is less than ideal. Guard yourself from becoming stagnant because I will be here to remind you that you, at one time, really wanted that job. Remember that? Live up to that fact before blaming anything or anyone else for the way you feel. Instead, get to work on being worthy of something better.

That's *The Way of The Conscientious Connector.*

NOTES

BONUS THREE

THERMOSTAT CHECK!
TURN COLD CALLING INTO WARM

It's all in how you set your Intention.

For some of you, cold calling is either part of your current job or someday it might be, just like meeting people for the first time at a network breakfast or a business meeting. Just the phrase 'cold call' can send chills up the spine of an otherwise very competent professional, but it doesn't have to be that way. It can, believe it or not, be the most fun you'll have if you are centered in your head and heart ahead of time to a better profile of yourself. For now I will assume cold calling and meeting new people is not a comfortable activity for you and I will share my take on things.

To do so, however, I may have to challenge you a little for your own good. Very few people enjoy, initially, the process of meeting new people because we all want to make the right first impression and not screw that up. We want it to go well and many of us put a ton of pressure on ourselves to not say the wrong thing. We worry about spinach in our teeth and we oftentimes hope beyond hope we won't spit when we speak or tip our glass or do anything else that carries with it the potential for a bad first impression. Am I close?

Here's what you should do: Get over thinking you will make a mistake or give off a bad first impression. Do that right now. How do you know that is even possible? How do you know, in fact, that the people you meet will think anything negative about you whatsoever? Who put that into your head in the first place?

If you are afraid that something bad will happen, you are already programming yourself to help ensure that it will. But, if you have a steady, rock solid foundation in place that tells you that you are smart, caring, cool, informed, worthy of their time and attention and you have great products/services that really help people have a better life experience, your whole demeanor will back that up because that is where you have programmed yourself to 'live'.

The other thing to remember is that most first impressions aren't all they're cracked up to be, anyway. Stand up at a breakfast meeting to introduce yourself and knock over four glasses of water and I am sure you will feel some embarrassment. It is in our DNA to run from embarrassing situations or to become obtusely defensive over common occurrences like that. But, has anyone else ever done that in your presence? Absolutely. Can you recall that happening? Probably not. The reason is because people don't pay as close attention to other people as they do to themselves. When you witnessed someone else knocking over their glasses of water, did that leave a permanent scar on them in your memory? Highly doubtful. So, if you cannot remember someone else doing that, why do you think the audience will recall with disdain the time you did?

We place way too much worry on such things. Relax. We're all fallible and yet we're all molded from the same perfection. Breathe and be grateful.

Now, let's get to the good stuff. The best way to get over being nervous about anything is to do that thing that makes you nervous over and over until it doesn't bother you so much anymore. Getting over it requires doing it. There are no shortcuts, but there are ways to approach it that I can help you with.

Think of yourself as a Broadway singer, gearing up to perform live at Carnegie Hall. How many times will you rehearse the song before the show opens to a live audience? The answer is that you will rehearse that song as many times as it takes for you to be comfortable singing it. There are no shortcuts to that process.

Cold calling, meeting new people at events and/or knocking on unsuspecting doors is what some term a necessary evil and they continue to program themselves accordingly. Most of us have to talk to strangers in one way or another in order to have a shot at finding a new customer or making a connection for our career, so some of us will invent ways to get through that process by cushioning the blow. Leads companies and telemarketers bear the brunt of that first contact in various ways, but after that so-called lead is there for you to call, it is still a stranger calling a stranger.

Note that it is still a defensive posture, still being treated as a necessary evil. That's what you can change in your demeanor as well as your approach to meeting new people whether it is over the phone or at a gathering.

The objective should always be this: Figure out how to change the scenario from stranger to stranger, to *friend to friend*. In order to do that you have to figure out how to be a friend to that person you are about to talk to. Get your information straight on why you are calling. Figure out what you can offer them that will help them with their job or their life. Is it just the product or service you offer that will make their life a happier life? Or, is your product like most others and you need to dig deeper to provide other types of value to the person you are talking to? Understand the ways you may be of service, especially if your product is a common one, like cable tv service or home furnishings. **Your mission should be that by the time you are finished with that initial call, they are thanking you for calling them.**

My good friend, golf coach and mentor Mark Heller worked two summers during his college years going door-to-door to sell books. He had a catalog, a winning smile, great personality and a determination to figure out a way to be welcomed into the home of a perfect stranger who answered the door when he knocked. It was hardball selling and straight commission.

Not only did he have to canvas neighborhoods, get in, get orders placed and collect checks, but he also had to go back a few weeks later to *deliver* the books he had sold them. And, at each one of those intervals, Mark's success hinged on the fact that the customer could change their mind and cancel the order. Add to that the fact that he would be dropped off in a neighborhood without a car for hours at a time and you can see why I appreciate the fact that this was hardball selling at its finest.

Mark told me that if he were 'on his game,' he would soon be welcomed back for cookies and tea because he had a way about him that allowed for perfect strangers to like him and want to help him earn money for college. Can you imagine yourself going out to a neighborhood, getting dropped off with sample books and order forms and systematically canvassing a neighborhood?

These days, a lot of that door-to-door work is done through telemarketers and direct mail, which is certainly a safer way to conduct business in terms of not having to stand there and be turned down in person. It is, nevertheless, sorely lacking in personal interaction when you cannot see the person's face while negotiating with them. Cold calling isn't for the faint of heart but it is, frankly, a marvelous training ground for anyone in sales.

I, too, experienced some serious challenges early in my career. I was a Regional Manager covering nine states for the Promotional Products Division of Rand McNally, the world's foremost maker of maps, custom coffee table books and the like. My job was to call on distributors and help them understand how to sell the Rand McNally products to their clients.

The challenge for us was that the products, while exceptional, were much more expensive than other products distributors could recommend to their clients. The products I represented often required much longer lead times, so it quickly became overwhelmingly apparent to my 11 colleagues and me that if we were going to get to keep our jobs, we had to *cold call like crazy*, find a person inside a company we could convince to take a look at the Rand McNally products, get that person to agree to a meeting with one of our distributors, then find the best distributor who was willing to take the appointment. We were not allowed to sell to the client ourselves because that would violate our agreement with our distributors. So I cold called 70% of my time. I called, left messages, followed up, called again, was turned down most of the time but had to keep going if I was going to hit my numbers.

That's hardball cold calling and, when I started out, it was nuts because I wasn't good at it. The urgency of my needs made me more aggressive and the people I called could hear that desperation in my voice. Not only was I calling them out of the blue, but if they so much as even *hinted* that they wouldn't be willing to meet with my distributor, I am sure they could hear my exasperation over the phone. Naturally, I was reluctant to keep doing something that made me feel bad, but I persevered and eventually got really good at it. I just had to figure out my positioning, my process, my way.

Positioning is Key

When I look back on it now and share this with you, I will be the first to tell you that my 'positioning' as I picked up the phone to make calls back then was all out of whack. My approach and my remarks were about *me and about my needs*, not the prospects'. I had numbers to hit, after all; kids to feed and things to pay for. I was, for lack of a better term, dumping my challenges onto a perfect stranger over the phone. I was asking them for the favor of helping me out. I call that *pathetic positioning*.

Remember - it's not about you. It's always about *them*.

My positioning was transparent. Those conversations sometimes lasted a mere minute before I heard the polite *no thank you* followed by the inevitable dial tone. Was that because they really weren't interested in my products or was it because they weren't interested in sharing my desperation?

I had to get past that to a place where the reason for my call was a *benefit to the person I called*. Without it, nothing good would come from this investment of time, energy, emotion and frustration. I had to be sincere, authentic and it had to be believable, because you can't fake this stuff for long.

Here's Some Good News

If your product or service is going to be of great benefit to the person you are about to call, the person you are about to call *wants* your information to be of benefit. They will want to hear about it. It justifies their investment of time spent with you. It makes them feel smart for doing so because what you are calling about is something that they need.

That's the approach to have.

- *They want to hear from you because you will enhance their life and help their company!* You need to get over the idea that people you connect with for the first time are always going to NOT be interested in what you have to say. People will pick up on that attitude and argue your limitations for you, so don't give them that to feed upon. If you learn how to present what you have to say in a compelling and interesting way, you must remember that they want you to have good information they can use. They want you to be successful. They want to have a reason to you thank you for the call.

- *Put yourself in their shoes.* The act of calling someone you do not know forces you to take a look at the process and put yourself in the shoes and heart of the person you are about to try to reach. You have to find 'empathy' in this process. If you have a product or service that you believe is a good product or service, that's the first step. If that confidence in what you are representing is there, people might give you the benefit of the doubt and listen to what you have to say, but only if there are compelling, potential benefits to *them* for spending time hearing about it.

- *You'll become familiar with various ways people put up their defenses.*

This information is worth gold to you for the rest of your career. Look for the lessons. All of us have similar feelings, most of us do not like to cold call and most of us aren't very good at it. The people on the other end of the phone want to know about things that will benefit the company, so they will stay on the phone with you for as long as the information is of benefit to them. That's all you can ask of someone over the phone. Likewise, that's all you can ask of someone standing right in front of you at a networking event. Be yourself. Be authentic. Talk from their perspective and not your own. You'll do great!

- *You'll pick up new connections with each call if you play your cards right.* This is arguably the biggest reason I am a fan of cold calling. With every new connection as a *Conscientious Connector,* you are adding more and more people who will likely want to help you in some way with a referral or a nice recommendation to others. Just keep building that database and impressing more and more other professionals and you will never be without people to talk to and follow up with.

- *You'll build for yourself a bigger and bigger fan club.* Even if the people you talk to never become your clients, you can still add them to your fan club. Remember that people move from job to job, company to company, region to region. **We get calls to this day from connections we made ten, fifteen years go.** Somebody keeps our information and, even though they couldn't use our services at the time, they liked us and kept our card, then called us when they moved to a new company.

Positioning, as you will learn from practice, not only can turn a cold call into a warm call but it can also create a contact to add to your database that will always want to help you be more successful. Trust me, this happens more often than you probably think. Not everyone you talk to will develop into a key contact that buys from you, but many of them will nevertheless instrumentally want to help you if you understand how to position each call. Further, each subsequent conversation you have will help build on that relationship.

First and foremost, and before you pick up the phone to call someone, understand how your service or product will help that person or that entity this person represents. If you do not have a compelling reason to call, why call? But, if you can come up with compelling reasons for them to consider your product or service, and I mean really compelling reasons, your chances of setting an appointment will increase dramatically, and, in that process, your cold call will turn much warmer. Turn up the heat by authentically investing in empathetic, foundational thought and research about how you will help someone before you call them. Think about that before you pick up the phone. Anticipate and be ready. It is your job to bring value, not just call to see if you can gain an appointment. There's a huge difference and how you do this has everything to do with how they will remember you later and regard you to others.

HOMEWORK

1. The very first thing you need to do is change a cold call opportunity into a warm one. Once you have done that, you are no longer making a cold call. List out all you can gather about the target you are about to cold call, including everything you can gather from the internet about the company, its history, the people you are about to try to reach and their competing companies. Practice with this information.

2. Next, look for any information you can gather from your sources that might provide that person with information *they* can use, regardless of whether you benefit. Perhaps you can read about their competitors and come up with information they may have missed. Perhaps your research will reveal information about changes in tax structures or a pending sale of a division. Anything you can use becomes a researched talking point. Remember, you are applying for an opportunity to be of service, just as if you were applying for a job within his/her company. It doesn't matter what that person's title is or their position; they represent something you want and you must respect their authority and their position in that structure at all costs or you will be out.

3. Review what it is that is compelling you to want to connect with this person. Is it your services? Is it your products? Are you absolutely certain that if this person actually agrees to talk to you or meet with you, that he/she will like what she sees and want to buy what you're selling? If you are the least bit unsure of yourself or your products/services before you make this phone call, I will tell you right now to not make that call because you are not absolutely certain about this. You are not prepared and you will be found out. Either figure out a way to get to absolute certainty or move on to someone else.

4. Congratulate yourself for practicing and practicing until this is no longer something you find the least bit intimidating, because that

will happen. Now you are a veteran and you know how to turn any cold call into a warm call by digging deep and finding reasons they should hear you out. When you reach that point, you will look back and wonder what all the fuss was about.

~~~~~~~

One last remark that is very important for you to hear: If you are in sales and your job is to penetrate accounts, (get in, figure out how to sell and get the order) then you have your work already cut out for you and you know what to do.

As for turning cold calling into warm calling, incorporate this training into what you already know. I am far more interested in you building a database of the right, sustainable connections that will continue to feed you leads and referrals than I am about your current batting average at making a sale. By improving your ability to connect you will build a better sales average naturally. One serves the other.

~~~~~~~

You read the book. Congratulations!

As a special thank you, if you will send an honest assessment of the book to Amazon, I will send you a special bonus download. It is offered to those who finished the book and agree to do the work, apply the lessons and change the world for the better. Just type in "Finished Conscientious Connector" in the subject line and email me at Dave@DaveRIbble.com.

POSTSCRIPT

I am grateful that *The Way of The Conscientious Connector* brought us together. We really never know where life will take us or, for that matter, who will become an influence on our journey, which is an exciting part of becoming a *Conscientious Connector*. Because you hold my writing and ideas in your hand, you have become a positive influence on me and I thank you for that. It is my hope that I will return the favor and become a positive, life-changing influence on you, too. Please plan to let me know how this information helped you.

If you picked this particular book because you knew you could use some solid advice and direction from a seasoned sales and marketing guy, let me also congratulate you for seeking information beyond what you were already familiar with. Most of your peers, competitors and the rest won't take the time to invest this way in their selves. But you did.

Always be learning more

I love speaking about and sharing my information with anyone who is open to learning more about the true art of this and the inherent benefits that come with such practice.

Occasionally, the invitations include a chance to speak to professionals who are unemployed and I usually accept because I like to keep my ear to the ground. This gives me yet another opportunity to interview them and keep up on current economic conditions. I already know, first-hand, what being unemployed is like and what it can do to damage a person's self-esteem. I know how I felt when I went through that. I have great empathy for others experiencing it.

During my time with them and while teaching, I also like to see what steps they are taking to improve their 'hire-ability'. For example, what are they reading? I will walk to the blackboard, pick up the chalk and tell them to shout out good books that they have read that helped them in some way. Unfortunately, few people speak up, not because they are shy, but because they aren't focused as much on improving themselves as they are focused on just getting by, and that is a dilemma all of us should be concerned with, even alarmed, because without continually encouraging the pursuit of learning new skills, the process stagnates. We cannot afford that if we want to see improvement in our collective capabilities.

This is why I am very glad that you have read my book and are hopefully taking steps to change your paradigm. You can lead the way. You can show others how this works and bring them into the fold with you. *The Way of The Conscientious Connector* is downright contagious because of the positive effects you will have on those you meet.

One caveat: Changes don't happen overnight, so prepare yourself for the very real possibility that you will have to practice *The Way of The Conscientious Connector* for a while. Remember, *people you meet aren't used to someone looking out for them like this.* They will have to adjust, like you, to this different way of approaching people, following up with them and searching for ways to help them. This will become a process you thoroughly enjoy, more all the time.

Likewise, people you only talk to over the phone or through email and social media will have to adjust to the new 'you' brought about by what you learned, here. I assure you, once they trust you are for real and you demonstrate to them what you have learned, you will start to see a different attitude from many, if not most, in their desire to help you, too. As we said before, by slowing down your process and learning more about how you can help others, your own progress will start to accelerate. I will be thrilled to hear from you as that begins to happen.

The greatest untapped source for creative, innovative thinking might just be that person staring back at you in the mirror. Give yourself a pat on the back and allow great ideas to come to you that you can share with others. The people you need to meet in order to advance your career are looking for you, too. But you probably won't recognize them until you start to practice this.

Continue to write in your journal and record the reactions you receive from others. This is your life, not a dress rehearsal. Do the work. Build on it and make this personal to you, for rewards await those who approach this in a truly authentic way. We will hit more home runs in our own lives when we practice each day at a higher standard of behavior; a standard that says each of us have opportunity for success and should be encouraged, not just manipulated for personal gain and then discarded. We must pursue this for more than just ourselves. It is how we are wired. It is how things are supposed to work. Jill Lublin, international speaker and the author of three best sellers talks in *The Profit of Kindness* (Career Press 2017, p46) about this: "The human species is designed to be in sync. We move to the rhythm of others, mirror the actions and moods of others, gravitate toward likeminded peers, and align with people who have the same sense of humor, beliefs and values. When we are with people who like us, we feel comfortable."

When you act in *The Way of The Conscientious Connector* you begin to be more comfortable talking to most everyone. You acclimate to the needs of the other person. You seek out and find talking points, common interests. You automatically pay more attention to how you can help them. When you give them your undivided attention you will expand *their* universe, not just your own.

Dave Ribble

ABOUT THE AUTHOR

Dave Ribble grew up on a 52-acre farm with his two brothers just outside Fairmount, Indiana and attended the same Fairmount High School as their parents. He played sports, was in a band and lived the typical Midwest life before moving to California and going to work for a time with Disney. Ribble is a graduate of his beloved Chapman University where he majored in Marketing and Business. An author, coach, facilitator, trainer and speaker, Dave is dedicated to helping people find more success and happiness in their lives.

For the past 30-plus years he has worked in various promotional marketing and consulting capacities and has served many companies in varied industries, which has afforded him a unique opportunity to interview clients, supplier partners and associates and to understand well what the average worker or CEO or VP of Marketing has to deal with each day; the constant challenges for most of us that are not all that uncommon.

Dave trains on the art of Conscientiously Connecting; needed and often requested training that is for individuals, professional entrepreneurs, corporate clients and organizations. The subjects he writes about continue to expand, as well, so look for more of Dave's writings on topics such as *Innovative Thinking, Overcoming Limiting Beliefs, Creating Better Relationships* and other subjects designed to empower and encourage best beneficial practices. He also writes for several magazines. Follow him on social media and sign up for his communication and marketing advice.

Ribble and his wife Gaye reside in Southern California and enjoy their extended family that, at last count, totals 12 grandchildren including triplets and three great-grandchildren. He enjoys reading, writing, golf, music and musical theater, travel and interviewing people he meets to learn more about how we can all support one another, *conscientiously.*

Visit DaveRibble.com for more information about his courses, training programs, to book him as a speaker and to suggest other subjects/challenges that you would like for him to address that would help and support you in your Business - Career - Life.

Made in the USA
San Bernardino, CA
18 October 2017